INFORMATION TECHNOLOGY
A Revolutionary Change

INFORMATION TECHNOLOGY
A Revolutionary Change
(In 9 Volumes)

Volume 9
(Understanding the Information and Communication Society)

Editor
RAMESH CHANDRA
Vice-Chancellor, Bundelkhand University, Jhansi (U.P.)

KALPAZ PUBLICATIONS
DELHI–110052

INFORMATION TECHNOLOGY: A REVOLUTIONARY CHANGE
(Information Technology)

Rs. 8000 (Set)
Rs. 900 (Each Volume)

ISBN: 81-7835-201-X (Set)
ISBN: 81-7835-228-1 (Vol. 9)

Published in 2003 in India by
Kalpaz Publications
C–30, Satyawati Nagar
Delhi–110052
E-mail: kalpaz@hotmail.com

Laser Typesetting at: Varsha Graphics, Delhi
Printed at: Mehra Offset Printers, New Delhi

Contents

Preface *vii*

1. **The Infotech Landscape** **1**
New Trends and Future Directions; Building of Infotech Skills; Preparing Students for IT Careers.

2. **The Internet Applications** **82**
Towards Electronic Democracy.

3. **ICTs and Media** **105**
Public Service Broadcasting.

4. **Freedom of Expression on the Net** **125**
Characteristics of the Internet; Privacy on the Net; Protecting Freedom of Expression on the Net; The Internet Promote Democracy; Government's Control on Internet Content and Access.

5. **Global ICT Scenario** **182**
The Internet and other Networks; Radio and Television; Sub Saharan Africa; ICT Infrastructure; Computers and Data Processing; The Status of ICT in Arab Countries; The Asia Crisis and ICTs; ICT and Central and Eastern European Countries; Impact of ICT in Latin America and Caribbean; Information and Library Services; The Inter University Network; ICTs and Western Europe and North America; Basic Indicators of ICT; The Canadian Information Highway; Information Policy for European Union.

Bibliography 301

Index 303

Preface

The emergence of the new online environment is part of a major transformation of our entire communications system. The second half of the 20th century has witnessed the global phenomenon of an information explosion. The development of different electronic technologies has made it possible for millions of people to have fast access to huge information resources stored in different places on the planet, to communicate with each other and to handle information presented in various forms.

Today's global networks create connections between people which span time and distance in ways the world has never before seen and with implications which are beginning to have major political, social, and economic implications. It also giving millions of people direct access to information in ways the world has never before seen. In today's 'reach out and touch someone' age, millions of people who would never put pen to paper to write a letter will spend evenings writing to dozens of people through their online connections. Electronic mail has given new life and new meaning to a profoundly traditional form of communication. Telecomputing may in fact be the last frontier of written literacy available which will incite students to traditional literacy skills.

If the information society is to be both open and universal it should develop along the principles embodied in the Universal Declaration of Human Rights. They are, among others, the right to freedom of expression, free access to information, the right to education and the right to participate in cultural life. Governments, industry and the civil society are seeking to apply these long accepted principles to the electronic information environment, but these efforts are hampered by major difficulties and challenges, including the critical issue of how to ensure fair conditions for developing countries, which are entering the digital age at a major disadvantage.

A number of international consultations are showing that clearer policy guidelines are needed in the increasingly open, interactive and global information environment. Such guidelines should cover all aspects of the global information networks—technological and economic, but also educational, scientific, cultural and social. Today, however, most national and international debate is concentrating on technological and economic aspects, because of their more immediately perceived impact, often to the detriment of other issues which will ultimately have a deeper, more fundamental significance in achieving an Information Society for All.

Editor

1

The Infotech Landscape

The emergence of the new online environment is part of a major transformation of our entire communications system. More than half of all Americans were hooked up to the Internet by the end of 2000, and within the next four years that number is expected to grow to 85 percent. Nearly nine out of ten American homes will soon be interactively wired. Most will connect through personal computers; but other devices, including digital TVs, game consoles, portable devices, and next-generation digital cable set-top boxes, will increasingly provide a link.

In many ways, teens are the defining users of this digital media culture. They are the first generation to grow up surrounded by and immersed in digital technologies. With nearly three-quarters of twelve-to-seventeen-year-olds online, teens surpass adults in their use of chat, instant messaging, and other forms of Internet communications. As is early adapters of these technologies, teens are as comfortable growing up with digital media as their parents generation was with the telephone and TV. This easy fluency among teens, in contrast to the typically greater hesitancy among adults, is shifting power relationships within the family.

Teenagers are not only helping their parents learn how to use a computer, they often guide their families purchases for computer-related products. Teens are also integrating interactive devices into their daily lives in unexpected, often inventive ways. Dubbed Webbersli or viewers by the media industry, many teens have already begun using the television and the computer simultaneously, far in advance of the so-called convergence of these two media. A host of new products is being created exclusively for teens, which may very well be the test market for the next generation of digital content and services. For example, teens desire to chat is spawning many new hand-held, wireless tech products that are designed primarily for instant messaging and chat, but which also feature interactive gaming, Internet access, digital picture and music storage, and personal information management.

The young people of today are also tomorrow's adults; how they consume and participate in new media will help determine the future shape and direction of the media system Teens are more than just consumers of media content; they are also active participants and creators of this new media culture, developing content themselves, designing personal Web sites, and launching their own online enterprises. As one trade publication observed, young people have not simply adopted digital media, they have internalized it. The behaviours, attitudes, and values that teens are embracing as part of their new-media experience could have significant impacts on the larger culture. New media technologies are making their way into American life at a time when teens have become a booming target market for advertisers and marketers. Spending among teenagers has increased steadily during the past several decades, rising dramatically in more recent years. Teen spending power doubled between the years 1960 and 1980, and tripled in the 90s. By 2000, 31.6 million teenagers spent an estimated $155 billion of their own money in the retail market. Teens not only spend money on themselves; they also wield tremendous influence over purchases made by their parents. The increase in families where both parents work, along with the aggressive marketing of adult products to children, have given teens much more power and responsibility in purchasing decisions of such big-ticket items as cars, family vacations, and furniture.

Indeed, the rise of teen digital media is part of a larger proliferation of new product categories and programs targeted at this valuable demographic group. This is a generation that has grown up in a marketplace that zeroes in on younger and younger audiences, employing synergy and cross-marketing among television and movie characters and products to create a ubiquitous commercial youth culture.

In the 1980s, children got their own TV networks, radio networks, magazines, newspapers, kids clothing brands, books, banking, and such high-ticket items as video games and other high-tech products. By 1995, notes market research expert James McNeal, virtually every consumer goods industry was somehow involved in marketing to children, either as a primary influence, or future market, or some combination of these.

Despite the rapid growth of this new digital culture, comparatively little public attention has been paid to it. When the spotlight has been cast on teens and new media, news coverage has tended to focus on the negative impacts. For example, after the 1999 shooting at Columbine High School, the world of cyberspace was seen as a dark and dangerous place that ensnared young people. News stories and congressional hearings occasionally provide frightening accounts of teens who have become unwitting victims of pornography or, even worse, of online predators who lurk in chat rooms.

Concerns about online pornography produced the Communications Decency Act in 1996, which was subsequently ruled unconstitutional, as well as two subsequent acts, which are currently facing court challenges. Dozens of filtering software products have flooded the market, promising to assuage parental concern by blocking out harmful content on the Internet.

But while parents, policymakers, and educators worry about pornography and predation, they also express optimism about the Internet's power to enhance educational opportunities and communication possibilities. Most Americans believe that children should enjoy equitable access to these powerful new technologies, prompting a range of public and private initiatives to wire the nation's schools and libraries in order to help bridge the ihdigital divide.

This contradictory discourse, with concerns about the hazards of the Internet on the one hand, and visions of its educational potential on the other, echoes earlier public attitudes over new media. Each new media technology brought with it great promise for social educational benefits and great concern for children's exposure to inappropriate and harmful content. As a consequence, even as this new medium is becoming a pervasive presence in teens' lives, it remains largely under the radar of parents, scholars, and policymakers alike.

The World Wide Web, as the centre of innovation and implementation for the new-media system. The Web sites, identifying the key features that characterize online content and activity for teens, and analysing the major industry trends that are influencing the design and direction of the new teen media culture.

Many research has documented a number of critical biological, cognitive, and emotional changes that take place during the transition period of adolescence. One of the most important is identity formation. As teens begin the exploration of their adult identities, they undergo a shift in self-perception. They begin thinking about their hypothetical future selves, often choosing from different possible identities, and trying some on for size. They also become intensely preoccupied with comparing themselves to others. As their self-identity undergoes these changes, teens are exposed to ever-greater levels of uncertainty and vulnerability.

Media have always played a role in this process. As teenagers spend less time with their families, outside influences become more important. The opinions of friends matter more; and diverse media, such as music, movies, magazines, and computers, become more powerful influences as well. Teens are active users of media, basing their choices on both interest and need. Because teen engagement with media usually intensifies just as parental influence is waning, the media can play a strong role in shaping teen attitudes, as well as their sense of self and the world.

The handful of studies that have been conducted on teens' use of new media suggest that accessing the Internet addresses many of the same needs served by traditional media such as entertainment, identity formation, high sensation, coping, and youth culture identification. However, the unique nature of the new digital environment presents an unprecedented array of possibilities for communication, interaction, and expression never before available.

No longer must teens serve strictly as consumers of one-way messages (as from television or radio). Online technologies offer new tools and new opportunities to become more actively involved in the exploration of identity, and to find expression for many different possible selves. Chat rooms, for example, allow teens to create personas quite distinct from their everyday identities, and to act them out in cyberspace.

The Internet and other digital media have created a new culture of simulation, is with profound implications for the development of identity. From scientists trying to create artificial life to children ,morphing through a series of virtual personae. But it is on the Internet that our confrontations with technology as it collides with our sense of human identity are fresh, even raw.

In the real-time communities of cyberspace, we are dwellers on the threshold between the real and virtual, unsure of our footing, inventing ourselves as we go along.

Electronic communication also relieves teens from typical gender role constraints that often influence face-to-face interactions. Susannah Stern's study of the home pages of adolescent girls concludes that home pages provide girls with greater opportunity to openly express thoughts, interests, and to create a public identity. Other studies have noted that young adolescent girls find the Internet particularly liberating because they are treated with a degree of respect missing in face-to-face conversations. For example, teen girls, who stereotypically are less talkative and assertive than boys, spoke freely and passionately in a computer-mediated forum. Scholars have also suggested that teens use the Internet not just to communicate with individual others, but also to participate in various online communities.

Particularly for those teens who feel uncomfortable or unaccepted in their (offline) lives, online communities provide extensive networks of like-minded others with whom teens can share their thoughts and experiences. For example, in a communications environment that feels anonymous, young people can reveal their fears and secrets.

Beyond the psycho-social concerns are a broader set of political and cultural issues. One that interests us is whether the Internet can contribute to greater civic and political engagement by youth. In his recent book, Bowling Alone, Harvard University political scientist Robert Putnam documents how each successive generation of Americans has been less inclined to vote than was its immediate predecessor. He worries that even with the proliferation of news sources in the mass media, young people today are substantially less knowledgeable about public affairs.

A 1999 study found, however, that although young people were in general much less likely to seek out political information than were older cohorts, they were more likely to use the Internet as their preferred means of access. And while voter turnout is lower among young adults, volunteering for community activities among adolescents is on the rise.

While a handful of notable youth media examples exist, much less is known about whether online political sites actually stimulates or serve merely as a virtual substitute for real civic engagement.

In focusing primarily on the content and services for teens on the World Wide Web, we acknowledge that the Internet is only one sector of a much larger new digital media system. However, that the technological innovation, experimentation, and evolving business practices that are taking place in the online context reveal a great deal about overall trends in the digital media. As more and more household appliances are connected to a digital hub, moreover, and as the use of portable wireless devices proliferates, the distinction between ionlinelo and inoffline will diminish accordingly. Thus we used the Internet as a lens through which we could take a snapshot of this evolving new-media culture.

The dynamic changes occurring on the Internet are part of a much broader set of economic, institutional, and technological forces that are shaping the entire digital landscape. Since we were interested in understanding these larger trends, we also conducted an analysis of the key factors that are influencing the design and direction of the new teen media culture, both on the Web and in other emerging media platforms such as wireless application protocol (WAP) portable devices and interactive television.

Web sites are being created under non-profit auspices and, in some cases, by teens themselves. In this arena, teens are engaging in community-building activities, volunteering for public service, and participating in various forms of political activism. Most of the research on how teens actually use the new media comes from the commercial market-research sector. Thus we investigated that sector, too, and obtained some of its findings through conferences and trade shows, as well as gleaning other pertinent data from trade publications.In the latter half of 2000, the economy of the Web plummeted, as venture capital quickly dried up amid projections of less-than-expected revenues.

New Trends and Future Directions

Computers are now capable of handling audio files with fidelity that rivals that of CDs, and the quality of streaming video, still in its early development, continues to improve. Televisions, in turn, are now being used to access the Internet, a trend that will grow with the introduction of new, more sophisticated cable set-top boxes.

Mobile phones, pagers, and personal digital assistants (PDAs) are now manufactured as Internet-ready devices, and videogame consoles are being designed as integrated home entertainment centres, with the ability to play movies and music as well as to surf the Web. And the Web itself will one day be bypassed, giving way to new forms of content and new means of delivery, including new ways to exploit the Internet. A study shows Internet's future pointed to four trends that were likely to usher in the post-Web world:

(1) the wireless revolution, with content tailored specifically for portable, mobile devices;

(2) peer-to-peer computing, featuring new software and services that will facilitate the exchange of data among PCs, including both collaborative projects from remote locations and distributed processing (harnessing several computers simultaneously across distances);

(3) instant messaging, expanded to include multimedia conversations across digital TV and wireless platforms; and

(4) machine-to-machine communications, automating tasks and undertaking negotiations on the user's behalf.

The Net is a platform around which we will build all sorts of really interesting products and services, explains Richard Newton, dean of the College of Engineering at the University of California at Berkeley.

Many of these new products and services will be delivered by a range of devices beyond the standard personal computer. Such appliances as personal video recorders (PVRs), third-generation (3G) mobile communications devices, and interactive television (ITV) via advanced set-top boxes will produce dramatic changes in the ways in which media content is produced, packaged, and disseminated and the ways in which revenues are derived in the process.

Not only is media content becoming accessible nearly everywhere, but the options concerning when, where, and how consumers access such programming are rapidly expanding. Rather than passively consuming the media in static and linear forms, consumers are already creating their own unique media experiences, using customizable PVR and ITV programming features, for example, or assembling personal music collections by downloading MP3 sound files from the Internet and in burning their own CDs.

The launch of the Digital Entertainment Network (DEN.net) in 1998 was accompanied by fanfare typical of the dot-com boom the television-like network was simply ahead of its time, before enough teens had access to high-speed broadband Internet service. And some industry observers concluded that the site self-destructed because of a weak business model, complicated by a scandal over lavish spending and other alleged improprieties.

Many experts view the recent fluctuations in the Internet economy as a period of readjustment in an over-hyped industry where venture capital has flowed in too often on the basis of rather shaky business plans. The Internet is undergoing a vast weeding- out, remarked one market research executive, noting that survivors are finding the right combination of business practices to enable them not only to stay afloat but to generate a profit.

But the starts and stops in the dot-com marketplace should not divert our attention from the inexorable movement of digital media into the lives of teens. This generation is growing up at the centre of the technological explosion that has transformed the media system. Their coming of age is occurring simultaneously with the growth and maturity of the new digital media culture. Their increased personal spending power, combined with their technological savvy, have made teens a particularly powerful target market for online businesses, generating a cornucopia of varied content and activities on the Web, tailored specifically to their interests.

Teenagers have embraced this new online world with great enthusiasm, responding eagerly to its invitation to share ideas, contribute content, and otherwise place their stamp on a media system that they themselves create and manage. Teens have also seized upon all manner of electronic gadgets from pagers to mobile phones to PDAs. And with the promise of Internet connectivity to all of these devices and others just around the corner, teens are marching into the future with the potential for unprecedented levels of communications and information retrieval at their fingertips.

The media world that teens inhabit departs in significant ways from the one their parents knew during their own adolescence. The digital media are challenging many of the conventions and institutions of the past, blurring or obliterating the boundaries between public and private, commercial and noncommercial, school and home, local and global.

The properties of the interactive media are particularly seductive to adolescents, tapping into many of their developmental needs, capturing their imaginations, and kindling their hopes and desires. Online communication tools enable instantaneous and constant contact with peers; personal home pages offer compelling opportunities for self-expression and identity exploration; and ubiquitous portable devices facilitate mobility and independence.

The Internet's extensive reach and its promise of anonymity create an environment that encourages information-seeking on a wide variety of topics inaccessible or taboo for earlier generations. Chat rooms and forums allow teens to engage in discussion and debate without fear of exposure. As the features and functions of this new digital online marketplace are being tested and refined, teens serve as subjects for continuous and pervasive market research, connected through electronic umbilical cords to a phalanx of companies that monitor their every online move.

As a consequence, a unique symbiosis has developed between the creators of this digital culture and its most avid users; today's teens are eager and willing partners in the design and implementation of an array of cultural products and practices. Their engagement with digital media is ushering in a new set of behaviours, values, and expectations that this generation has internalized and will carry with them into adulthood.

With the whirling pace of change in communication technologies as we move toward an increasingly converged media environment, it remains vital to keep abreast of these developments. There is an urgent need for further research on the role that new media are playing in the lives of youth. We find it very troubling that so much of what is known about how teens are interacting with the new digital media is confined to the proprietary domain of market research, where it is either completely off-limits to outsiders or priced so prohibitively as to be inaccessible to the public.

Except for a handful of scholars, the academic community has failed to respond in a timely or effective fashion to the dynamic changes in the media environment of young people. Conventions and constraints within academic institutions keep scholars far behind the rapid pace of change in the media. For example, traditional methods for studying mass media content do not lend themselves easily to analyses of Internet content and services. As a consequence, many scholars are hesitant to tackle the methodological risks of conducting such studies.

For example, with the variety of options available for plugging in, teens have adapted, in part, by developing the ability to engage in several activities simultaneously. But no one knows what this means for the depth of their processing or whether the high level of stimulation from a variety of media affects attention span, although these are concerns that have been raised among parents and educators. Additionally, the access to boundless information without leaving home is unique.

Adolescents are not a monolithic group, after all. There are not only personal differences, but income, ethnic, geographic, and sexual differences within this highly diverse group of young people. The way these various subgroups relate to the new media may differ sharply from what is known in the existing research literature.

Since so much of this new-media culture is rooted in very sophisticated technologies, we need to understand more fully the inherent properties and capabilities of these new digital tools, and how they can be harnessed most effectively to serve the needs of children and adolescents. We also need studies of the institutions that are creating this digital culture, both its commercial and its noncommercial sectors.

Multidisciplinary approaches are needed, combining the contributions of historians, sociologists, anthropologists, and economists, who can study new media in all of their dimensions. Although longitudinal studies of the impact of media are important, we also need focused, policy-relevant research that addresses specific issues and needs. Sometimes this research may not be entirely conclusive, and the fluid nature of the media system may pose methodological challenges to researchers. But the need for serious appraisals at this critical, early stage of the new media's development seems clear.

The new-media environment for teens is primarily commercial in nature, positioning youth as consumers of popular culture and as a market for a multitude of products and services. In some respects these trends are logical extensions of what has been happening throughout this century, with the increasing number of products and services created for and marketed to youth, fuelled by the rise in young people's spending power.

But the nature and extent of marketing in the online world is unprecedented, with the digital media intensifying many of the existing trends in the commercialization of children's lives. At every turn, from home to school to shopping mall, teens encounter various efforts to involve them in commercial transactions. By exploiting the interactive capacity of the online media to involve youth themselves (wittingly or not) in the marketing of various products, marketers have taken a qualitative leap in their use of sales tactics to shape and influence teen behaviour.

In addition to the merger of content and commerce, and the ease of buying products online through e-commerce (which will become even easier in new interactive TV implementations), the push toward impulse buying is made stronger.

The new media have spurred an alphabet soup of commerce, including e-commerce, t-commerce, and m-commerce (covering the worlds of the Internet, television, and mobile communications). In a culture that is already commercialized and market-driven, the ready availability of instant gratification (and delayed payment) online raises questions about the new media's impact on young people in particular and the quality of our culture in general.

Many teenagers work at after-school jobs, often to pay for the many consumer goods and services targeted directly to their demographic. These trends have raised concerns among parents and educators, as many high school students find it difficult to work and keep up with their schoolwork. Consumer groups note with alarm that credit card debt is rising among young people.

New digital marketing strategies will very likely compound these trends, as ubiquitous marketing tools on wireless devices, in wired classrooms, and through interactive televisions will target teens throughout the day and night with seductive appeals designed to encourage impulse buying, and with special digital credit devices to facilitate instantaneous purchases.

Consumer protection policies will be needed to ensure that teens are not unfairly taken advantage of in the digital marketplace.

Teens are the most avid participants in such programs, which pay them both to post a view bar or payball at the bottom of their screens while they surf the Web, and to recruit other into the program. The viewbar exhibits various advertisements and companies monitor the amount of time users spend on the Web (and thus, ideally, watch ads on the viewbar) and pay them an hourly rate.

Similar programs pay teens to use branded e-mail programs or to listen to streaming audio programming. Not only do teens take advantage of this easily way to make money online, but many become marketers themselves by posting entire pages that list pay-for-surf companies, as a means of generating additional payments for referrals. Although these are strictly voluntary programs, regulators should examine this form of marketing closely and consider possible policies against any unfair practices targeted at underage youth in the digital environment.

Teen privacy protection is a particularly urgent concern that merits public attention and consideration for policy formation. Often, the concept of teens' online safety is framed as protection from stalkers and insulation from online pornography or other inappropriate material. While these are legitimate causes for concern, the collection of personal data for commercial purposes is more pervasive. Thus we need to broaden the concept of online safety to include the maintenance of personal privacy.

Younger audiences (or even adult audiences, for that matter) may not understand that when they provide personal information online, they may be compromising the sanctity of their own personal privacy.

When a Web site such as Bolt or Thirsty prompts teens to share their names, addresses, and other information in the interest of incommunity, or when teens give in to the very natural adolescent tendency to share personal information as a means of expressing themselves and bonding with others, they stand to lose much more than they gain.

Coupled with other databases and profiles both online and off, the isolated bits of information that teens surrender in registering for site membership and contests, or in the course of online chats and discussions, may add up to a complete loss of privacy.

Market research also plays a role in this regard. Teenagers who freely discussed what they liked and disliked about the Ford Focus advertising campaign in the Ford-sponsored car section of Bolt may not have realized that their feedback (and quite possibly their names and other personal information) are now the property of Bolt. Such data can be sold to other market researchers who are a part of the $1.5 trillion industry of direct marketing and advertising databases.

Moreover, even if such Web sites post privacy policies that explain that they are, indeed, collecting teens' personal information to use as market research or sell to other companies, it is questionable whether teens will search for such policies.

Children under the age of 13 are currently protected under the Children's Online Privacy Protection Act (COPPA), which took effect in 2000. COPPA prohibits commercial Web sites and online services from collecting personal information from these children without parental consent and proper notification.

To date, however, teens are not afforded any privacy protections in the digital media. As content and services for teens continue to migrate to cell phones and other smart wireless devices with global positioning systems (GPS), threats to their privacy will grow.

Public concerns over privacy are already on the rise, prompting a proliferation of congressional hearings and a number of legislative proposals. A coalition of consumer groups formed this year to promote the need for privacy policies, especially for the digital media. The particular concerns of adolescents will need to be included in any legislative or regulatory remedies.

The central role that market research is playing in the digital teen culture is of special concern. Never before has there been a medium with the ability to tap into the needs, desires, interests, and behaviours of children and youth. Never before has there been such an intertwining of the machinations of the marketplace with the activities of young people.

Some of the market research practices such as the creation of online focus groups disguised as chat rooms may well be deceptive, a matter that the Federal Trade Commission (FTC) should investigate. Close attention should be paid to these online market research practices as well as those being developed for other digital technologies.

Parents, health professionals, and policymakers will need to be particularly vigilant as marketers continue to focus attention on younger and younger age groups, grooming the so-called for their role as teen consumers. The American Psychological Association has been looking into the questionable role played by some child psychologists who sell their services to market research firms, and is developing ethical guidelines for the profession.

While technologically savvy and comfortable with digital media, children and youth may not be as sophisticated as they need to be to protect themselves from manipulative and exploitative marketing and data collection practices in this new interactive world. Clearly, there is a need for comprehensive consumer education in the schools, with a curriculum that is sufficiently flexible to stay current in this rapidly changing marketplace.

The digital media also create unique opportunities to harness the power of technology as a positive force in the lives of children and youth. However, the full potential of the digital media will not be realized unless there are clear public and private policies to help guide their development. In order to achieve this goal, we need a new framework for thinking about the media and their relationship to children and youth.

For example, thousands of scientific studies (and considerable federal money), as well as countless articles in the popular press, have been devoted to assessing the relationship of televised violence to antisocial behaviour.

While these issues are important and will remain so in the future, the emergence of digital media provides an opportunity to define some new goals for the media system, and to take steps to ensure that these goals are realized.

On the one hand, the Internet has fostered many opportunities for community- building, participation, information-seeking, and collaboration. All of these activities can contribute to the development of the necessary attributes for citizenship. On the other hand, the rapid and pervasive commercialization of the digital media may be moving the culture in the opposite direction, encouraging values, attitudes, and behaviours that are aimed at grooming and consumers rather than effective citizens.

But there are a number of challenges that must be met if we are to see the emergence and survival of a healthy youth civic sector in the digital landscape. The dominance of the for- profit model on the Web raises serious questions about the continued viability of the truly noncommercial content and services that are integral to the authenticity of an alternative online culture.

As the Internet continues to make its transition to the next generations moving from slow, fixed dial-up connections to broadband access, interactive television, and wireless mobile devices the noncommercial civic media initiatives that are visible on today's Web may either be marginalized or may disappear altogether. Foundation grants, government support, and contributions from the private sector will all be needed to sustain non-profit, civic, and grassroots sites. Only with the effort of informed and active citizens, and with public policies that are conducive to the development of an online civic sector, will such support mechanisms be put in place.

A number of efforts in this regard are already underway, involving schools, libraries, public broadcasters, and other community organizations. Some of these projects (e.g., the Digital Promise) are concerned with identifying sources of funding for the production of noncommercial civic, educational, and cultural materials online.

Other projects are designed to test the online civic-sector concept at the community level. Still other projects (e.g., the Communitarian Network), primarily academic in nature, explore the philosophical underpinnings of the in common concept. What is missing in all of these efforts (and there are many others) is a means of coordinating them in some fashion, helping to create a critical mass of civic content online that will serve both local needs and national interests.

Finally, despite the rapid penetration of the Internet into American homes, there remains a troubling in digital divide that threatens to leave many youth behind in the technological revolution of the twenty-first century. Even though programs such as the the -rattler are making it easier for less-advantaged schools and libraries to gain affordable access to the Internet, the rapid introduction of broadband technologies may undercut the positive impact of these policies. More youth may have access as Internet penetration continues to grow, but the quality of that access may suffer in comparison to new premium services that are being introduced. As a result, a new digital divide might emerge, separating those with rudimentary, dial-up access from those who enjoy sophisticated, state-of-the art communications. The content of the new broadband universe, moreover, will reflect these inequities.

Such is the ambivalent picture that inevitably results from a serious appraisal of the new Web culture. Attractive in its ease of use, its ready access to seemingly boundless information, its open invitation to users to submit their own content, potentially even strengthening the bonds of community, the Web also raises serious concerns.

Fortunately, the digital age is still very much in formation, and the answers to these questions await our active participation in fashioning the kind of new media system that will serve the public interest as effectively as it generates private profits. We stand, in short, on the threshold of a new era. We have a unique window of opportunity to ensure that the potential benefits of the new media for teens and children are fully realized, while the harms and negative impacts are minimized. To achieve this goal, however, we will need a broad-based movement, enlisting all those who care about the quality of the media culture, both to explore and assess the system we have today, as well as to envision and enact a more promising system for tomorrow.

Building of Infotech Skills

The impact of the rapid creation and adoption of IT on the U.S. economy, describe the demand and supply trends for the core IT occupations and "Descriptions of Core Information Technology Professions" IT labour market. Over the past several years, the nature of America's information technology (IT) work force challenge has been the subject of much debate. There are many conflicting views of the challenge, and even among those who agree on the nature of the challenge, there are conflicting views of what the best solutions are. The perception of the challenge tends to be shaded by the perspective of the observer.

For the most part, industry sees the problem as a worker shortage. Companies believe that there simply aren't enough people in the IT occupations to meet the growing demand. Employee groups and advocates for employees, on the other hand, believe there are enough trained technical professionals in the United States, but industry has not tapped these existing labour pools.

And economists argue that the IT work force challenge is the expected result of the rising importance of IT in our economy and the consequent demand for highly-skilled core IT workers, and that, in the long run, market forces will fix the problem.

The Office of Technology Policy finds merit in each of the perspectives. However, it is our conclusion that the true nature of the challenge is more complex than any of these views individually, and that the challenge is driven by the unique nature of IT and its pervasiveness throughout the U.S. economy and our society. Two factors are chiefly responsible for creating the IT worker challenge. First, there has been sustained rapid growth in the demand for highly-skilled IT workers-demand that has accelerated in recent years. This demand is the product of the Information Age-virtually every segment of the American economy has embraced IT for the productivity improvements it brings to existing business functions, as well as for the new capabilities, products and services IT enables.

The ubiquity of IT can be seen almost everywhere: in the shift of business's equipment investment into information technologies, in the unprecedented emergence of the web as a venue for commerce and communication, and in the proliferation of computers in businesses and homes to name a few. As a result, demand for highly-skilled IT workers leads all other occupations and is expected to continue in the years ahead.

Second, the variety and complexity of software and hardware products and their applications, together with the unique business requirements of each industry, have created "spot" demand for workers with unique combinations of IT skills, experience and industry knowledge-expressed often by employers as needing "the right person, with the right skill, at the right time." The combination of time-sensitive competitive pressures and limited-time need for employees with unique combinations of technical skills, business skills, and hands-on experience has led many employers to pursue "buy" decisions in this labour market, rather than "make" decisions (to hire, then train for the task). Thus while there is a need to address the growing demand for highly-skilled IT workers, there is the additional challenge of meeting the unique demands of this niche labour market.

In a broad sense, the term "information worker" can be applied to data entry personnel, auto mechanics who use computer diagnostic equipment, medical technicians who operate CAT scan equipment, and loan officers who use computers to assess creditworthiness, as well as computer programmers, systems analysts, and computer scientists and engineers.

Office of Technology Policy analysis shows that the difficulty in meeting the national demand for IT workers is primarily for those with higher-end skills. The core IT occupations are differentiated, generally, from other IT and IT-related jobs by significantly higher skill and educational requirements.

The ability to conduct a quantitative analysis of IT employment is limited, to a large extent, by the availability of data, especially consistent longitudinal data that enables analysis of trends. Through its Occupational Employment Survey, the Department of Labour collects employment data on the four IT occupations that comprise our definition of core IT workers, and uses that data for its biennial ten-year projections of occupational and industry employment.

In addition, the Current Population Survey (CPS)-conducted jointly by the U.S. Department of Labour's Bureau of Labour Statistics (BLS) and the U.S. Department of Commerce's Census Bureau-provides data on core IT workers in two occupational categories: "computer systems analysts and scientists" and "computer programmers." While accounting for three of the core IT occupations, CPS data does not provide detailed information on the number of computer engineers.

The National Science Foundation does not consider computer programming as a science or engineering occupation, and therefore its Scientist and Engineer Statistical (SESTAT) data system does not fully account for the total number of computer programmers in the United States.

Computer scientists generally design computers and conduct research to improve their design or use, and develop and adapt principles for applying computers to new uses. They are distinguished from other computer professionals by the higher level of theoretical expertise and innovation they apply to complex problems and the creation or application of new technology.

Computer scientists employed by academic institutions work in areas ranging from theory, to hardware, to language design. Some work on multidisciplinary projects, such as developing and advancing uses for virtual reality. Computer scientists in private industry work in areas such as applying theory, developing specialized languages, or designing programming tools, knowledge-based systems, or computer games. Included in the "computer scientist" occupation are database administrators and computer support specialists.

Database administrators work with database management systems software, coordinating changes to, testing, and implementing computer databases. Since they also may be responsible for design implementation and system security, database administrators plan and coordinate security measures. Computer support specialists provide assistance and advice to users. They interpret problems and provide technical support for hardware, software, and systems. Support specialists may work within an organization or directly for a computer or software vendor.

Many others specialize in analysis, application, or design of a particular system or piece of the system. Network or systems administrators, for example, may install, configure, and support an organization's systems or portion of a system. Telecommunications specialists generally are involved with the interfacing of computer and communications equipment. Computer security specialists are responsible for planning, coordinating, and implementing an organization's information security measures.

Computer engineers work with the hardware and software aspects of systems design and development. Computer engineers may often work as part of a team that designs new computing devices or computer-related equipment. Software engineers design and develop both packaged and systems software.

Systems analysts use their knowledge and skills in a problem solving capacity, implementing the means for computer technology to meet the individual needs of an organization. They study business, scientific, or engineering data processing problems and design new solutions using computers.

This process may include planning and developing new computer systems or devising ways to apply existing systems to operations still completed manually or by some less efficient method.

Systems analysts may design entirely new systems, including both hardware and software, or add a single new software application to harness more of the computer's power. They work to help an organization realize the maximum benefit from its investment in equipment, personnel, and business processes.

Computer programmers write and maintain the detailed instructions, called "programs" or "software," that list in logical order the steps that computers must execute to perform their functions. In many large organizations, computer programmers follow descriptions prepared by systems analysts who have studied the task that the computer system is going to perform.

The transition from a mainframe to a primarily PC-based environment has blurred the once rigid distinction between the programmer and the user.

Increasingly adept users are taking over many of the tasks previously performed by computer programmers. A growing number of sophisticated software packages allow users and systems analysts to write programs.

The sweep of digital technologies and the transformation to a knowledge-based economy have created robust demand for workers highly skilled in the development and use of information technology. While there has been explosive employment growth in the U.S. software industry for more than a decade, the demand for workers who can create, apply and use information technology goes beyond the IT industry, cutting across manufacturing and services, transportation, health care, education and government.

Technology has contributed almost half of the Nation's long-term economic growth since World War II. And IT is the most important enabling technology in the world today. It is responsible for new products and services; creating new companies and industries; revitalizing existing products, services, and industries; providing new venues for commerce; enhancing our ability to manage information and to innovate; and improving our productivity, quality of life, and national standard of living. IT is changing the way we live and work, and transforming the economy at a fundamental level. The evidence is ubiquitous:

— Information technology's share of the U.S. economy nearly doubled between 1977 and 1998, growing from 4.2 percent to 8.2 percent. Information technologies contributed more than a third of real U.S. economic growth between 1995 and 1997.

— The cost of computing-measured in millions of instructions per second, or MIPS-fell 98.5 percent from $230 in 1991 to $3.42 in 1997. And the price per MIPS is expected to fall below a dollar this year, and to about one-fifth of a cent within a decade. This decline in computing costs is credited with reducing inflation by more than a full percentage point in 1997.

In 1994, three million people used the Internet. Year-end 1998 figures indicate more than 147 million people worldwide were accessing the Internet at least once a week from home or business. The number of Internet users is projected to grow to approximately 320 million by 2000, and to 720 million by 2005.

Traffic on the Internet is doubling every 100 days. This rapid growth in traffic is generating demand for both hardware and software, as well as for skilled IT workers to implement and manage these systems. Between 1998 and 2003, U.S. business-to-business commerce over the Internet is projected to grow from $48 billion to $1.3 trillion, with an additional $1.8 to $3.2 billion in global e-commerce; and U.S. consumer sales over the Internet are projected to rise from $3.9 billion to $108 billion.

For years, economists have expressed skepticism about IT's contribution to economic growth and productivity improvements. In recent years, many economists have come around. Today, one of the Nation's leading economists, Federal Reserve chairman Alan Greenspan, is an enthusiastic supporter of the vital role of IT in the U.S. economy.

The rapid acceleration of computer and telecommunications technologies is a major reason for the appreciable increase in their productivity in this expansion, and is likely to continue to be a significant force in expanding standards of living into the twenty-first century.

Ways in which employers tap the labour market, and the decisions they make about hiring and training investments, are affected by the business environment in which they operate. Today, the business environment for IT product and service producers is having a significant effect on employer approaches to the recruitment, retention, and training of highly-skilled IT workers.

In the decades following World War II, the U.S. high technology enterprise was dominated by government spending in defence and space. Dominant employers of highly-skilled technical workers resided in industries characterized by product life cycles measured in years, not months, such as the defence and aerospace industries.

Later, with the development of commercial computers, new IT industries began to play an important role in the labour markets for highly skilled technical workers, with the growth of computer hardware makers such as IBM, semiconductor manufacturers such as Texas Instruments and Intel, and service companies such as Electronic Data Systems. These large and stable firms had the time and incentive to serve as the training grounds for highly-skilled technical workers.

Many of these workers then brought their knowledge and skills to small and medium-sized high technology firms connected to these industries, and founded and staffed the new entrepreneurial firms that fuelled America's growing IT industry.

Today, the defence and aerospace industries have been downsized and are experiencing slow or no growth, and U.S. IT hardware manufacturers have globalized. At the same time, the computer and data processing services industry-consisting of software producers and IT consultants-has experienced a remarkable period of growth, with employment growing sixfold from 1976 to 1996.

The employment growth in this industry is a product of the phenomenal demand for IT related-products and services that not only enhance the productivity of current operations, but also create new products, services, and firm capabilities. Software and its applications are often the critical driver of these improvements. Today, the computer and data processing services industry is, by far, the largest employer of highly skilled core IT workers, employing more than a quarter of all workers in these professions; in 2006, the industry's share is projected to rise to nearly 40 percent.

Growth in science and engineering jobs is beginning to reflect this shift. Time is one of the most critical competitive factors for companies for whom IT is their core business. While product and technology life cycles have decreased markedly across all industry sectors, time pressures are most intense for these IT product and service producers. These companies confront life cycles or project deadlines that are measured in months or Internet years. For example, at Hewlett Packard, new products earn their greatest revenue in their first year on the market and, by their second year, revenues are already tapering off. Nearly two-thirds of the company's revenues are generated from products less than two years old. Moreover, early market entry provides a critical competitive edge. In many cases, the first competitors to the market with a new product are likely to capture most of the market share.

For example, in some key areas of packaged software-Internet browsers, word processing, spread sheet, page layout, and e-mail-two producers account for the lion's share of the market. Competitors who are among the first to the market capture the critical flow of funds generated by those markets that is needed to pay the costs of developing the next generation of technology and products.

Sometimes they become the de facto standard. If a company fails to reach the market in time, the lack of revenues to invest in development poses a serious risk that the company will eventually fall at the hands of more nimble competitors.

The pressures of time-based competition are often felt more acuteiy by smaller firms which may lack the buffers that larger firms have, such as a broader product portfolio from which to generate revenues or a larger staff available for retraining and deployment to projects.

In industry segments characterized by fast-paced creators or innovators of IT products and services, jobs and companies change rapidly, with a high rate of creative destruction. In this group, a few firms will grow into large, dominating competitors. Some will be acquired by other firms. Many will die in the creative destruction process. It is important to note that the development of software is highly labour-intensive.

A principal way to accelerate software development is to devote more human resources to the process. In addition, rapid technological change makes it more difficult for companies to predict future resource requirements and introduces greater uncertainty into the business environment. Therefore, companies may not be able to ascertain their specific skill needs very far into the future.

Another major competitive factor concerns the production of hardware versus the production and application of software.

Developing and producing high-tech hardware is highly capital intensive, requiring expensive manufacturing plants and other facilities. This is a relatively high barrier to entry into the business, a barrier that tends to limit the number of competitors. In contrast, software development and application can be carried out from a home basement, with a few computers and desks.

Both the pressures of time, and product and service proliferation, play an important role in the market for IT workers. The critical element of time argues for hiring workers who already possess the needed technical skills and experience, who can work productively at once. Otherwise, when faced with a six-month product life cycle, a training period as short as six weeks for a new IT worker or team represents one quarter of time-to-market.

In that scenario, an employer risks missing the market window altogether and, thus, the stream of revenues needed to keep the company in high-tech competition. Similarly, an extended breaking-in period for an employee increases the chance that a customer's project deadline will not be met. Product proliferation creates the need for IT workers specialized in particular technical skills and their application.

The information technology industry is advancing at a whirlwind pace; with product cycles and time-to-market periods shortening, and demands for continued innovation and productivity growing with each passing day. What we will offer next year has not been invented today.

Among employers of IT workers, some focus on the development of new IT-related products and services, or perform projects under contract to other firms. These employers, for which IT is the core business, are the ones that must often contend with very short product life cycles and intense competitive pressures, or pressure from customers to bring projects in on time and within budget. Often, these employers, such as those in the computer and data processing services industry, have a high level of IT worker intensity in the work force.

Other employers of IT workers focus on the application of information technologies to enhance their core businesses in other fields, such as in insurance, banking, retail, or manufacturing. These firms have lower IT worker intensity, and typically enjoy longer life cycles in their use of information technologies. These different types of IT employers confront different business challenges, which affect the way they recruit, retain, and invest in IT workers.

The mix of knowledge and skills required can vary significantly from one IT job to another, in terms of the specific technical skills needed, industry knowledge and experience, and other qualifications in areas such as project management, communications, and organizational skills. Thus IT workers qualified for one job may not qualify for another.

Certain technical skills may be in high demand or "hot," or be new skills-such as today's Java programmers, and computer security and e-commerce specialists-with employers having difficulty recruiting and retaining people with those skills. Also, IT is changing rapidly, which causes companies to frequently need different skill sets.

Today's IT labour market appears to be tighter at the high-end, with the competition for talent especially intense for workers with specific "hot" skill sets, often in combination with appropriate experience. Those with hot skills are seeing fast rising salaries and commanding a salary premium above those whose skills are in less demand, more dated, or more generic. Those with multiple hot skills and relevant industry experience are seeing especially fast rising compensation.

Many employers, especially those for whom IT is their core business, demand job candidates with exact skill fit, requiring no additional training. Faced with short product life cycles, customer deadlines, and competitive pressures that leave no time to spare, such employers want workers with the right skills and experience who can be productive right away.

With numerous combinations of technical skill sets and fields of experience, part of the IT labour market appears to operate as a series of niches requiring specialized, higher skill sets. Even if a company receives many resumes from which to choose to fill its job, the right candidate, with the right skills and experience may not be in the resume mix.

For example, one IT company had hired 1,000 engineers after receiving 22,000 resumes, or a selection rate of about 4 percent. A technical recruiter lamented that they had gotten 300 applicants at an IT job fair, yet did not find anyone qualified for the job for which they were recruiting.

As time has become an increasingly important factor of competitiveness for many employers of IT workers, the time available to retrain existing employees or train new employees in the skills needed for new projects has diminished. In its recent report on the supply of IT workers, the Computing Research Association (CRA) states that "companies are forced by short product life and short product development cycles to hire new employees or reassign existing workers in ways that do not require a lot of break-in training before they can be productive."

In this environment, many companies have concluded that they cannot afford the time penalty and the uncertainty associated with "making" the employees they need (through training or retraining). Many employers are, instead, pursuing a "buy" strategy, seeking the exact skills and experience they need for a particular project and paying a premium for that.

The CRA report acknowledges the need for looking outside the company to find the required technical skills, saying that the business environment "makes it difficult to retrain an existing employee for a significantly different job. Thus employers are sometimes forced, by competitive pressures, to lay off workers of one type and hire workers of another type. Or they may refuse to hire anyone who does not already possess the needed skills.

These employer practices receive harsh criticism at times from labour unions and some government officials, but to some degree this is a rational and perhaps necessary reaction to the realities of the marketplace. There is, of course, a time risk associated with seeking to recruit and hire the candidate with the exact skills and experience, especially in a tight labour market. Outside hires also lack important, company-specific knowledge, and may be less committed and loyal to the employer.

Companies also pursue buy decisions for other reasons. First, in fast-growth IT companies, often every core IT worker is deployed on current projects leaving none available for retraining. Second, in a dynamic, fast paced, highly competitive environment such as IT, the technology paths are often uncertain, making it very difficult to project future skill needs.

Though the "buy" strategy generally requires paying a premium for the requisite skills, companies are able to reduce the risks associated with the uncertainty about their future skill needs, while reducing or even eliminating the cost of training. At the same time, employers can be reasonably assured that new hires are able to hit the ground running.

As with other investments, companies generally invest in training because of the returns it brings through improved performance. However, the current IT business environment and its effect on the highly-skilled IT labour market increase the risk of training investments and reduce the likelihood of capturing an acceptable return on the investment.

The tight IT labour market-a function of both the rapid demand for core IT workers, generally, and the need to fill specific niches- has created an environment in which many companies seek to find the people they need by luring talented IT workers away from their current employers using a variety of mechanisms. These inducements encourage job-hopping among IT employees, creating another major disincentive for companies to train or retrain workers. Companies that invest in the training of employees to upgrade their IT skills may create an attractive target for poaching by other companies, putting at risk both the employees and the companies' training investment.

Employers who apply information technologies in support of their core businesses in other fields often have more stable employment environments and longer IT life cycles and, thus, have greater ability to "make" their skill base by investing in training. However, since they share the same labour pool with firms whose core business is IT, they are buffeted by the actions of others. They, too, risk poaching of their employees and may also have to pay premiums to acquire and retain certain IT skills, especially the ones most in demand.

In some companies, training and education are offered as benefits to employees (to attract or retain them) who understand they must keep their skills current if they are to remain viable in the IT labour market.

As many companies have turned to a buy strategy to gain the critical skills they need, they have undertaken a wide range of strategies to attract and retain workers-from the commonplace to the extraordinary. Unlike so many occupations in which job stability is a hallmark of success, the business environment in IT has created a labour market in which job hopping serves as a means to gain the vital technical skills needed for career opportunities. Acquiring new skills allows them to move within the entire IT work community for opportunities, rather than solely within a particular company.

The impact can be seen in how quickly IT workers move from one employer to the next, and how intensely they are recruited. The average job length is four years for IT staffers and five years for IT managers. More than two-thirds of IT professionals have been contacted by a headhunter in the past year-an average of three times each in just the past six months. The recruitment is even more intense for the hot skills. For example, three out of four staff members, and nine out of ten managers in data mining report being contacted by recruiters in the past year. And in super hot Silicon Valley, the average length of stay at a single job is 18 months, according to Digital Nation.

IT workers ranked "challenge of their job, responsibility" and "job atmosphere" ahead of "base pay" as what mattered the most to them about their jobs. Quality of working life issues, job stability, and having the opportunities to gain critical skills through job assignments dominated the responses. Still, monetary compensation ranks high among the tools used by companies to recruit and retain employees. Among the more common tools employed: signing/performance bonuses, salary premiums for hot skills, stock options, referral fees, royalty fees, child care, flexible hours, telecommuting, training and education, tuition reimbursement, time off/extra vacation time, gyms and exercise facilities.

A sutdy said about the reported high rates of vacancies in IT companies and other IT-worker intensive organizations. Vacancies are a normal part of business, the result of turnover and the time it takes to fill a job. In industries and occupations that are experiencing sustained, rapid growth, and relatively high rates of labour mobility, vacancies should not be surprising. If it takes between 35-70 days to fill different positions, and the company is experiencing rapid growth, and if a specialized type of employee is being sought, vacancies are to be expected. A tight labour market compounds the challenge.

Not all employers of IT workers enjoy a well-oiled and nimble human resources department, with sophisticated and creative recruitment methods, and a streamlined hiring process. Many small companies do not have human resource departments at all, and hiring functions may be performed by technical professionals who have little or no knowledge and experience in human resources practices.

Many companies contract with recruiting firms to fill their jobs, but many of these recruiters lack the technical knowledge to do much more than follow the technical specification the hiring firm provides.

Making the labour markets work better-in terms of effectively identifying the critically needed skills, rapid identification of potential candidates, and streamlining the internal hiring process-could help reduce the time it takes to staff operations and reduce vacancy rates. Finally, it should be noted that recruitment of skilled IT workers is not limited to companies. Many states see a highly-skilled IT work force as a major tool to encourage economic development.

The loss of skilled IT workers to others is also a concern of economic development officials. For example, the Hudson Valley, New York area is losing IT professionals to contract work for employers in other areas. It was noted at the Hudson Valley town meeting that the northern New Jersey market pays IT professionals 10 percent more and the New York City market pays 25 percent more.

Some people see information technology as a tool to keep the residents from moving to other states for job opportunities. U.S. Senator Kent Conrad expressed his concern about the isolation of small towns around the country stating, "There is a need to keep the best and brightest in North Dakota. This is the biggest concern of parents. IT is an opportunity to provide these jobs."

Some employers of IT workers are looking to foreign workers to meet their skill needs. Whether or not to allow larger numbers of skilled foreign workers to enter the country in order to meet employers' demands for new IT workers is a contentious issue.

The allowable number of H-1B visas, which allow skilled foreign workers to work in the United States for up to six years. Although H-1B visas are "non-immigrant" visas, they are often used as a stepping stone to permanent immigration. In some cases, foreign students enter the United States on a student visa, receive an H-1B visa after graduation, and then seek permanent employment-based immigration.

Nearly half of the people who become permanent employment-based immigrants convert from H-visa non-immigrant status. Prior to 1998, the number of H-1B visas had been capped at 65,000 workers per year. The IT industry has increasingly used H-1B visas. In 1995, only about a quarter of temporary skilled foreign workers were in IT-related fields; by 1997 about half were in IT fields. Largely due to the increased use by the IT industry, the H-1B cap was reached for the first time in August 1997.

The IT industry led a major effort to increase the H-1B visa cap. IT industry needs more skilled foreign workers to help meet skill shortages, an inability to find workers has limited growth in the IT industry and other parts of the economy that need IT workers, the IT industry needs an international work force to meet the needs of international markets, the IT industry needs to be able to attract the best and brightest workers from around the world, and the alternative to bringing foreign workers to the United States is to move work overseas.

H-1B workers cause wages in IT occupations to be lower than they would otherwise be, reducing the incentive for U.S. residents to enter, or stay in, these occupations; thus immigration can create a self-perpetuating demand for more immigration, and the H-1B program has been abused by firms, which have brought in foreign workers to work at less than the prevailing U.S. wages.

In late 1998, the Congress and the White House agreed to compromise legislation that would temporarily increase the H-1B cap and also attempt to curb abuses in the program. The law also provides for the collection of a $500 fee for each H-1B application in order to create a fund for low-income student scholarships and training programs.

The National Science Foundation will administer the newly established Computer Science, Engineering and Mathematics Scholarship Program, providing student scholarships to enable the achievement of higher education degrees in IT-related disciplines. The law also includes new provisions intended to prevent abuses of the program. For example, H-1B dependent employers must attest that they are not laying off U.S. workers for similar jobs and that they have made significant efforts to recruit U.S. workers.

In the midst of a tight labour market, there are numerous anecdotes of middle-age technical workers having difficulty finding IT jobs. Data from the National Science Foundation indicate, however, that the employment profile for computer and math scientists closely parallels that of the overall science and engineering work force.

The IT industry is young and fast growing compared to many other industries and, thus, has a younger worker demographic profile which may contribute to the perception that it is not a hospitable environment for mid-career workers. The difficulties faced by mid-career technical workers have been widely reported in IT magazines 26 and this issue was raised at several of the town meetings. There are a number of reasons mid-career technical workers may face barriers in the IT labour market. The IT industry is populated by many younger workers. Approximately 75 percent of computer systems analysts and scientists, and nearly 80 percent of computer programmers are under the age of 45.

Many managers in the IT industry are in their 20s and 30s, and may be uncomfortable hiring or managing older and more experienced workers. A Network World survey of 200 readers with some hiring responsibility showed that younger network managers are less likely to hire older workers than younger workers. Almost half of respondents 20 to 30 years of age had never hired a person over the age of 40.

Many IT companies have operating modes that require long and intense work hours, and mid-career workers, for example those with family obligations, may be assumed to be unwilling to work these long hours. Some employers may hold the perception that mid-career workers expect higher pay for doing the same work that younger workers do. There is a perception that mid-career workers may not be current with the latest skills, may not be as flexible in doing different kinds of work, and may be less innovative, compared to younger workers. Some employers may have concerns that mid-career workers will cost the company more in insurance premiums, due to age and higher likelihood of having covered family members. On the other hand, many mid-career workers have kept up with the latest skills (or could easily obtain them), are innovative, and are willing to work long hours for market pay rates. Many mid-career workers have a breadth of experience that could benefit many young IT companies.

Some mid-career unemployed and underemployed engineers may find difficulty in obtaining employment because they expect higher wages or, while they may be highly-skilled and experienced, they may not have the specific technical skills that employers want. On the other hand, it is likely that some mid-career engineers who have appropriate skills and are willing to work at market wages are overlooked because of the perception-not the reality-that older workers cannot do the job.

It should also be noted that many of the IT jobs that are the hardest to fill are those in non-IT industries, in government, and in schools. Many of these types of organizations do not seem to have the same youth-oriented culture that characterizes many entrepreneurial software companies, and would welcome mid-career technical workers.

The 1998 American Competitiveness and Workforce Improvement Act, which increased the number of skilled non-immigrant foreign workers allowed to work in the United States, requires the National Science Foundation to contract with the National Academy of Sciences to conduct a study assessing the status of older workers in the IT field, including a consideration of the existence and extent of age discrimination in the IT work place. Many mid-career workers have a breadth of experience that could benefit many young IT companies.

In an uncertain business environment, faced with rapid technological change, many employers seek flexible means of staffing their projects. Employers use independent contractors or temporary workers employed by staffing companies as a mechanism to meet their need for IT workers in this dynamic environment.

In the case of contract workers, the workers are not considered to be employees and are responsible for paying their own payroll taxes and unemployment insurance. In the case of temporary workers, the staffing companies are responsible for their employees' wages and legally required payroll deductions, and may provide some benefits as well. Using either independent contractors or temporary workers has advantages for the employer. Employers can get the specific skills they need for a temporary project without hiring people that might need to be laid off later. Employers can also check out people on a trial basis before deciding whether or not to hire them. And companies do not have to pay for expensive benefit packages. Contract or temporary work can also be advantageous to some employees.

Independent contractors with skills in high demand can get paid at a higher rate than most employees, and some workers desire the greater flexibility and variety that can come from temporary or contract work. Temporary work may also let employees gain work experience that may make them more marketable. On the other hand, many employees who accept such arrangements may prefer to have permanent employment. The IT industry has been expanding its use of various types of temporary workers.

According to the National Association of Temporary and Staffing Services, total wages paid for assigned technical workers (a category that includes computer programmers, computer systems analysts, designers, drafters, editors, engineers, and illustrators) grew from $1.9 billion in 1991 to $4.7 billion in 1998. The increasing use of temporary workers has implications for the training of IT workers. When a company uses temporary or contract workers, it is generally purchasing skills for immediate use, and has little or no motivation for investing in training for that worker.

The incentive and responsibility for investing in training lies clearly with the individual worker, and, to some extent, with the temp agency. Temp agencies do invest in training. A 1998 survey by the National Association of Temporary and Staffing Services indicated that staffing firms expended $720 million for skills training in 1997, training 4.8 million individuals.

The Court of Appeals panel held that workers who are employed by a temp agency can also be considered common-law employees of the company that directs their work, and, as such, are entitled to participate in company benefits. This ruling will clearly make long-term employment of workers through temp agencies more expensive and less attractive to employers, and is likely to slow the use of independent contractors and temporary workers.

Outsourcing technical skills should allow the proliferation of technical consulting companies and staffing operations that can offer a wider range of opportunities to individuals. These operations should also be able to capture a greater return on investments in training because they can provide better career paths for technical employees, focus their retention practices, and provide internal mobility, thereby reducing turnover.

As information technology has emerged as a fundamental driver of global business and economic growth, there has been explosive growth in the demand for IT professionals. For more than 15 years, employment in the core IT occupations- computer scientists, computer engineers, systems analysts and computer programmers-has grown at an astounding pace. The growth rate for computer scientists and systems analysts has even accelerated in recent years.

In addition, employment in the computer and data processing services industry 83 -which employs the largest number of IT workers and has the highest proportion of IT workers in its work force-has experienced rapid employment and revenue growth.

Current Population Survey (CPS)-a joint project of the U.S. Departments of Commerce and Labour-shows the number of "computer systems analysts and scientists"-which includes computer engineers- and "computer programmers" soared from 719,000 to 2,084,000, an increase of 190 percent, more than six times faster than the overall U.S. job growth rate of 30.4 percent. Computer systems analysts and scientists have shown the most rapid growth, 433 percent, during this period. In contrast, computer programmers grew by 38.4 percent, much closer to the overall U.S.

For more than 15 years, employment in the core IT occupations- computer scientists, computer engineers, systems analysts and computer programmers-has grown at an astounding pace. The growth rate for computer scientists and systems analysts has even accelerated in recent years.

Though the overall job growth rate for the country has remained steady, the core IT occupations have grown at an even faster rate in recent years than for the 15-year period. Annual average growth for computer systems analysts and scientists was 11.8 percent and 2.2 percent for computer programmers during the 1983-1998 period, according to CPS data. Between 1995 and 1998, computer systems analysts and scientists recorded an annual average job growth rate of 16.4 percent, while computer programmers scored a 3.7 percent annual average job growth. Thus employment growth for IT occupations seems to be even stronger in recent years than in the past.

There are three primary Federal government data sources for information about the U.S. information technology work force-the Current Population Survey (CPS), the Industry-Occupation Employment Matrix (I-O Matrix), and the National Science Foundation's Scientist and Engineer Statistics (SESTAT) data system. Each source uses different methodologies for collecting data and arriving at estimates of the number of these workers. Despite the different methodologies, there is general agreement that the size of the core IT work force in 1998 was approximately 2.1 million.

Some computer engineers are captured in "Computer Systems Analysts and Scientists" occupation, though others are captured under the occupational title "Electrical and Electronic Engineers." Computer systems managers are captured under the occupation "Managers and Administrators," of which 498,000 are engineering, science and computer systems managers.

The three fastest growing occupations in the 1996-2006 employment projections are core IT occupations. Computer scientists, computer engineers, and systems analysts are each projected to more than double during this period.

Compared to the other core IT occupations, computer programming has a slow projected growth rate over the ten-year projection period. Several causes have been cited as underlying factors in this relatively slow growth:

— *Offshore contracting of code writing*: Once the higher-level work involved in software development-design, identification of key variables, specification of program modules for manipulation of data, and determination of operation flows and linkages needed to carry out a set of desired tests-has been accomplished, lower-level coding work can be broken into many separate pieces and the work distributed. Increasingly this type of work is being outsourced to low-cost regions of the world, such as Bangalore, India.

— *Automation of code writing*: Tools such as CASE (Computer Aided Software Engineering), a collection of automated tools and methods, assist software engineers and reduce the need for programmers by increasing productivity through automation of manual tasks, improving quality through automated checks and reminders, incorporating standardization, and by providing complete and accessible documentation. In effect, this transfers the programmer function to higher-level software engineers.

— *Advanced programming languages/Object-oriented programming*: The transition from a mainframe environment to a PC environment blurred the distinction between programmers and users. As prepackaged software has found its way onto desktops around the country, end-users have become increasingly capable of performing many of the functions that previously resided in the sole domain of programmers.

Employers pursuing more bang for their salary buck are seeking employees from other IT or IT-related specialties-such as computer scientists, electrical engineers, and math majors-who also have strong programming skills. While they may not carry the title "programmer," programming is an essential, often core, part of their responsibilities.

In the IT core occupations, in particular, past BLS projections often have been on the low side, often significantly underestimating their growth. For example, in their 1994 to 2005 projections, BLS projected the number of new core IT workers needed for new jobs and to replace those exiting the profession to average approximately 95,000 a year. In their next round of projections, that average grew to approximately 138,000 a year-an increase of 45 percent, even though the 1996-2006 projections include nine of the years included in the previous projections.

BLS's projected annual average growth rate for core IT occupations between 1996 and 2006 is slightly lower than the actual growth rate in the preceding decade, despite the economy's growing reliance on information technology.

In US, although Current Population Survey (CPS) data are not directly comparable to OES-based data, CPS data show tremendous growth in IT occupations since 1996. According to CPS data, the increase in computer systems analysts and scientists/ computer programmers during the first two years of the projection period exceeded the average pace anticipated for the core IT occupations in the 1996-2006 projections by more than 50 percent. Viewed in terms of growth rates, CPS data indicate these occupations grew at a substantially higher annual average growth rate than BLS projected for core IT workers during the 1996-2006 period.

The service sector, in general, and the computer and data processing services (CDPS) industry, in particular, will lead growth in the core IT occupations according to BLS projections. The service sector 38 is expected to account for the lion's share of growth in the core IT occupations during the 1996-2006 period. By 2006, the service sector is projected to increase its employment of computer systems analysts, scientists, and engineers by 177 percent and computer programmers by 47 percent.

In contrast, the manufacturing sector is projected to experience comparatively slower growth in the number of computer scientists, computer engineers and systems analysts (approximately 44 percent), and a 20 percent decrease in the number of computer programmers.

IT occupational growth in the service sector will be led by the CDPS industry, according to BLS projections. CDPS is, by far, the largest employer of core IT workers. In all, the CDPS industry is projected to account for 55.8 percent of the total employment growth in IT occupations between 1996 and 2006. The CDPS industry also has the highest IT worker intensity of any industry. In 1996, more than one-in-three CDPS workers were in the core IT occupations, by 2006 that ratio is projected to grow to more than two-in-five.

IT worker intensity-defined as the percentage of an industry's work force composed of core IT occupations-provides a guide to which industries are most reliant on these workers and, by extension, which might be affected most by tight IT labour markets.

When IT worker intensity and size of the IT work force are taken together, a picture emerges as to which industries' competitive performance would be most adversely affected by difficulties in hiring highly skilled IT workers. The computer and data processing services industry stands out starkly as an industry with much at stake in the supply of IT workers. But not only is the CDPS industry affected by the supply of IT workers, the unique characteristics of the industry and its work environment significantly affect the national pool of IT workers from which all industries must draw.

The core IT work force has a much different demographic and educational composition than the civilian labour force as a whole. In particular, core IT workers have a much higher level of educational attainment, a higher proportion of male workers and are more likely to be employed in the service sector; the finance, insurance, and real estate industries; and manufacturing.

Most characteristically, core IT workers get their education from four-year colleges; however, there are a wide range of other education and training grounds for IT workers generally, including: two-year associate degree-granting community colleges, which provide grounding in applications as well as basic theory, and vocational technical education programs. Most jobs in the core IT occupations, however, require a four-year degree or equivalent skills.

There are approximately one million college graduates whose education has included significant preparation for IT work, most of them holding bachelor's level degrees or higher. Specifically, the analysis counts approximately 783,700 college graduates in the United States with bachelor's degrees or higher in information technology fields-computer and information sciences or computer engineering-through April 1997. It includes graduates with bachelor's degrees in electrical engineering that reported second majors or minors in computer science or related IT specialties. In addition, OTP estimates approximately 105,000 additional college graduates with IT degrees through June 1999.

The National Science Foundation's SESTAT database provides a window into the educational background of core IT workers who have a bachelor's degree or higher. An analysis of the recently released 1997 SESTAT data shows that 42 percent of the core IT work force with degrees has an IT degree, while another 4 percent completed an undergraduate minor or second major in computer science or computer engineering, for a total of 46 percent. An additional 40 percent hold a degree in another engineering, science, or mathematics discipline. The remaining degreed IT workers hold degrees in business and other disciplines.

Beyond its relationship with 1,900 commercial training companies, Microsoft is working with 1,000 academic institutions around the world to achieve this extensive training capacity. While approximately 900 of these academic institutions are located in the United States, Microsoft expects that the fastest growth in education partnerships in 1999 will be outside the United States.

Some study suggest that the combination of fast employment growth, rising compensation and low unemployment rates may signal a tight labour market. In contrast to the strong quantitative data showing the rapid growth of the core IT occupations, evidence of strong rising compensation for these occupations is mixed. While it seems clear, from both government and non-government data, that the compensation level for IT professionals is both high and rising, the question remains whether rising compensation is unique to these occupations and the result of a tight labour market, or whether it is part of a more general trend generated by a very prosperous U.S. economy.

Government experts suggest that the variance between the government and private wage surveys is generally the result of various factors including sample size and survey methodology (design of samples, use of well-constructed and tested questions, methods of obtaining higher rates of sample responses), concluding that the government data is likely to be significantly more accurate. Though there are mixed signals on compensation for the core IT occupations generally, analysis by the Commerce Department's Office of Technology Policy indicates a consensus in several areas:

— *IT worker salaries are high and rising*: Those with hot skills are seeing fast rising salaries and are commanding a salary premium above those whose skills are less hot, more dated or more generic. Those with combinations of multiple hot skills and relevant industry experience are seeing especially fast rising compensation.

— *Starting salaries are rising fast*: Food counter workers have benefited from a 6.4 percent average annual salary increase, driven in part by an increase in the minimum wage from $4.25 per hour to $5.15 per hour during this time period. The increase in the minimum wage also contributed to the overall work force's 3.0 percent average annual salary increase.

Computer systems analysts' and scientists' salary increase during this period was equal to that of the overall work force, but higher than professional specialty occupations as a whole, and lawyers, physicians, and teachers in particular. Computer programmers enjoyed an even greater increase in salary during this period, posting an average annual salary increase of 4.3 percent, despite the fact that demand for computer programmers has been, and is projected to be, much slower than for other core IT occupations.

However, the higher average annual salary increases for computer programmers are supportive of the Office of Technology Policy's conclusion that skills in the hot programming areas are in high demand and being rewarded accordingly. 1997 National Occupational

Employment and Wage Estimates, OES data does not allow for an analysis of wage trends because the OES survey only began collecting wage data in 1996. However, the information from OES provides a good snapshot of employment and wages for the core IT occupations.

The Institute of Electrical and Electronics Engineers-USA (IEEE-USA) 1999 Salary and Fringe Benefits Survey. IEEE-USA reports in its 1999 Salary and Fringe Benefits Survey that the purchasing power of its members has reached an all-time high, surpassing the previous high recorded in its previous biennial survey.

In particular, IEEE-USA's 1999 Salary and Fringe Benefits Survey finds that the primary income-base salaries, net earnings from self-employment, and commissions and bonuses-of IEEE members working full-time in their areas of professional competence rose 13.9 percent to $82,000 between 1997 and 1999, compared to a 3.3 percent increase in the Consumer Price Index in urban areas for the same period.

New entrants into the core IT occupations have benefited from high increases in starting salary offers during the past three years, according to the National Association of Colleges and Employers. NACE has collected data for many years on starting salary offers for bachelor's degree holders across a wide range of occupations, including three of the core IT occupations-computer scientists, computer engineers, and computer programmers.

NACE data provide a window into the long and short-term behaviour of starting salary offers. OTP analyzed starting salary offers for the IT professions and several other professional specialties-accounting (private), financial/treasury analysis, design and construction engineering, manufacturing and industrial engineering, and research and development-to identify longer term and more recent trends.

Compared to other professions, IT workers have enjoyed faster growth in average annual starting salary offers during both the short and longer term. In contrast, the national unemployment rate-which reached a 42 year low of 4.2 percent in March 1999-is still three times as high as the unemployment rate of the core IT occupations.

State and Regional Perspective on Supply, Demand and Salaries supply and demand conditions for different types of workers in each region, or whether they are due to differences in the kind of work performed in occupational categories among the regions.

The National Science Foundation's SESTAT database provides regional salary information on core IT workers for those with degrees in computer and information sciences (regardless of their occupation), as well as for those employed as computer and information scientists. The Pacific region has the highest median salary in both categories, $55,000 for those employed as computer and information scientists, $53,000 for those with degrees in computer and information sciences. The United States needs to do a better job at encouraging and preparing young people to enter technical education and careers.

Town meeting participants identified the image of the technical professional as an important factor in shaping young people's attitudes about careers in science and technology. Many people have a distorted, negative image of IT workers, scientists and engineers, perceiving them as highly intelligent, but socially inept or absent-minded "geeks" or "nerds." The media play an influential role in shaping these public perceptions.

Women and minorities are infrequently portrayed in technical roles; typically, scientists and technologists are portrayed by white males. The print media also perpetuate such images. Many children and adults embrace these stereotypical images, and have limited exposure to the wide variety of careers and people in the IT, science and engineering fields. In preparation for the IT Work Force Convocation, a group of students from Missouri in the sixth and ninth grades was asked to draw a picture of an IT worker. Prevalent among the images were bow ties and bald heads, pocket protectors, pants that were too short, and nearly all of the IT workers portrayed wore glasses. Of the 160 pictures of IT workers submitted by the students, only 16 of them portrayed women.

Television offers many examples of real life scientists and engineers. The PBS program NOVA features technical professionals from a wide range of disciplines. Natural scientists are frequently featured in programs about nature and animals. Today, many local television weather forecasters are meteorologists and offer snippets of information about meteorological science. Still, participants in the national dialogue suggested that efforts are needed to improve the image of the technical professions.

This would include explaining the important contributions science and technology make to our economy and quality of life. Identifying and highlighting role models could help young people and their parents learn that technical workers are normal people who perform a wide range of interesting and exciting jobs in science and technology. Participants also suggested that industry and government open a dialogue with the entertainment industry, as well as the national and local media to encourage these influential shapers of image to improve their depiction of technical professionals, and expand and improve the quality of national and local science and technology reporting.

Government and the private sector should work together to support and develop national information and advertising campaigns to improve the image of the technical professions, and communicate the portfolio of skills needed to thrive in the new economy. Information products in a variety of print, video, and digital media should be tailored to reach parents, students, teachers, and guidance counsellors. Messages should focus on the vital role science and technology play in the economy and our quality of life.

Materials could explain that most jobs in the future will require some technical skills, and that science, technology and IT work involves a broad array of exciting careers. The campaign could identify and highlight "normal" role models, including women and minorities, what they do, and their contributions to society.

Industry and government-at the Federal, state, and local levels-should establish a dialogue with those who heavily influence perceptions about people who make and use science and technology. At the national level, industry and government could establish a dialogue with the entertainment industry and the press to improve the image of technical professionals and the portrayal of their work in television, movies, and the printed media. State and local government officials could join regional businesses in establishing a dialogue with local media to encourage a more positive portrayal of technical workers, and expanded coverage of the community's science and technology activities and those who participate in them.

Technology-intensive companies and organizations could invite members of the community in which they reside to visit and see how such organizations work, how they use technology, their working environments, and their contributions to the economy and quality of life. The Federal government could expand its efforts to promote Federal scientists and engineers as role models, and publicize the exciting diversity and value of their work.

Prepearing Students for IT Carrers

For lack of knowledge and interest in such careers, students may fail to take the appropriate courses in math and science needed to help prepare them for a technology-intensive workplace in a rapidly changing economy. Young people form opinions about careers before they graduate from high school, and middle school is seen as a key decision-making point. Many students receive little information about the wide range of interesting and exciting careers in science and technology, the industries that develop and use science and technology, or the education and skills needed to pursue technical jobs. In recent testimony before the Senate Judiciary Committee, an academic expert said, "Currently, few students in high school are aware of what it is that computer scientists do, what academic skills are required, the challenges and activities on the job, and what the economic rewards are. "

Parents play one of the most important roles in influencing children's career choices. For example, a group of students in the third, sixth, ninth, and twelfth grades was asked: What or who has influenced your decision about what you want to do or be when you enter the work force. At every grade level, parents were identified as exerting the most influence over career choices. Yet, parents often lack information that would enable them to encourage their children to choose a career in science and technology.

Teachers and school counsellors are providers of career information, but may also lack knowledge about science and technology-based industries. A recent Harris Poll commissioned by the American Association of Engineering Societies confirmed a lack of public awareness of the technical professions. In the survey, 61 percent of Americans felt that they were not very well or not at all informed about engineering and engineers.

Due to a lack of career information and encouragement, and few positive role models, many students at an early age dismiss the notion of or never develop an interest in a science or technology career. Information on Careers and Industry. Company visits for middle school students were viewed as a good way to introduce them to technical careers and high-technology work settings. Maryland high-tech organizations sponsored a technology career fair to bring middle school students and their parents together with companies to discuss the kinds of careers that are available. An Arizona industry representative suggested that kiosks be placed in libraries which provide information about a region's industry clusters and the jobs in those clusters, so students and parents can become familiar with job titles and content.

Career planning tools include self assessment exercises, and other general career planning and management information and tools. Each Cornerstone Partner Society has developed a career web site with information on each field and current career options. The 3M Foundation and Minnesota State Colleges and Universities sponsored the development of the Technical Careers Tool Kit. The tool kit provides educational and motivational materials to promote awareness of career opportunities in technical fields and the importance of two-year post-secondary technical and career education.

The kit is now being marketed to employers and educators nationwide and is designed to help them work together to create cooperative programs that provide students with exposure to today's work-places and technologies. The kit contains video presentations and background materials. The videos show successful School-To-Work activities in action, including workplace visits, internship programs, and high-tech professionals in the classroom. The videos highlight successful school and business partnerships and demonstrate how such activities can trigger enthusiasm among employees.

TECH (Technical Teams Encouraging Career Horizons) is one of 3M's Science Encouragement Programs. Teams of women and men scientists visit junior and senior high schools to inform students-especially girls and minorities-of career opportunities in science and engineering, and of the need to maximize their career options by studying math and science in school. Each year up to 250 TECH volunteers reach 8,000-10,000 students. Most of the schools are in the St. Paul area, but TECH has recently expanded to involve the 3M Austin Centre in Texas and there are plans to set up TECH programs nationwide.

To make the route to high-technology careers more transparent, state and local governments, and educators could identify K-16 pathways to IT and other technical careers, highlighting career ladders, job market data, and skill requirements. Education and training opportunities could be identified or developed to help students move along these pathways that lead to careers. Businesses could sponsor/cooperate on work-focused IT, science, and engineering projects, at school or the company workplace, with projects focusing on the use of the computer. Schools could develop after-school and summer courses in IT, science, and technology, and encourage students to participate in the development and maintenance of school-based IT infrastructure. K-12 faculty and businesses could work together to create curriculum, and have technical professionals from local high-tech industries speak to students, or teach a class or short course.

The U.S. Department of Education makes a major investment in programs to strengthen math and science education, and to prepare Americans for technology-based careers. To improve math and science education, the Department focuses on improving teaching quality through teacher preparation and effective professional development, upgrading curricula by providing schools with good information and resources, providing learning support for students who need extra assistance, and building a research and evaluation base. The Department also is working to connect U.S. classrooms to the Internet, and ensure that all Americans will be technologically literate. Efforts involve helping ensure teachers are prepared to integrate technology into the curriculum, and use the new teaching and learning styles enabled by technology, as well as demonstrations of innovative uses of technology for education and training. The Department leads efforts to prepare students for high technology careers, for example through school to work programs, and to open the doors of college to more students through a range of financial mechanisms.

The growing use of computers on the job and the high growth in computer-related occupations have made computer skills an important component of most students' educational portfolio.

In many industries, the number of workers who use a computer at their job now ranges from 50 to 85 percent. IT is being widely deployed in the U.S. K-12 educational system. Today, there are about six students for each computer in K-12 schools, though student access varies.

Efforts are springing up to help build IT infrastructure in the K-12 education system. For example, U.S. Tech Corps is a national non-profit organization dedicated to improving K-12 education at the grassroots level through the effective integration of technology into the learning environment. TECH CORPS recruits, places, and supports volunteers from the technology community who advise and assist schools in the introduction and integration of new technologies into the educational system.

A student's own interest and skills are influential in career choice, and computer use in K-12 provides early exposure to IT and the opportunity for skill development. The development of students' computer skills is increasingly integrated into instruction, for example studying chemistry using spreadsheets and simulations.

According to the National Assessment of Education Progress, 54 percent of U.S. fourth grade math teachers use computers for math/learning games, and 27 percent of eighth grade math teachers use computers for simulations and applications. In the assessment, more Computer use in K-12 provides early exposure to IT and the opportunity for skill development.

There are a growing number of programs aimed at developing students' information technology skills. For example, in 1996, local community leaders in Omaha, Nebraska recognized that many young people were not obtaining the academic and cultural skills required to compete in the metro area's growing technical labour market. At the same time, local IT companies reported increasing difficulty in recruiting for many high skilled, high wage positions.

A number of efforts are designed to help develop teachers' computer skills. The International Technology Education Association (ITEA) is the professional organization of technology teachers which strengthens the profession through leadership, professional development, membership services, publications, and classroom activities.

ITEA conducts various professional development programs:

— The Technology Teacher, Technology and Children, The Journal of Technology Education, TTTe, Curriculum Brief, and a variety of other publications and videos provide teaching directions, instructional ideas and networking opportunities.

— Ten primary committees coordinate all aspects of technology education and sponsor dozens of meetings, conferences and exhibits each year.

— An active honours and awards program recognizes outstanding teachers and programs (K-12) from states, provinces and countries that are affiliated with the Association. ITEA also presents award certificates and supports other programs which recognize outstanding efforts in the technology teaching profession.

— A public policy program provides information to government agencies, associations and other special interest groups concerning technology education. The Association strives to provide an understanding of the importance of technology education to the future growth and wellbeing of all nations.

Steps to Improve Schools' Capacity for IT Skills Development:

— Expand technical education/IT infrastructure in schools:

— Businesses could donate IT equipment, software, and IT-related services to schools and keep them up to date.

— Strengthen teacher training in IT:

— Create and implement IT curricula in schools of education.

— School systems could reward liberal arts teachers who integrate IT into curriculum, as well as reward teachers who obtain IT certifications and remain in teaching.

— Businesses could work with schools to develop "teaching the teacher" programs in which high-technology industry's technical staff conduct training workshops for teachers.

Challenges in Preparing Post-Secondary Students for the Information Technology Work Force

There are number of challenges to better prepare college students for the high-tech work force, including: increasing student opportunities for relevant technical education and skills development, increasing faculty exposure to high-tech industry, ensuring that curricula are up-to-date and impart the knowledge and skills employers need, and ensuring adequate IT education and training infrastructure.

Students need greater knowledge of the work environments to which they will move after graduation. This would increase their understanding of the skills needed to play a productive role in the high-tech workplace, and help illustrate the relevancy of what they learn in the classroom.

A number of efforts to increase student exposure to the world of work were discussed. A large high-tech company in Washington state described an effort in which faculty would teach theory during the class and then software engineering students went to the company to work on a real project-with real software engineers and a real technical manager-applying what they learned in class.

For example, In US, the University of Maryland formed a partnership with a private IT school which created an intensive five-week training program to teach COBOL to students of all ages to address the year 2000 problem.

Businesses are recruited to sponsor students' training and to hire them upon completion of the program. Participating businesses also contribute to a scholarship fund. After a stint at the sponsor company, a student can draw from the scholarship fund to pay for up to four years of tuition toward a bachelor's degree.

There is concern that fewer college students will pursue graduate level IT studies, opting instead for lucrative job opportunities as IT workers in industry. The "seed corn" problem could result in insufficient numbers of faculty to train the next generation of students, as well as fewer U.S. master's and Ph.D. graduates for advanced, cutting edge IT work.

There are different steps to increase student Opportunities:

— *Expand student opportunities for technical education, training, and experience*: Businesses could provide funds for science and technology scholarships for high school students, college students, or current workers who commit to working for a contributing company or in states and regions where the private sector's need for IT workers is growing.

— *The business and education communities should develop more hands-on work-study opportunities*: The Federal government could work with community colleges and computer science/engineering schools, local business communities, and others to establish an IT/e-commerce extension service in which students studying IT assist small and medium-sized firms with IT planning, implementation and problem solving.

— Barriers (i.e., recognizing class credits) to matriculating from two-year IT programs at community colleges to four-year IT programs at universities should be reduced.

The Global Wireless Education Consortium (GWEC) was established in 1997 to increase the quality and quantity of technicians, engineers, and IT specialists to meet the demands of an expanding wireless communications industry. Industry members work with colleges and university partners to develop up-to-date wireless technology curriculum. GWEC provides its members with industry/educator developed wireless curriculum packages for adaptation by two-year, four-year, or Master's level academic programs.

GWEC industry members also offer students pursuing wireless education in GWEC partnership schools the opportunity to compete for paid intern-ships and co-ops with GWEC member companies in the Practical Work Experience Program (PWE). The PWE program is developed by schools and industry members to enhance the wireless education of students pursuing computer science, engineering or technician related fields of study. Faculty attendance at industry sponsored training courses and training materials are also provided to member schools without cost. One hundred participants attended a faculty workshop held in the summer of 1998, and the number of participants is expected to double at the 1999 summer workshop.

The National Science Foundation is playing a leadership role in strengthening curriculum for technical skills development at the Nation's community colleges. The Advanced Technological Education (ATE) program promotes improvement in technician education delivered at the undergraduate and secondary school levels. Focused on both national and regional levels, it provides funding to support curriculum development and program improvement for technicians being educated for the high performance workplace of advanced technologies. Curriculum development encompasses the design and implementation of new curricula, courses, laboratories, and instructional materials. Students enrolled in ATE programs at two-year colleges typically earn an associate degree in a science or technology discipline qualifying them for employment or transfer to a four-year institution. Program improvement encompasses faculty and teacher development, student academic support, and formal cooperative arrangements among institutions and other partners, such as industrial internships and cooperative experiences.

One of the ATE Centres of Excellence is the Northwest Centre for Emerging Technologies (NWCET) in Washington state. NWCET has developed a set of skill standards for eight career clusters in information technology. Key in the retraining of incumbent workers is NWCET's participation in Washington State's Worker Retraining Program, a program that provides financial aid to those who have been laid off from their jobs which allows them to return to school to obtain marketable skills.

The National Science Foundation is playing a leadership role in strengthening curriculum for technical skills development at the Nation's community colleges. The Advanced Technological Education Program promotes improvement in technician education delivered at the undergraduate and secondary school levels.

Each year, NWCET helps to provide retraining to hundreds of individuals who continue on to successful careers in the IT industry. While industry needs the skills often produced in short-term intensive skills training programs, such programs may not provide enough emphasis on the underlying knowledge and problem-solving needed for a rapidly changing business and technological environment. If workers do not possess the underlying knowledge and skills, their specific technical skills will become outdated in a few years.

A growing number and wide variety of programs have been established to upgrade the skills of the current IT work force. These include internal company training programs, training programs provided by technology vendors, private training schools, community college and university-based programs, Federal and state programs, and others. Many of these programs focus on developing the skills of low to mid-level IT workers, and include certificate programs at community colleges in areas such as network technician and web design, as well as popular vendor certification programs, for example, those focused on Microsoft and Novell products. These programs provide a limited set of technical skills in a short duration, compared to the knowledge, skill development, and time commitment required for competency in high skill jobs such as computer scientists and computer engineers.

For highly skilled IT jobs-where job growth is the fastest, labour markets tightest, education and training pipeline the longest, and where employers are often exacting in the skills they need-many employers prefer to pay a premium to hire a worker who already fits a specific education and skill profile. Many employers want employees with experience, in addition to technical skills, making it difficult for workers who may acquire technical skills in demand, but lack experience in their application.

Since providing IT skills for the current work force requires educating for broad knowledge and skill, and training for specific technologies, educational providers need to examine ways to match the method of skill upgrading to the speed and depth of reskilling needed. IT workers also need information on technological trends, and the skill needs that will flow from them, so they can pursue options for keeping their skills relevant to the market place.

A representative of an IT professional society said "Internet-based learning networks offer a particularly effective, convenient, and potentially more affordable alternative to conventional classroom and laboratory-based instructional programs..." Some concern was raised about the ability to use Federal financial support for training from for-profit training providers.

To be eligible for certain kinds of Federal financial aid, including Pell grants and guaranteed student loans, an education and training provider must meet certain requirements, such as being accredited, being authorized to do business in the state where it offers education and training, having been in business for two years, having programs that result in a credential, and offering programs of some minimum length. These requirements follow provisions of the Higher Education Act, and exist in large part to help prevent fraud and abuse.

For-profit schools can and do meet these requirements, including some computer training programs that result in certificates. However, a substantial number of computer training programs are not currently eligible for Federal financial aid. They may not have been in business for two years, or they may not meet the instructional time requirements. Many schools have not tried to meet the standards, such as accreditation, required for Federal financial aid. In a hot area such as IT, schools that have enough students and are making ample money without access to financial aid may have little motivation to go through the steps required to qualify for the aid.

Some communities are implementing more comprehensive approaches to training workers, and linking them to potential employers. The Northern Virginia Regional Workforce Development Coordinating Centre acts as a regional information clearing-house for individuals seeking IT jobs and skills, as well as employers seeking assistance in finding qualified workers with critical IT skills. The centre works with employers to create education programs to produce qualified workers, as well as with potential employees to help them identify careers and training programs linked to current and future job openings in the IT field.

The web site provides a data base of technology training and education providers, a listing of links related to IT assessment and career development, listings of job vacancies, and information on financing IT training and education programs. As of May 1999, 1,109 students are receiving training at four regional colleges, 614 have completed IT training and 192 students have been placed in IT or IT-related positions. The Summer Technology Program which focuses on developing technology-related interest in middle school students in Northern Virginia had 230 student participants in 1998.

Specific skills include computer repair, computer-related design and drafting, and business machine repair. For dislocated workers who need new skills for jobs in demand, one-year retraining scholarships are provided through the JobLink program for individualized programs of education and training at colleges, technical colleges and training institutes. Between July 1997 and June 1998, the program filled 1,701 jobs with 1,144 employers.

Employers should establish and participate in consortia or collaborate in other ways to develop regional training infrastructure and provide worker training. This could be accomplished by businesses alone, or in partnership with the local and regional education community, and other stakeholders. The Federal government could provide matching funds to organize and facilitate cooperation among firms in developing these alliances, as well as participate in alliances as an employer in areas where IT workers are needed to fill government jobs.

To expand the size of the IT labour pool, there is growing interest in tapping nontraditional sources of labour, and training workers from these groups for IT jobs. A representative of an IT professional society suggested that the pool of workers available for IT jobs is broader and deeper than commonly thought. This includes college graduates with science and engineering degrees, college graduates with nontechnical degrees, downsized and older engineers, non-degreed technicians with the potential to increase their skills, and mid-career workers.

Microsoft is working to recruit and train those leaving the armed services, many who have acquired good technical skills during the course of their military training. The Microsoft Military IT Career Initiative-a partnership between Microsoft authorized training providers and career placement organizations-provides resources and guidance for those interested in pursuing a post-military career in IT. This includes: a skills assessment to determine what type of IT career a candidate might be suited for and what training would be needed, technical training programs, financial assistance, and job placement services.

There is also interest in moving highly-skilled, mid-career technical workers who have been displaced into the IT professions. For example, the Massachusetts Software Council Fellowship Program (SCFP) Inc. is a private non-profit corporation providing displaced, but highly skilled workers to the software industry through retraining and education. Initiated in 1993 under the sponsorship of the Massachusetts Software Council and the Commonwealth of Massachusetts, the SCFP provides a bridge for mature professionals who are making a transition from other technical industries to find careers in the software industry.

The integrated learning approach includes a five-month on-site company project experience and weekly seminars to keep the Fellows current on issues unique to the software industry. Classes start approximately every two months. More than 450 individuals have graduated from the program and have been placed in companies. Graduates earn a starting salary that is 93 percent of their previous wages and reach their previous salary or surpass it within a year's time. Positions into which graduates are placed include software engineers, quality engineers, customer support, marketing and sales, and technical documentation.

The underrepresentation of women and minorities in the professional IT work force stems partly from their underrepresentation in the technical education pipeline that leads to these jobs. Women leave high school about as well prepared in math and science as men. In computers, however, according to a report by the American Association of University Women's Educational Foundation, while 30 percent of high school boys take a computer science course, 25 percent of high school girls do.

Only 2 percent of high school girls take a computer applications course, compared to 6 percent of boys. While women earn more than half of all bachelor's degrees, they are less likely to earn degrees in science and engineering than men.

The science and engineering selection rate- those earning degrees in science and engineering as a percentage of the total bachelor's degrees awarded in all fields-is much lower for women, 29 percent, than for men, 41 percent. This suggests that increasing women's participation in the education pipeline that leads to many IT jobs may require efforts to get more college-bound women to choose science and engineering as a field of study, especially computer science and engineering disciplines.

There are many efforts underway to increase the awareness and interest of girls in science and technology careers. The Girl Scouts of the U.S.A. has a variety of programs to increase the interest of girls in science and technology by providing fun yet valuable hands-on learning experiences. Starting with the youngest program age level, girls can participate in projects and earn awards involving computers and technology. Older girls can interact with positive women role models who are active in science and technology careers. Some local Girl Scout councils sponsor career exploration and "Walk-A-Day in My Shoes" internships in which girls can find out what it is like to work in a professional career by spending time side-by-side with a mentor in a local company or organization. Local councils often collaborate and coordinate these type programs with the outreach activities of other organizations like the American Association of University Women.

Some of the underlying factors contributing to the underrepresentation of Black, Hispanic, and Native American students in the technical education pipeline are different than those for women. In 1996, large differences remained at all grade levels in the math and science achievement scores of Black and Hispanic students compared with Whites and Asians.

Native American students generally scored closer to the national average than did Black or Hispanic students. There are disparities in the types of math and science courses taken. Forty-four percent of Black, 46 percent of Hispanic, and 41 percent of Native American high school graduates have taken chemistry. Less than 20 percent of Hispanic and Black high school graduates have taken physics.

Racial and ethnic minority college freshmen declare science and engineering as a major at a rate equal to or greater than White college students. Black and Hispanic college students earn bachelor's degrees in science and engineering at rates roughly equal to White students but less than Asian students. There is some difference in the rate at which different ethnic and racial minorities earn engineering degrees, as a percent of all achelor's degrees awarded. Of racial and ethnic minorities who earn bachelor's degrees, Blacks and Hispanics earn them in computer science at rates equal to or greater than White or Native American students.

The High School Computer Competition is a mentoring program for minority high school students sponsored by local chapters of the National Black Data Processing Associates. There are more than 1,660 active student members. The goal of the program is to provide students with information about computer history, terminology, theory and programming and to provide hands-on experience in Visual Basic design, coding, documentation and testing. The program is targeted to students in the ninth through eleventh grades. Mentoring and educational assistance is provided to students at computer training camps during the winter and spring months of the school academic year.

In July 1998, the Office of Technology Policy launched a web site on the IT work force. Through the web site, which lists more than 200 resources, visitors can learn about high-tech work force initiatives across the country, tap valuable information resources, and network with other people who can offer insight and opportunities for collaboration.

For example, companies can explore ways that other companies have used to develop a skilled work force. Individuals can get information on scholarships, internships, training, and job banks. State and local government agencies can find out what other governments are doing to build a high-tech work force.

During the IT Work Force Convocation held in January 1998, the Education Department announced $6 million in grants to expand employer involvement in school-to-work programs. Among the awards since made has been a grant to a school-to-work project cooperatively sponsored by the National Alliance of Business, the Information Technology Association of America, and the

Education Development Centre, Inc. The goal of the project, the Techforce Initiative, is to highlight and expand IT employer involvement in School-to-Work or School-to-Careers activities nationwide by facilitating and supporting the efforts of individuals and organizations committed to building IT-focused School-to-Careers partnerships.

Major activities of the project include managing a Learning Network of Centres of Excellence for IT and School-to-Careers, organizing regional symposia for IT industry leaders and educators around the country, developing champions for IT School-to-Careers within the industry and educational communities, and widely marketing the great role and potential of IT School-to-Careers in addressing the IT workers/skills issue.

In Spring 1998, two Department of Labour supported information systems, America's Talent Bank and America's Job Bank, were integrated to create an $8 million nationwide network linking employers and job seekers into one Internet-based system. America's Job Bank's computerized network can now link state Employment Service offices to provide job seekers with the largest pool of active job opportunities available anywhere and nationwide exposure for their resumes. For employers it provides rapid, national exposure for job openings and an easily accessible pool of candidates.

In addition to the Internet, the job openings and resumes found in America's Job Bank are available on computer systems in public libraries, colleges and universities, high schools, shopping malls, transition offices on military bases worldwide and other places of public access. With the debut of Version 4.0 of America's Job Bank in April 1999, approximately eight to nine million individual job searches per month are being reported. In July 1998, the Labour Department awarded $7.7 million in grants for demonstration projects, in partnerships with employers and training providers, to train dislocated workers for technology-related occupations and industries. Awards were made to eleven organizations throughout the country, which will use the awards to retrain and prepare workers for careers requiring information technology and other advanced technology skills.

Under the terms of the American Competitiveness and Workforce Improvement Act of 1998, the Department of Labour has been authorized to support new innovative skill demonstration programs to solve labour shortages. Approximately half the revenues generated by the $500 fee that U.S. employers pay for each visa application under the H-1B nonimmigrant skilled worker program will be used to make awards to private industry councils, including regional skills alliances, to demonstrate cooperative industry/ community-based approaches to work force skills development.

The American Federal government is not only engaged in addressing the national IT work force challenge, but its own IT work force challenge as well. Viewed as a single employer, the Federal government is among the largest, if not the largest, employers of core IT workers. In 1996, the Federal government employed 67,857 core IT workers; by 2006, BLS projects the number to climb to 96,704. In addition, it is estimated that almost half the Federal IT work force may retire or otherwise leave the Federal service during this period.

Facing an expanding IT work force and the need to replace large numbers of its current work force, the

Federal government faces a daunting challenge in meeting its own IT work force needs. In 1998 the Federal Chief Information Officer's Council (CIO Council) established a multi-agency working group under its Education and Training Committee to help address this challenge by identifying ways to recruit, retain, and re-skill IT professionals, both technicians and managers. The Federal government's role as one of the largest employers of IT workers in the Nation means that its IT worker recruitment, retention, and re-skilling strategies can play a significant role in shaping the policies of other employers and, thus, indirectly contribute to meeting the national IT work force challenge.

2

The Internet Applications

The origin of the Internet in 1969 can be traced to cold war research. The United States Department of Defense Advanced Research Projects Agency (DARPA) set out to create a robust mechanism for computer-based communications. The original network was called ARPANET. Its objective was to construct a communications network able to withstand disruptions that would take place in the event of nuclear war.

The network was designed to allow multiple destination paths and to enable lower-level communications software to utilise alternative paths at will. In addition, the network offered a built-in mechanism for load balancing as well as the ability to bypass inactive circuits. Initially the Internet provided four basic network services: remote access (Telnet), file transfer (FTP), mail, and news. To promote education and research activities, access was generally free. The concept of a free public network, rather than a private, commercial one, was a clear part of the culture surrounding the network. Academics and students used the network to exchange information, to share software, and to discuss and debate issues. During the 1970s, other academic organisations around the world began to construct similar networks to ARPANET using the same software available in the United States. The military, in particular, realised that it would need to create a more secure network than the experimental ARPANET. The military wanted to maintain its own secure telecommunications system and also maintain links to the public networks. To make this possible, an *internetting* project was initiated to link together these networks; hence the name the Internet.

An inter-networking protocol was developed to work with the original transmission control protocol. This combination of transmission control and an Internet protocol, abbreviated to TCP/IP, is the dominant standard for computer-based communications today. The benefit of the TCP/IP standard is that it is supported by virtually every computer and software manufacturer in the world. Whether the intention is to publish material or services for world-wide access or to confine them to an organisational environment, a wide choice exists in hardware and software. By enabling a rich interconnection of computing and communication environments, TCP/IP offers a simple mechanism for communicating from both present and future information systems. By 1986, the National Science Foundation (NSF), an independent government agency established to promote science and engineering, had taken the lead role to put together a high speed backbone with a transmission rate of 1.5 Megabits per second (Mbps). It established a mechanism for regional and local commercial providers to offer access outside government and academic communities. Government subsidies helped to support the technology while demand grew. By 1989, backbone speeds were increased to 45Mbps.

In April 1995, NSF support for the Internet backbone was withdrawn and the Internet is now operating using commercial telecommunications providers. The level of traffic generated on the Internet has been growing rapidly. One of the most remarkable features of the Internet is the flat fee policy. In the flat-fee model, users are charged for the size of the 'pipe' or maximum rate of transmission rather than the actual amount of data transmitted. For modem users, of course, charges may be based on connect time. While allowing users open access to any site, the Internet enables world-wide communication without the overhead of a toll system similar to the long distance telephone network now in place. The institution of long distance charges on the Internet would be impractical, since it would be impossible for users to predict the charges resulting from a given connection.

The World Wide Web and the Internet are commonly considered to be synonymous. "In actuality, the Web is a collection of protocols and standards used to access the information on the Internet. On the other hand, the Internet is a physical medium used to transport the data. The World Wide Web defines and unifies the 'languages' used to retrieve data on the Internet." The World Wide Web was introduced in 1991. Developed at CERN, a particle physics research centre in Switzerland, the WWW is a distributed hypertext system that operates on a client/server model. Web servers store available documents as plain ASCII text. These documents contain markup tags and follow a standard known as Hypertext Markup Language (HTML). The hypertext feature of

HTML provides support for linkage instructions, or URLs (Universal Resource Locators), and allows direct access to pages on other Web servers. In contrast to earlier connection-based protocols, the Web permits a seamless connection to any Internet address. The client programs that run on the user's computer, providing access to the Web, are known as browsers. The Mosaic browser, written for graphical user interfaces, became the prototype for many imitators, such as Netscape Navigator. This software family supports a mixture of text, sound, graphics, images, video, animation and binary (executable) files.

The information provided to users by Web servers is not limited to static files. Several methods exist to forward requests to other server processes that are able to extract information from large database systems and format it for the user. This technique permits simple transaction processing and is the foundation for electronic commerce via the Internet. Software developers have been working tc advance the capabilities of the Web by creating special viewers. For example, there are special viewers for *Postscript* documents or for executing multimedia presentations. Viewers are usually given away free by software developers, in hopes of marketing their development system. For the past two years, Sun Microsystems has been promoting an Internet development system called *Java,* that permits platform-independent software to be executed directly via the Web. More elaborate software tools, such as three-dimensional virtual reality generators, require far more bandwidth than the standard text-based Web page. With enhanced display features, the Internet is an attractive marketing medium with a wide global audience.

If the Internet becomes an effective means to distribute information, the viability of the technology will be a public concern. Current issues of concern to developers of Web sites include changes to the telecommunications infrastructure, security, copyright protection, and universal access. The evolution if not resolution of these issues will impact the future development of available information services and will have an impact on the appropriateness of this medium for government. The condition of international telecommunications infrastructure is a critical determinant of the viability and utility of government Internet-based services. It has therefore been the principal focus of state attention in deliberations about the Internet. Deregulation has been seen as a key tool in many countries seeking to upgrade their telecommunications infrastructure. However, a balance of state and market will still be required in many circumstances, though with the state taking a more promotional than regulatory role.

The experience of the United States is indicative of the political difficulty in balancing state and market. Due to the prior interests of Vice President Al Gore, the Clinton Administration was instrumental in focusing public attention on the idea of a future National Information Superhighway in 1994. The administration produced a *Strategic Planning Document* that placed the highest priority on information technology because "any nation that dominates information technology will be a leading superpower of the 21st century." The administration sees an active role for government, citing the prior success of the state in the development of a High Performance Computing and Communications (HPCC) programme, sponsored legislatively by then Senator Gore in 1986. This program was responsible for the development of the high speed (45Mbps) Internet backbones that are in place today. However, the continuing federal budget deficit combined with opposition from congressional Republicans to government interference in the free market process has limited activities to existing research projects. Although these projects involve US$2bn-worth of federal research funds, this is a scant commitment when applied to a nationwide communications infrastructure. In 1996, the US Congress passed The Telecommunications Act. The act attempted to reduce government regulation and control, recognising that communications technologies had advanced to the point where the transmission medium no longer defines the type of service. The act did not provide government funding for constructing an infrastructure.

By placing responsibility for managing the Internet backbone with telecommunications companies, the commercialisation of the Internet is likely to accelerate and a period of change and competition is underway. Of course, that is not a guarantee that competition will continue to be the norm. There is a high cost associated with building independent data networks that reach every household. The consolidation of competitors may restore local monopolies that restrict the range of services available to the public. The large infrastructure investments increase the likelihood that competitors will merge until several massive communication service providers dominate the industry. The providers might be far different from traditional communications providers, as the experience of television indicates. While AT&T dominated the telephone industry before its break-up in 1984, it controlled only the transmission medium, not the content. Broadcast television stations have, in effect, controlled the use of their channel license and in so doing have concentrated on the lowest common denominator for programming. Cable operators, although forced to provide limited public access on their systems, have followed a similar path and while many systems routinely advertise more that 100 channel capability, a large percentage of these channels are dedicated to pay per view and premium entertainment services.

The danger of entertainment-oriented system design is that it allows for a high speed channel in one direction only, thereby limiting information providers to those organisations who control the source of the high speed data stream. In the US, then, there has been a massive expansion of the telecommunications infrastructure, but the interaction of government and commerce remains an area for conflict, with a continuously shifting boundary of responsibilities. The same outcomes of conflict and shifting responsibilities are seen world-wide, and they will ultimately determine the extent to which an infrastructure exists to support government use of the Internet.

To support commercial and governmental transactions the Internet must offer a secure environment in which such transactions can take place. In a packet switched network the precise path from one site to another is unknown; therefore, the possibility exists for those packets to be examined, imitated, or diverted, resulting in the loss of personal information that may be used to commit fraud. The developers of Internet software have been working to construct secure transaction systems. However, public trust remains low, and some government agencies have also become involved. The development of secure network systems using large key cryptography has been opposed by law enforcement officials in a number of countries, notably the US. US government regulations, for example, have prohibited the export of cryptography technology since World War II. The fear is that if criminals obtain technology from which information cannot be decoded, it would be impossible for law enforcement officials to track their activities.

Government security agencies have asked that a second key be available that would permit the equivalent of government wiretapping. However, the global nature of the Internet makes it highly unlikely that a security system with a *back door* known only to the US government will be universally adopted. In addition to security, an increase in electronic commerce as well as other types of transactions raises concerns about privacy. The information collected about users in an all-digital environment is potentially immense and the ability to develop personal profiles from past transaction records could result in instances where life and health insurance are denied or employment is refused because of such profiles. The full impact of participating in an electronic marketplace that can be monitored and analysed has yet to be fully understood.

The ease with which digital information can be replicated has threatened the viability of conventional copyright laws. Information is no longer bound to a physical object such as a book or a vinyl disk that is difficult to reproduce. Digital information can be replicated with no loss of quality. Software tools can be used to modify or transform content from one form to another. The material may be transmitted quickly to any location on the network. At the same time, there needs to be a further clarification of what constitutes fair use. Fair use has traditionally allowed the transfer of material purchased and has allowed the purchaser some degree of ownership over the material. However, many software and content developers have taken the position that only the original purchaser has any right to use material and has no right to transfer it to others. If this concept had been applied to books, there would be no libraries, and books would have to be burned rather than sold or given to others.

If access to the Internet becomes essential for conducting ordinary day-to-day business, then it will be necessary to ensure that the average citizen has such access. The doctrine of universal access has, for example, been behind regulatory efforts to maintain low local phone rates at the expense of business users who pay the bulk of long distance charges. The strategy has been successful in a number of countries, with near universal access for phone services being achieved in many of the industrialised nations. At present, the costs of obtaining Internet access are too high to bring about universal access and the computer systems used are too difficult to set up and manage. The minimum functionality that will constitute access has been changing and will continue to do so. On the one hand, access is becoming easier, with options to use TV sets for display and alternate access methods such as satellite and coaxial cable. On the other hand, data transfer requirements continue to rise with the complexity of online materials. Universal access, therefore, is a moving target. Whilst access rates are likely to improve, universal access is still a long way off.

Before the advent of the Internet, collocation was a key success factor for rapid product development. When key team members from the various functions sit next to each other all day, information transfer is frequent and rich - very "high bandwidth". Formal meetings keep the project on track and establish goals and commitments, while informal meetings around the coffee pot allow people to build trust and teamwork and to discuss ideas or get help with problems.

Internet technologies allow remote, virtual collaboration in ways that were not possible just a few years ago. To use these tools successfully, product development teams must have a complementary IT infrastructure, matching tools, and the appropriate leadership, as well as the incentives and discipline to work together in a new way. These virtual teams - not "collocated" but "co-wired" - offer distinct advantages. For example: In a "co-wired" environment, people can also communicate frequently, both formally and informally. Formal meetings should be held regularly to keep the project on track and coordinate actions. In addition, informal communication channels, such as chat windows, should be very easy to learn and to use. The CAD design tools must be compatible among all team members, so that communicating design ideas and innovations is seamless. Most virtual collaboration software allows for automatic recording and tracking of the proceedings of meetings. Action items are written down and indexed. Repositories of knowledge are available that make the inventory of knowledge much more visible. Most virtual project teams have a knowledge manager position to care for this inventory. Collocated teams could take advantage of these same techniques, but few have the discipline to do so.

A co-wired product development team requires a communication infrastructure of two layers - a collaboration layer and a control layer. The collaboration environment includes areas for four levels of communication: project management, real-time design sharing, structured discussion and social and brainstorming spaces. The control layer builds and stores the knowledge inventory. The various design tools should smoothly connect these two layers. If they are properly organized and managed co-wired teams can develop products faster than collocated teams. Some types of communications, such as team building meetings, should be face-to-face or via video-conferencing, whereas other types such as technical exchanges can happen in real time or virtual time over the Internet, or by email. The meetings and communications should be "bandwidth-matched" to the needs at the time. Co-wired, virtual teams can take advantage of global expertise and diversity with very flexible capacity. The infrastructure and leadership of co-wired teams must provide for fast acknowledgement of communications, mutual understanding of each communication and a path for commitment and actions. The leader of a virtual, collaborative team should invest significant time in achieving the trust and social inclusion of all team members. The leader's goal is to align goals, processes, skills and tools across the team. Remote team members should be treated with the same respect and given the same promotional opportunities as collocated team members.

The next crest of the Internet wave will come from markets that are already well along the way with the most capacity for upside surprises, since their social structures and communications infrastructures offer few barriers. There are more adults with intentions of going online than there are adults with Internet access. Far from being dead, the Internet has a large growth potential everywhere, but progress is destined to be slower than its most enthusiastic advocates might have envisioned a few years ago. To expand the reach of the Web in developing countries, he says, public venues—libraries, schools, offices and Internet cafés—will have to play a more crucial role. The widespread availability is a long way off in the most populated areas of the world.

The Internet offers a unique opportunity to streamline the delivery of government services, enhance communication with its citizenry, and serve as a catalyst for empowering citizens to interact with government. The growth in popularity and ease of access to the Internet appears to coincide with pressures from public interest groups and some legislatures for more access to public information. The need for some governments to embrace this new technology is in part driven by the legislative mandate that all agencies provide public access to information. Meeting the requirements of this mandate often proves difficult using the *ad hoc* methods and controls of the past. Despite the passage of freedom of information legislation in many countries, there is still a resistance to sharing information by people within government who want to limit access to their data.

Development of the World Wide Web (WWW) has created a platform-independent mechanism for the transfer of documents, the ability to search large databases, to enter basic transactions, and even the ability to run applications. Governments are often frustrated in their efforts to co-ordinate and manage information by the wide variety of hardware and software platforms owned within the public sector. Internet technology offers a unifying platform on which the collection of data for internal and external use can be built. It has been adopted by hundreds of thousands of content providers and tens of millions of users.

The presence of a large user community makes a compelling case for the preparation of an information framework that takes advantage of this technology. In a very short period of time, many government officials will realise that the growth of Internet technologies will have a major impact not only on how information is presented to the public, but on how business is conducted among government agencies and the general public. Internet technology may set the stage for the online public services of the future.

Towards Electronic Democracy

In today's wired world, the interactive citizen is one of the fundamental cornerstones of change. The Internet has put new power into the hands of the citizen. Governments can no longer simply be dispensers of information, even in sophisticated forms being developed by many governments. But governments have not been passive observers and are rising to many of the challenges. New technologies are being used not only to deliver services to the public but also to enhance government administration and facilitate businesses. At this stage of development few governments have effectively been able to involve their citizenry electronically in the democratic process. Many governments have been effective dispensers of information, which often passes as a means of enhancing the democratic process. There are many government initiatives seeking to help citizens to get online, seek feedback on government reports online, and develop listservs and discussion groups to elicit the views of the citizens. There are also many groups actively participating in online activities in the hope of influencing government policies. But for the most part, governments are far behind the activities of citizens online around the world. Those actively engaged in online activities involving social or political change see the Internet as a medium to foster, enhance and change the way people have traditionally engaged in the democratic process.

Much of the enthusiasm and hope for new forms of democracy and citizen input into public issues, sound very like the gushing optimism expressed about the potential of television in its nascent years. It is not yet known if the potentials offered by the Internet will be met.

The Internet has been a tool of enrichment for large numbers of our populations. It has allowed diversity, the rise of the entrepreneur, the mushrooming of home businesses, the bringing together of family and friends through instant communications, the Internet has been a voice for many who for too long did not have the means to express themselves because prior mediums of the expression of communication have been controlled by the few.

The Internet has been many things to many people. New, advanced medical technologies and scientific breakthroughs have lengthened our average life span and brought us better health and lifestyles. On the Internet, there are pockets of dissent and discourse. there are many who use the new technologies for learning, to facilitate their businesses, to get a service, whether from government or business, play games with each other over long distances, keep in contact through email and a thousand and other good usages that can benefit the individual. We know the benefits, we know of the attempts of many professionals who seek to use the Internet to both gain knowledge and dispense and share knowledge. Perhaps, the most important feature of the Internet is that it has allowed individuals to communicate in ways not available before. This is an important new channel through which communication, ideas and knowledge can flow.

It can be persuasively argued that throughout history all new technologies have changed the way the world lives and operates as a society. Transportation brought the world together and television resulted in the global village that brought all of us on the planet closer together as a people. Now tourism is the world's second largest industry with millions of people on the move all around the world, experiencing and sharing in other cultures. Of course, these millions are mostly from the rich nations. It appears we see nothing wrong in going to exotic and culturally challenging parts of the world, in the quest for something new and exciting and the next best thing to experience, and then pay scant attention to the many more millions of poor. Ironically, many will argue that tourism brings needed dollars and helps these economies. But even this does not ring with the hallowed sound of truth as studies show that those who benefit most are the western multinational recreational chains and others who sell their wares globally to all and sundry. Whatever the opinions or views of individuals and governments in society it is evident that we need a far deeper debate and discourse over the impacts of technologies. There are concerns over ensuring all citizens have universal access to the Internet, there are serious, abiding anxieties about the digital divide that is occurring throughout the world.

Privacy laws, to protect people's information and endow on their certain rights over their own personal information, are spreading. But the implementation of such laws is but one small step. Articulation of these issues is just the start. We need deeper discourse. Ironically, it is this medium that affords the opportunity to bring such discourse forward. This is why online e-Democracy is so important as this activity represents the power of this technology and how it can be used to embrace democracy and involve people in the social, economic, cultural and political issues of the day. This is a tool that can give people, the individual citizen, the power to influence public policy.

Governments are slowly coming to realize that there is an undercurrent of democratic change going on in the world. The face of democracy is beginning to change and a few thousand at the moment are doing it. But this is a change that has the potential for growth. Many changes do occur in society when people speak out and spark debate. It is now time for such a discourse over the future of technology. We need to develop a philosophical base about all these new technologies so society drives technology and not technology drives us. Many governments are moving to electronic governance. In this context governance can be seen as both a means to using new technologies to deliver services to the citizen and ways in which to change and improve the efficient methods of administration within governments themselves. Another element looked at in this section is the means as whereby governments will increasingly be able to involve citizens in the democratic process of government. At this stage of development few governments have effectively been able to involve their citizenry electronically in the democratic process. For the most part, governments are far behind the activities of citizens online around the world, who see the Internet as a medium to foster, enhance and change the way people have traditionally engaged in the democratic process.

Governments tend simply to provide information on their web sites and use the Internet, and other technologies, to deliver services electronically. The prime example of this is the US White House site which is primarily an information tool and conduit to executive agency web sites. It was only in January 2000 that President Clinton announced that government had to be interactive with the citizen. The dispensing of information, without substantial input from the citizen, is not a real interactive transaction. Yet, the Internet in and of itself is an interactive medium. Individuals on the Internet understand this and, for growing legions of people, it is becoming a force that is changing the nature of democracy as we know it today. But this is just part of the wider picture of developments in electronic democracy. In fact, individuals and groups are coming together online around the world to influence policy. Politicians are also using the web. In the United States every Presidential candidate has a web site. There are also alternative web sites by interested citizens or groups who want to have their say about the candidates. There are also other groups who are offering sites which will present in-depth analysis of the issues in the upcoming presidential and congressional elections as well as elections at the local and state level.

The online world of democratic activism is growing around the world. This section looks at the emerging trends in electronic democracy, how citizens active online are changing the nature of democracy as we have understood it, and how governments are going to have to tap into this emerging trend. This section shows the distinction between online democracy, and what its participants are achieving, and electronic governance. In the wired world, the online citizen is increasingly playing more and more of a role in the democratic process. There are now hundreds of groups involved, from the community and local level to the national and international stage, in some way working to have an influence on government policies and programs, and on societal issues of our age. Because of these changes, the process of government will soon no longer be controlled from the top and micro-managed by a few when it comes to public policy. In the changing wired world, citizens are voicing their say. Governments may not necessarily be listening, but the thousands upon thousands of people engaging in discourse on the thousand and one issues of the day are certainly listening to each other. This is resulting in powerful currents of change which are only beginning to manifest themselves.

Electronic democracy is not about citizens voting on a multitude of referendums as laid out by governments. It is citizens engaging in the political process in means chosen by individuals. The new democracy we see surfacing is more the expression of individual voices that congeal into a collective whole over ideas that the society of peoples online develop into a consensus. And while a consensus might be formed on major issues, people are still in a position to express their individual thoughts and ideas (even if they range from the erudite to the opinionated). In this emerging world we see the evolution of a true populist democracy (albeit a small one at this point in time). Although people's ideas do not necessarily have to be acted upon individually, the means exist for individuals to communicate freely to an audience. That audience can be large or small, but it represents a freedom for the individual that has not existed up to this point in time. The mass media still hold the reigns of mass communication. It is still important to get that letter to the editor published so you can reach a wide readership. But with this new medium of the Internet you can write something and it will reach the level of interest in the audience out there. Because the Internet as a medium is becoming the tool through which the nature of democracy itself is changing and taking new shapes and forms, it is important that governments understand this phenomenon. Increasingly, public officials and elected politicians are going to be faced with not only an informed citizenry but a citizenry that wants to be engaged in the decision making process in some form or another. An analysis of the numerous groups springing up on the Internet on a multitude of issues illustrates that there are voices out there that governments are going to have to tap into.

In the wired world, individuals can now make their own choices as to which authorities and information sources they will accept. This is leading to a greater democratization of knowledge, empowerment of the individual, and the potential for more informed interactions between the citizenry and organizations, including government. Moreover, since individuals now have ready access to a variety of information resources, organizations have to adopt new proactive measures to compile and disseminate information in a competitive information environment.

A citizenry that is able to seek and obtain information and knowledge from any place in the world through the Internet will, in all likelihood, also expect more from government. One of the means that people can collectively work together to bring about change is through the strategic gathering, absorbing and using of information. Online groups and online activists, researchers and others involved as information professionals, instinctively understand this. It is the understanding of the nature of information and how it influences us as individuals that is going to bring the next big shift in society. As the Internet takes hold in our daily lives, and begins to take a new and ubiquitous shape and form, the need for governments to develop information policies to suit the changing nature of these technologies is becoming more evident. In much of the developed world, the Internet is a communications force that is growing.

According to NUA plc, a company in Ireland, that tracks the growth of the Internet and the implication of our growing information technology infrastructure, as of the end of the year 2000, 60% of the population in the United States and Canada will have some form of online access to the Internet. This can be in the office, the home, an educational institute or some public space, such as libraries, community halls, Internet cafes and other public venues. In the United Kingdom, over 50% of the population now enjoy some kind of Internet access. There, much of the growth of the Internet has been stimulated because many companies offer Internet access free. The citizen pays only for local calls.

In Europe, the whole question of measured rates is a serious issue, as many contend, this does impede not only access to the Internet, but, even if there is access, then the individual has to be careful about how long one is online. This is because the cost factor can act as an inhibitor to accessing the Internet and the amount of time spent online. However, despite these problems, there are now over 200 million people online around the world. We are now awash with information in our new cyber environments. There are currently billions of pages out on the world wide web. There is so much information that no single search engine can go out and suck up all the information an individual might be seeking. In fact, there is such a proliferation of information that many search engine companies now do not give total access to everything that is on the web. What some of the search engine companies are now doing is giving priority to companies who pay to have their company or organization show first on a search, when a given topic or key word is entered into their search engine.

When entering cyberspace, the challenges for the citizen who wants an open and accountable society, both from government and the private sector world, are now many. The success of our new information technology environments is going to depend on how much say and control citizens will have on information in the decade to come. Information is shaping our world. We now live in the Digital Age, in which information, in a global knowledge economy, has become the supreme commodity. Information is not only a piece of barter for the business world to use for competitive and commercial value. Information is now a precious commodity for the citizen. In our new Internet environments, citizens are increasingly demanding more privacy rights to protect their personal information. However, there is also a contradiction here, as at the moment, citizens are sharing and using personal and aggregate information more than ever before. But in a cyberspace environment, the citizen is becoming increasingly sophisticated in understanding the impact that information can have on one's life.

The Information Age appears to be bringing more demands for accountability. In the years to come, the public will come to expect more and more accountability, in the form of enlightening information, from private sector organizations. The Internet is an open network, which has created open environments. With this openness has come a demand for certain rights, to ensure the inherent democratic nature of the Internet is maintained. This idea is now spreading into society as a whole, resulting in demands for more and more accountability from all our public and private sector organizations. Thus, it appears that the next wave of information rights will spread out to the private sector. As the average citizen becomes armed with more knowledge, then it will be private sector organizations, along with governments, who are going to have to become more forthcoming about the information held in their organizations.

In an information-intensive society, citizens want more from both governments and the private sector alike. There are numerous ways that governments at the local, regional and national level can facilitate these new forms of democracy that are emerging. One is to take the example of Canada. The Canadian government, through their Community Access Program (CAP) has a goal to establish over 10,000 public access sites in rural and urban communities across Canada. Launched in 1994, CAP has already established over 4,200 sites in approximately 3,000 rural and remote communities and is a key component of the government's "Connecting Canadians" strategy - aimed at making Canada the world's most connected nation." The program is now being expanded to include urban centres with populations over 50,000. CAP matching funds of up to $17,000 per site are available to eligible applicants such as educational institutions, public libraries, community organizations, and municipal and territorial governments. The community funds can include cash or "in kind" contributions such as facilities, equipment and staffing of public access sites. This is a good model to be followed not only by national governments but international organizations.

If we are to handle the digital divide between those who have the opportunities to be online and the vast numbers of people who cannot necessarily afford the costs of going online, it is going to be essential to level the playing field. In any populist democracy it is important that initiatives embrace all the people. At the moment it is estimated there are only between 150 and 200 million people online. These are small numbers where our world population has exceeded 6 billion people. International organizations could also provide programs to educate people on usage of the Internet. Education then leads to individual usage. It will, naturally, vary from individual but through knowledge of how to use the Internet people can be participants in this new trend in democracy as they see fit. Such programs can embrace many peoples around the world and ensure that the users who most benefit are not just those in the affluent, industrialized countries.

3

ICTs and Media

ICTs have produced an unprecedented profusion and diversity of media. They have also opened up territory where the most powerful media are in cutthroat competition, and risk either crushing the weakest actors under their weight or leaving them jobless by the wayside. The reason is that the control and use of these new technologies require capital and capabilities of such enormous scale that, on the wealthiest of the consumer media markets, they inexorably lead to further concentration. However, is that this concentration is occurring just when thousands of new and independent media are bursting into disorderly life, in contrast with the previous era of one-party systems and the state-controlled monopoly of information.

In Africa in particular and in the countries of the former Soviet Union, the stranglehold of the state on the media has been broken, at least in the written press. There is a paradox within that paradox. In countries where until recently only one party predominated, the transition to democracy has been propitious for the media, whereas the return to democracy in the countries of the Southern Cone, and the end of apartheid in South Africa, have seen the disappearance of many titles that used to support the fight for freedom. It may be that periods of transition are more auspicious to pluralism and media diversity than the advent or return of democracy.

The transnationalization of media groups complicates the task of certain regimes that seek to hide the 'opposite point of view' from their people and merges together a number of cultural, political and journalistic models. Despite the fact that the new media in many countries have played the role of contradicting the party line, their globalization has not necessarily introduced the worldwide adoption of the values (human rights, freedom, tolerance) that their most ardent supporters believed they represented. Indeed, in certain countries, 'media interference' has, on the contrary, provoked even harsher reactions from authorities or countries with an identity crisis. While the objections of authoritarian regimes are fairly easy to overcome in the name of the principles of freedom, those put forward by democratic countries on the fundamental conception of freedom of expression - and above all on its limits - are worthy of particular attention.

The debate between the champions of free speech, based on the model of the First Amendment to the Constitution of the United States of America, and those who wish to impose stricter limits on the freedom of expression in the name of the struggle against racism, discrimination or war, lies at the heart of the information revolution. In this respect, technology has contingencies of its own, for the freedom of speech specific to one country is not necessarily that of other nations, who may define this notion by other norms. Freedom of expression is precisely one of the issues concerning labelling and filtering systems for Internet sites which are supposed to protect the public, and especially children, against inappropriate messages.

The Internet has a decisive role to play, because it escapes the technical and legal barriers set up by governments far more easily than the satellite television programmes picked up by dish antennas. The Internet is both a medium with its own audience, and a source of information for the other media. It is also a 'creator' of information flows, since it enables individuals and groups hitherto marginalized to become involved. Oppressed or isolated ethnic communities, underprivileged social groups, local social movements, banned political parties: all find in the Internet a means of entering onto the world stage, of presenting their situations in their own words, of expressing their claims independently of governments and the channels laid down by the large media groups. This role of the Internet is reinforced by e-mail, which also forms a new broadcasting medium. 'Virtual communities' have therefore become - a reality. The Internet also enables contact to be made with a new, younger audience, already prepared by experience with video game interactivity to plug into the cyberworld. These features have led some observers to the rather hasty conclusion that the Internet is the antidote to the dominant power of the media giants, the absolute weapon against state control and censorship, and the instrument of a new, more participatory form of citizenship.

New technology, however, does not eliminate conflictual relations or financial considerations. The large and most frequently visited Internet sites are already the prerogative of the established media groups. The communication giants present in the other media have purchased access providers or data banks. In most of the countries in transition, the costs of computer equipment and access subscriptions continue to be major obstacles which de facto exclude a large majority of the population from using the Internet.

Corresponding to this explosion in the scope of knowledge and scale of communication, are the new forms of state censorship. With limited success, governments have multiplied measures to prevent the media from crossing borders by banning dish antennas or foreign radio broadcasts. They even hope to dampen the liberating or contentious repercussions of the Internet by erasing 'hostile' sites using labelling and blocking systems, sanctioning access providers which tolerate them, and multiplying administrative or financial obstacles in order to limit the number of users. Democratic states are not necessarily the least repressive. The new media also offer new methods of information manipulation, which is the other face of censorship. Counselled by international public relations agencies, masters in the art of abusing information and communication techniques, authoritarian governments or large corporations with controversial business activities turn these new media around and use them against those who saw in them no more than an instrument of freedom. China has created its own site specializing in human rights.

In many countries, it is not the state which poses the greatest threat to the freedom of expression, but the 'new powers', non-governmental organizations which are taking over the work of state violence, either against it or with its connivance. In recent years, an increasing number of journalists have been the victims of mafia groups, paramilitary gangs and extremist religious factions. Increasing areas of the globe under the control of such groups have once again slipped out of range, thereby limiting the capacity for data collection at the source.

The new technologies are a poor weapon when armed gangs seal off an area and terrorize its people. More and more private individuals and public corporations are bringing court actions for slander or damages against even the most respectable programmes and publications, thereby attempting to intimidate them. Some of these lawsuits are legitimate, because freedom of speech must be balanced against other rights such as nondiscrimination, respect for privacy, or for a person's reputation and honour, but they are increasingly seen as a means of harassing the media and limiting public debate.

In the United States, they have been given the eloquent name of 'slapp', for strategic lawsuits against public participation. The privatization of censorship is also occurring at the distribution level. Closely supervised by self-appointed guardians of morality, or ethnic or religious groups, certain chain stores refuse to display and even sell certain books, videos or CDs. Internet access providers exclude sites deemed to be dangerous or harmful, and some public libraries, at the risk of blocking legitimate sites, have installed filtering software in order to prevent their younger customers from having access to obscene products. But the use of keywords enabling 'obscene' sites to be detected can just as easily block access to sites fighting pornography, defending the rights of women and children, or describing violations of human rights.

Technology in these instances is simply a new battlefield for groups which have always defended censorship in the name of morality, nationalism or religion. Now that the media have become commercialized, they worry about damage to their public image and try to avoid publicity which might keep them from being seen by general audiences. Censorship self-censorship - may therefore be the result of the supposed reactions of consumer groups or lobbies which are the noisiest and best organized. This situation also leads producers to steer clear of topics which are too sensitive or too controversial, thereby limiting the public space necessary for genuine debate and diversity. Hence a truly new paradox: just when technology is capable of pushing back the frontiers of censorship virtually to infinity, society is redefining the 'acceptable' limits of freedom of expression, through legislation or by adopting speech codes which are sometimes extremely strict, thus outlawing points of view which are deemed politically incorrect.

Public Service Broadcasting

In recent years, powerful media groups have grown still more powerful, not only in the countries of the North, but also in many countries of the South. The number of these media groups with their different levels of influence, ranging from global to regional, to national, to local, is in itself decreasing from year to year as a result of various mergers, takeovers and alliances. Concentration is horizontal, combining different media (the written press, television, etc.) and/or vertical (ranging from film studios to television channels and cinemas). It also sanctions a convergence of content (information and entertainment) and technology (the same content simultaneously supplies the written press, the audiovisual sector and the Internet). In certain countries, sometimes more than half the national circulation of daily newspapers is controlled by just one press group.

In most countries, local monopolies are the rule, and in these cases the newspapers are often part of powerful national or international groups, such as Gannett or Knight-Ridder in the United States or the Hersant group in France. Backed by their press power, these local enterprises usually extend business activities to the audiovisual sectors, as well as to publishing and advertising, and in so doing engulf neighbouring countries: instances include the German press in Austria, the French press in Belgium, and the Swedish press in the Baltic countries. Rupert Murdoch's News Corp. is an edifying example of the trend towards vertical and horizontal concentration, because the company is present in practically every media form, and covers the entire information chain: News Corp. has bought not only the exclusive rights for broadcasting sporting events, but also the subject of the information itself, i.e. the sports clubs, to ensure a more prestigious content and therefore a captive audience for its sports channels.

Mass media behaviour is to a considerable extent anchored in everyday events, in routine habits and customs. The relationship of the broadcasting media to viewers and listeners has become deeply rooted in their personality and behaviour. These are factors opposed to change, and they favor constancy and permanence. For this reason, the mass media of the future should be examined from the standpoint of constancy as much as from that of change and revolution. The radio and television media incorporate a large number of key elements which hardly alter or which change very slowly. On this basis, the forecasts which seek to see beyond the new media revolution can be founded upon assumptions that emphasize continuity.

A number of elements and success factors in the future of public service broadcasting are precisely of this kind and they are just as significant as are the opportunities for change. Many researchers regard television as a manifestation and symbol of so-called modernized Western society. They claim that television has replaced the traditional 'user interfaces' which included a variety of socio-societal structures such as place of residence, social class, religion and profession. For audiences in Western societies, radio and television have become a value- and culture-specific arena which reinforces personal identity. Radio and television channels broadcast programmes with elements of familiarity, belonging and continuity. They provide their audiences with identifiable points to which they can relate personal memories, common experiences of delight and pleasure or of anguish and sorrow.

The broadcasting media have thus become the single most important 'user interface' for personal identities and for experiencing what is perceived as being 'personal' in modern culture. In a recently published report, the Future Committee of the Finnish Parliament has stressed that experiencing something as one's own is one of the most important value bases of the information society.

Unless people find intellectual, community, environmental or material values with which they can identify in the networking and diversifying media, change is likely to lead to confusion and chaos rather than to the moral strengthening of the community. The strong influence of the broadcasting media on the everyday life of cosmopolitan societies is most probably based upon such feelings of personal recognition.

In modern communities, people are increasingly experiencing in their lives solidarity and events which are familiar to them through the mass media. This goes a long way to explaining why people from very different backgrounds, spheres and professions follow the same programmes and events at the same time. Viewing television and listening to radio, people manifest their solidarity and feel that they belong to a group. Today, this belonging often concerns national or regional cultures, but it can also relate to global togetherness. The principal broadcasting channels with a sense of responsibility must endeavour to meet the feeling and meaning of the audiences' common experience.

Critical tensions between various groups in societies are heightened when the programmes put out by the mass media channels do not provide a real response to the need of individuals to experience something as their own. Under these circumstances, feelings of alienation and of cultural and social discrimination are reinforced. Broadcasting programmes can thus be socially 'dysfunctional', as witnessed in some countries where people's power took over the public media, set up alternative media, or rejected the information put out by the official media. In 1990, when Gorbachev was seeking to keep Lithuania as part of the Soviet Union, the public proclaimed loudly that the country had been independent since 1921.

Pluralistic media are fundamental to the value systems of democratic societies. In order to exercise the basic values of freedom of speech and expression individuals must be able to obtain and acquire knowledge and information that is significant to them personally, created by the community itself and independent of those in power.

Public service broadcasting, as it originated in Europe, was created to serve these goals. Its ideal was to provide citizens with media that would be independent of both government and economic control. Public service broadcasting has thus always emphazised the significance of public control, reflected in the fact that it is accountable to the audience in a way in which the commercial media are not, even when they are popular. The principle of accountability implies that audiences can demand that the media provide programming that is important and significant to them on a personal level. The corollary is that public service broadcasting is also based upon the concept of an active, developing and self-fulfilling human being.

Public service broadcasting has traditionally been given the mandate to produce programming with informative, educative and also entertaining content. It has been expected to meet the needs of the various facets of the personality in a balanced way so as to provide a whole image of the individual. Broadcasting technology spread to Africa and Asia, often as a part of colonization. For this reason, public service radio, and later television, tended to serve the interests of the colonizing powers and later those of the newly independent national regimes, rather than those of the general public for whom they were originally established. Thus historically, in many of these countries, the public service mandate was often subservient to the whims and caprices of those in power, and was viewed as a primary tool for ensuring continuance in power.

In South Asia, one generally sees an entrenched government control over radio and television despite a colonial legacy of a BBC-type of public broadcasting code such as in India and Sri Lanka, along with a free press. But in other countries of the subcontinent, like Pakistan, Bangladesh and Nepal, one sees a situation similar to that in Eastern Europe, where some state broadcasters continue to work only as propaganda agents of governments despite the maturing of these democracies. In Nepal, in contrast, the government produced a communication policy paper in 1990, followed by a revised broadcasting act in 1992. Since then, several new FM stations have been granted a licence to broadcast, including Radio Sagarmatha, an independent station run by a consortium of NGOs. Their programmes do indeed reflect the community's concerns: environment, education, culture.

In view of the prospects opened up by developments in technology, it may be asked whether the ideals set up by public service broadcasting are still sustainable. This question arises because audiences today can use advanced communication technology to access those media contents which they think will best meet their various communication needs. Communicating via network media and the Internet, audiences now have unrestricted access to those sources of information that were previously beyond their reach, behind, inter alia, a variety of media gatekeepers. It may be argued that communication built upwards does away with the need for public service broadcasting which, despite everything, is always constructed by programming planners and gatekeepers.

It is true that in the network society the individual has an unprecedented opportunity to obtain access to virtually any source of information though this opportunity is not available equally to everyone. The Internet era has multiplied the individual's opportunity for accessing new, geographically distant sources of information which are not dependent on fixed-time programming schedules. The limits of time and space are disintegrating. In particular, the Internet has opened up the borders of the world to its users and promoted the unrestricted movement of information in a manner that is without parallel in world history. It has also facilitated genuine debate among people united by a common topic or interest.

Many information networks are complementing the diverse sources of news used by broadcasting. One of these is the International Freedom of Expression and Exchange Network (IFEX), and particularly noteworthy is the work of the Pacific Islands News Association, which issues news alerts concerning the media in this region.

The number of computers connected to the Internet is still growing rapidly. In July 1998, there were 36.7 million computers connected to the Internet worldwide. In Finland, there were 100.53 computers per 1,000 inhabitants connected to the Internet. However, the worldwide communication network and information gateways are, by their very existence, creating the need for the pendulum to swing the other way. As both the sources of information and the number of connections multiply, the need for meanings that unite also grows. One of the most important challenges of the information society, beyond making information available, is to enable analytical interpretation of it and to facilitate understanding.

In the networked information society, public service broadcasting should emphasize the contribution to its prestige made by the high level of interpretation and analysis which is part of its mission. Those working and communicating in the various networks need both knowledge and certainty about their own points of departure. Only a communicator who is certain about his or her own self can engage in a fully reciprocal communication process with others.

The elements of public service broadcasting that are emphasized in the information society are pluralism, independence, and, finally, communication, which strengthens identity and instills understanding about the meaning of citizenship. The sense of self and identity are reinforced when the members of a society and a culture are given the opportunity to obtain information that is relevant and important to them. The growth and vitality of this sense is often simulated by fictional material and storytelling: films, serials and series, music, entertainment and humour.

Public service broadcasting best carries out its mission in the information society when it provides all segments of the audience with cultural material to reinforce a positive sense of identity and self. Public service broadcasting must become more aware of this key characteristic and must emphasize it as a core element of its mission.

Boundaries are being broken down, the roles of states are changing, many operations are being globalized and contexts are becoming more complex. Decision-making in matters affecting citizens is becoming more distant and is, in many cases, no longer recognizable. Political citizenship generally means that people are capable of understanding matters affecting them and their relationship to such matters.

An integrating and globalizing world, where decision-making is often faceless, offers a particular challenge to the media. In order to enjoy full citizenship in the information society individuals must be able to obtain information on matters affecting them personally and to feel that they can influence such matters. This is quite a different matter from the consumers' opportunity to obtain the communication services which they require.

Citizenship in the information society also signifies that individuals can increasingly and naturally participate and do business electronically. Finland has sought to promote the conditions and opportunities for electronic public dealings and participation by citizens. The fulfilment of civil obligations, dealings with welfare services, study, library visits, relations with the authorities and other such matters will soon be managed remotely. Such forms of interactivity should also be promoted by public service broadcasting. In a democratic information society populated by active citizens, encouraging the ideals of citizenship and of civil duties and rights is particularly important and should therefore be a core element of the future mission of public service broadcasting.

Citizenship in the information society implies that individuals have the right to relevant and reliable information. Under these circumstances, the number of sources of information is less important than the reliability and relevance of the information to which citizens have access. Citizenship is closely tied to equality, and all members of the community must have an equal opportunity to obtain basic information service. On the eve of the information society, we should reassess what is meant by basic information services. For example, is equal access to communication networks one of the basic rights of the citizen of the information society? If so, how is it to be implemented? Can it be achieved only through relatively expensive hardware investments, or can equal connection and basic services be implemented by means already available to the overwhelming majority of the public?

As far as public service broadcasting is concerned, all these questions are significant. This raises the original question of whether the information society is for eveyone, or for only a few. In operational terms, the question is whether there are realistic and practical governmental and entrepreneurial policies and strategies to ensure that networks and services are expanded to reach all countries, or whether these polices and strategies are market driven and profit based. If profit is the sole or principal motivation, are decision-makers deliberately excluding large segments of the world's population by consciously employing a policy of social exclusion? This would undoubtedly run counter to the ideals and objectives of public service broadcasting and related media. Furthermore, such policies would be self-defeating since they negate the objective of universal access to information and communication media and are not even favourable to the new concept of global marketing!

Because digital broadcasting technology allows for new ways of registering and monitoring communication, it is all the more important that the privacy of individual citizens as communicators be respected. Individuals can be equal players in the public political arena only if they can be certain of respect for their privacy and integrity. Political systems must be able to guarantee this protection if they are to earn the trust of their citizens. In a multiple-source and increasingly complex situation, the ethics of communication should also require journalism to be firmly based on reliable and objective argumentation. In a multi-channel world, the prestige associated with reliability for all channels will increase and will also be subject to more critical exposure.

In recent years, public service broadcasting the world over has seen economic resources diminish. Nevertheless, over the next few years, digital technology will require appreciable financial investments in both technology and programme content. Even for many large companies, such expenditures present a difficult financial problem. In this context, it has been suggested that the public service broadcasting companies ought not to invest too much in digital technology, but rather focus for the time being on dealing with the basic analogue broadcasting media. This choice would nevertheless be fatal for both public service broadcasting and for society as a whole. Without the slightest doubt, the basic point of departure must be that public service broadcasting should not only enter the digital era, but should take the lead in exploring the new possibilities which the information society offers to all media.

Digital technology allows public service

broadcasting to carry out its mission more effectively and in a more focused way. Digital broadcasting technology can provide public service programming to several different audience groups simultaneously. Some countries are developing digital services in the belief that new digital channels targeting niche audiences will complement and enrich the programmes already offered by the basic channels, but will neither displace nor replace the full service programmes. For the cultural and value reasons discussed earlier, viewers and listeners will continue to feel the need for general channels in the future. At the same time, their demand for in-depth and even highly detailed information which can be supplied via special channels or via digital television user-oriented network services will increase.

Public service broadcasting companies should be involved increating a new audiovisual communication culture in which traditional broadcast products converge with new media and multimedia products. In the public service range, these products can be presented either in parallel or as specific elements of programmes. Audiences are expecting public service broadcasting to play a prominent and visible role in the new media. Several public service broadcasting companies have developed, inter alia, Internet services, and their success has been encouraging. For example, the BBC's Internet services are the most popular network services at the moment. The appeal of the public service companies 'Internet pages is based on the fact that the audience has an image of these companies which stresses reliability, diversity and quality. In the chaos of the media world, consumers are on the look out for organizations or 'portals' through which they can access reliable, interesting and significant sources of information.

The changes in both the content and programming structures of public service broadcasting represent a major operational challenge which will affect not only the operating and production methods within companies, where digitalizing production technology is creating new opportunities, but also the relationship to the content production sector operating outside radio and television. Public service broadcasting companies will survive the challenges of the digital era only if they are able to create collaborative networking with both the new media technology sector and the content production sector.

Many sectors of society can contribute more than can be imagined to content production for the digital broadcasting media. It is natural that in the past, education, social services or the science sector, for example, did not perceive themselves as being close to the audiovisual production sector. Today, however, they are already producing a variety of ambitious new-media audiovisual products, which could well form one part of the new broadcasting content.

The public service companies must now invite new organizations in society to cooperate in digital production. To a large extent this is a question of motivation and example, and public service broadcasting should take on a pioneering role particularly in the areas of culture, science, education and welfare. This role should also to extend to making information society services available to citizens and households.

One universal obstacle to the advancement of the information society is the reluctance of citizens to use the new electronic services and information technology in general, even though the benefits of such use are clear. The fears of and negative attitudes towards electronic information ought not to be underestimated. Public service broadcasting should, as a part of its information society role, provide new services that emphasize the citizens' point of view, and this in turn will encourage an adaptation of public service broadcasting to the environment of the future. Moreover, the image of reliability, independence and public accountability associated with public service broadcasting offers a good basis to start moving in this direction.

For many members of the broadcast audience, the transition to an information society is still an abstract, or even unacceptable, vision. They are concerned about the undermining of human interaction and about the possible increasing alienation of large, less affluent segments of our societies. In many countries, those retiring from active life in 1999 will live, on the average, for about twenty years in the emerging information society, and it may be asked whether their needs will have been taken properly into account. Others are concerned about the overemphasis on the commercial and marketing aspects of the digital future.

However, for many, the so-called information society represents new opportunities just for huge global businesses. Public service broadcasters will undoubtedly understand the importance of market revenue in developing new services. However, the value base of the information society - just as for any society of whatever period - should not be business oriented, and public service broadcasters should take an intellectual lead in the public debate on these matters. Such a debate should not be an abstract discussion of the objectives and structures of the information society, but should include concrete demonstrations of services which viewers and listeners can utilize every day in public service broadcasting programmes.

In providing a well-balanced and structured range of old and new services to the audiences, public service broadcasting should present an understandable and approachable view of what the information society means in the audience's everyday life. As is the case with existing public service broadcasting, it would be difficult - and even undesirable - to try to define in detail which concrete operations and services these new products should provide in the future. The public service mission is not a list of quantifiable tasks. A society defines what public service broadcasting means in each particular context and this is often expressed as a broadcasting law. The statement ratified by the member states of the Council of Europe defines public service broadcasting as an essential factor in pluralistic communication accessible to everyone and hence as a central factor of social cohesion in the information society. This guideline is also valid for the production of new digital and multimedia services.

4

Freedom of Expression on the Net

The Internet is uniquely decentralized, global, abundant, inexpensive, interactive and user-controlled. In US, the campaign finance laws were developed for the centralized, scarce, and expensive media of radio, television and print. The Internet supports a diverse range of content—text, graphics, audio and video; chat rooms, moderated and unmoderated email lists, and "newsgroups;" and World Wide Web sites endlessly and seamlessly linked on a global basis—much of it spontaneous and independent from campaign committees and the political parties. Initial efforts to apply the Federal Election Campaign Act (FECA) to these new and varied Internet communications have yielded troubling results, threatening to burden.

In US, the Internet fosters what the Supreme Court has called a "never-ending worldwide conversation." As such, the Court has held, expression on the Internet is entitled to the highest level of protection under the First Amendment. It would be worse than ironic if rules designed to deemphasize the unfair advantage of money, to broaden the diversity of groups that can have an impact on the election process and to "return our electoral process to the people" were applied to deter individuals from using the "electronic soapbox" of the Internet.

More recently, there has been a hint of change from the FEC, with bolder calls from some individual Commissioners for redefinition of the campaign finance law's application to the Internet. We support such calls, and we urge the Commission - to the maximum extent possible within the terms and exceptions of FECA - to recognize that a large portion of the political activity in cyberspace does not merit regulation. Ultimately, however, it will likely require a Congressional amendment to FECA to protect individual advocacy and remove any cloud from this most democratic, open and inexpensive of mass media.

In US, the Centre for Democracy and Technology is a public interest organization dedicated to developing and implementing public policies that protect and enhance civil liberties and democratic values in the new digital media. We are not experts in campaign finance law and we have not taken a position on legislative proposals concerning campaign finance. However, we have made it one of our priorities to defend freedom of expression on the Internet.

CDT staff were among the first to articulate the ways in which the architecture of the Internet serves core First Amendment values by increasing access to diverse information sources and minimizing the need for government content regulation.

CDT helped organize the Citizens Internet Empowerment Coalition, which challenged Congress' first attempt to control content on the Internet, the Communications Decency Act (CDA). We brought the

Internet into the courtroom in Philadelphia, demonstrating its unique features to the three judge panel hearing the CDA case. US user-controlled vision of the Internet proved central to the Supreme Court's landmark ruling in Reno v. ACLU, holding that the Internet was a unique medium entitled to the highest First Amendment protection. It is from that perspective that we have become concerned about the implications of the FEC's initial efforts to apply the campaign finance law to the Internet.

In evaluating the First Amendment standards applicable to any medium of communication, the Supreme Court has long recognized that "differences in the characteristics of new media justify differences in the First Amendment standards applied to them." The Supreme Court found that the Internet is a unique medium, distinct from broadcast, print, and cable. The Court described the speech outlets of the Internet as "vast democratic fora" and a "new marketplace of ideas," which "provides relatively unlimited, low-cost capacity for communication of all kinds," the growth of which "has been and continues to be phenomenal." The Court recognized that it is the very breadth and variety of speech over the Internet that gives the Internet its extraordinary communicative power:

This dynamic, multifaceted category of communication includes not only traditional print and news services, but also audio, video, and still images, as well as interactive, real-time dialogue. Through the use of chat rooms, any person with a phone line can become a town crier with a voice that resonates farther than it could from any soapbox. Through the use of Web pages, mail exploders, and newsgroups, the same individual can become a pamphleteer.

Characteristics of the Internet

Architectural and economic characteristics of the Internet make it a medium uniquely suited, if properly fostered, to achieving the marketplace of ideas which the First Amendment is intended to support and through which our democratic ideals can best be realized. These unique characteristics must guide the application of campaign finance rules to the Internet.

— *Decentralized*: Traditional mass media's system of limited distribution channels sets up a gatekeeper system controlled by a relatively small number of entities. In contrast, the Internet's architecture is decentralized and distributed. It is a network of networks consciously designed to function without gatekeepers.

— *Global*: The Internet provides immediate access to information from around the world. With simple email, it is as easy and inexpensive to send a message to another continent as to the building across the street. Search engines on the World Wide Web list local and foreign sites without distinction. Those wishing to avoid government regulation have shown the ability to quickly "mirror" content on servers outside the reach of censors.

— *Abundant*: The Internet can accommodate a virtually unlimited number of speakers. Thus, while the architecture of mass media creates scarcity, the Internet's architecture places little limit on the amount and diversity of information that can be made available. As the Supreme Court stated, "Unlike the conditions that prevailed when Congress first authorized regulation of the broadcast spectrum, the

Internet can hardly be considered a scarce expressive commodity. It provides relatively unlimited, low-cost capacity for communication of all kinds... ."

— *Inexpensive*: Existing campaign finance law reflects the economics of the mass media: speaking effectively is expensive. In contrast, on the Internet, "talk is cheap." The Internet sustains a level of speech among individuals and loosely organized groups unparalleled in other media. It is the first electronic medium to allow every user to be a publisher. Users can reach and create communities of interest despite geographic, social, and political barriers, enabling nearly everyone who wants to espouse political opinions to do so. Armed with an email account, an individual can send a mass emailing to hundreds of thousands of individuals with little expense. At one of the many portal services, individuals can create Web pages to discuss their likes, dislikes, wage a campaign against a corporation, flak products, or express their political views - for free.

— *Interactive*: Unlike the one-way transmissions typifying most radio and television, the Internet is bidirectional in nature. It allows responsive communications from one-to-one, from one-to-many, and from many-to-one.

— *User-controlled*: Unlike television and radio, which offer individuals little opportunity to make decisions about what information they receive, the Internet is a user-controlled medium. As the Supreme Court found in striking down the Communications Decency Act, individuals are not assaulted by information on the Internet but rather enjoy an unequalled ability to direct and control the information that they come in contact with.

In US, the 1996 presidential election witnessed the beginning of Internet-based political activity. Both the Clinton-Gore and the Dole-Kemp campaigns used Web sites to distribute information, solicit volunteers, and highlight campaign activities. What was more important, however, than the major political parties' adding the Internet to their campaign strategies was the way in which the Internet served as a platform for informal, unorganized, grassroots political discussions of a breadth and variety rarely witnessed in the off-line world.

The Internet provides individuals and informal organizations the ability to communicate inexpensively. From their virtual platforms, individuals and organizations are publishing newsletters, advertisements, voters guides and other election-related materials; creating dynamic forums that support issue-based organizing, interactive discussions, and political advocacy; and registering voters. The Internet can lower barriers to participation.

Small groups and minor parties, among the first to use the Internet, are currently engaged in long-term affiliation-building activities online. Foreshadowing the significant future role of the Internet in political campaigns and the national political dialogue, the Web has been credited as a decisive factor in recent.

In addition to broadening the number and diversity of speakers, the Internet creates opportunities for new forms of speech. Real-time dialogues can be hosted, creating a parallel to the town hall meeting without the time and expense. Conversations can be held outside of real-time, as postings on Web sites form "threaded" discussions on specific topics, which can be archived and returned to at any time.

The Internet also provides voters with an efficient and timely method to gather information about candidates. It has been suggested that many voters make uninformed choices or become frustrated and drop out of the process not because they do not care about the outcome of an election but because becoming informed takes too much effort.

The Internet has particular advantages in enabling voters to obtain information, compare candidates, review voting records, and hear from third-parties through easy-to-find resources. Voters can access information when they want it. 10% of voters have already used the Internet to gather information they used in a voting decision. Exit poll respondents said that the information they found on the Internet was simply not available in traditional mediums. They also highlighted the convenience of the Internet and the sheer volume of information available.

The Federal Election Campaign Act (FECA), adopted in 1971 and significantly amended in 1974, seeks to quantify the cost of political speech, limit the amount of money collected and spent on campaign-related activities, and enable public scrutiny of the impact of money on campaigns and elected officials through disclosure of the identity of contributors.

In general the law establishes:

— Contribution limits: Federal election law limits the amount of money individuals and groups can contribute to candidates, party committees, and political action committees (PACs). In particular, the law limits an individual's overall contributions at $25,000 per calendar year and sets caps on contributions: to a candidate at $1,000 per election; to a national party committee at $20,000 per calendar year; and to other political committees at $5,000 per calendar year. While "contributions" are thus limited, "independent expenditures" by individuals or groups are not·

— Prohibited contributions and expenditures: The law prohibits corporations, labour organizations, federal government contractors and foreign nationals from making any contributions and expenditures to influence federal elections. It also prohibits contributions to federal elections in another person's name and prohibits cash contributions in federal elections of more than $100.

— Disclosure requirements: Candidate committees, party committees and PACs must file periodic reports disclosing the money they raise and spend, and generally identifying the source of contributions. Candidates must disclose and attribute contributions from PACs and party committees and they must identify individuals who contribute more than $200 per year.

— Identification requirements: While "independent expenditures" by individuals or groups are unrestricted, where any expenditure finances communications expressly advocating the election or defeat of a clearly identified candidate or soliciting contributions through any general public political advertising, the communication must identify the party responsible by name and indicate whether or not it is authorized by the campaign.

Existing campaign finance law is based on several assumptions that reflect the nature of traditional mass media. First and foremost, the law assumes that speech is expensive and that therefore money inextricably determines the amount and impact of political speech.

In contrast, the Internet greatly reduces the cost of speech. Because the initial start-up costs of becoming a speaker on the Internet are relatively low and, once the investment is made, the difference between communicating to a single individual and communicating to masses of individuals is marginal, the effect of money is vastly diminished in the online environment.

In addition, the campaign finance law assumes that the content of political speech (at least the political speech that matters) will be conducted by a relatively small set of entities created to influence elections. The law assumes that there is a distinction between speakers and listeners, that the speakers will be the candidates (and their committees and parties), and that most citizens will participate in the campaign process not by speaking but by contributing money.

Under this traditional scenario, to the extent that individuals become involved in the political process as "volunteers," it is assumed they will not be speaking, but rather will be disseminating material (mainly printed material) produced by the campaign in the form of leaflets that volunteers will stuff into envelopes or deliver door-to-door. On Internet, in contrast, anybody can be a speaker. A "volunteer" can create a Web site as good as the campaign webmaster's.

There is another difference between the traditional mass media and the Internet, one having to do with the role of advertising. Television and radio work on the advertising model: advertisements pay for the content. By and large on television and radio, the content is not political in nature.

Most content providers on radio and television are studiously apolitical in their programming. To the extend there is content regarding politics, it is in the form of news, which is exempt from FECA. By and large, on television and radio, the only way that political speech is broadcast outside of the news is in the form of very expensive paid political advertisements.

On the Internet, the distinctions between content, news and advertisement are very different. There is a great deal of content not supported by any advertising. Some content on the Internet is supported by advertising, but it is different in two crucial ways, especially in the campaign context.

On the Internet, most political content is not in the form of paid political advertisements; it is in the form of freestanding Web pages. On the Internet, there is no disincentive for political content. By and large, candidates do not spend a lot of money on the Internet for paid political advertisement that support the content of others. Rather, to the extent that candidates "advertise" on the Internet, they do it the way everybody else does, with banner adds that do not carry content, but that try to attract viewers to click away from one content page to another content page (i.e., the candidate's).

One way to assess the application of campaign finance laws to the Internet is to try to map the asserted goals of campaign finance regulation onto the new medium. Doing so illustrates how the goals of campaign finance would be best achieved by not regulating much of the campaign and election-related activity on the Internet.

Supporters of campaign finance restrictions argue that the role of money in politics fosters inequality in our democratic system. The original supporters of FECA feared that well-financed political action groups thwart the one person, one vote principle. The goal of FECA was to "broaden the diversity of groups that can have an input on the election process" and to "return our electoral process to the people." Current campaign finance reformers share this goal.

The Internet is an inherently equalizing force for non-candidates and minor candidates to participate in campaign discussions in ways previously reserved to well-funded candidates. Because it is open and inexpensive, the Internet empowers all users with the ability to speak to a large audience. A single wired individual can be powerful: one man organized over 100 campus protests against the Republican Party's Contract with America from his basement computer.

The Internet is unlikely to reduce the amount campaigns spend on radio and television. But certainly, the Internet does not significantly increase the amount of money spent by campaigns, and does not impose large additional fund-raising demands on politicians and candidates.

Online, voters can easily check distorted candidate or organization statements. A search for a candidate name is sure to deliver not only the candidate's views on an issue but critiques and criticisms of the can did ate's position as well as other relevant information. Proponents of campaign finance reform often raise concerns about the expense and delay of responding to distorted claims made by incumbent candidates or moneyed interests in traditional media.

The expense of responding online is relatively low. Through linking and searching, opposing points of view and responses to a candidate's claim will be simultaneously available to the voter. Special interest groups can and will spend money on Internet political efforts, but individuals and smaller groups can inexpensively build Web sites responding to or critiquing candidate and interest group statements.

Given the global nature of the Internet, this is one goal that no amount of regulation can achieve. Restricting outside influence to local elections is probably made substantially more difficult by the Internet. Because the Internet is a global medium, an out-of-state voter or organization utilizing the Web for political advocacy is just as likely to influence an election as an in-state voter or organization. Web sites overseas will be beyond the reach of U.S. regulators.

The FEC has clearly established that disseminating information about federal elections through the Internet can be subject to regulation under the Federal Election Campaign Act. In 1995, the FEC ruled that a Web site distributing information, run by an independent, "virtual PAC" is a form of "general public political advertising." The FEC has found that an individual may have to report to the government in order to create a Web page expressing support for a candidate, that hyperlinks may constitute political contributions, and that providing free Web sites to all candidates is a prohibited corporate contribution.

Hypertext links form one of the distinguishing characteristics of the World Wide Web. In 1998, the FEC concluded that "links" constitute a thing of value and that a link on a corporate site constitutes an illegal corporate contribution.

The most important FEC ruling on nonpartisan online political activities is Advisory Opinion 1996. Online service provider CompuServe wanted to offer free Web sites and member accounts on a "nonpartisan basis" to all federal candidates in order to allow the posting of position papers and to facilitate responding to questions from voters via email. CompuServe told the Commission that it typically charged $9.95 per month for the service but provides free accounts to many journalists, schools, charities, government entities, and non-profit organizations.

In response, the FEC ruled that the free accounts would be considered prohibited corporate contributions to federal candidates. The Commission had previously permitted a cable television station to give free airtime to candidates. That fell under the exemption for news stories or commentary by media outlets, but CompuServe did not qualify for the media exemption. Neither CompuServe's contention that the Web sites would add value to the CompuServe service nor the fact that the accounts were similar to those given to other non-profit entities allowed CompuServe to escape the law against corporate contributions.

Financial information provider Bloomberg later asked the FEC to review its proposal to conduct electronic town meetings with federal candidates on its Web site. In the Bloomberg proposal, journalists were to moderate the discussions, which would be available for later broadcast on Bloomberg television.

The FEC ruled that Bloomberg was a "news and commentary provider via computer linkages" and was "performing a newspaper or periodical function for computer users." The Commission said that the

Bloomberg proposal differed from CompuServe's because the "means of presentation [were to be] controlled by a press entity." Because Bloomberg was only exempted as a "wire service," the question of whether any exclusively Internet-based company can be defined as a media company remains unanswered.

In Advisory Opinion 1997-16, the FEC made its first ruling on organizational activities on the Web. The Oregon Natural Resources Council Action (ONCRA) wanted to announce candidate endorsements of its affiliated PAC , Oregon Natural Resources Council Action Federal PAC (PAC), to its members on the ONCRA Web site instead of by mail. The FEC ruled that the group could not list its endorsements on the site unless it instituted a screening mechanism to ensure that it was only accessed by members. Corporations, including non-profits groups, can communicate endorsements to their members, but if they communicate to the general public it is considered an illegal corporate contribution. PACs on the other hand can make endorsements, contributions and expenditures with regard to Federal elections subject to the limits and disclosure requirements of FECA.

If the FEC determines that Exley or another Web user spent over $1,000 in support of a candidate, the user will have to register as a political committee. Those who are required to register must provide their name and address, appoint a custodian of books and a treasurer, and report all bank accounts and funds to be used for political activities. If any contribution to the political committee exceeds $200, such as a computer, the committee must also have records of the contributor's occupation and employer.

Similarly, if the FEC strictly enforces the election law's limits on association with the official campaign, many activities such as collecting information from campaigns for inclusion on a Web site, linking to the official campaign Web site, or other minimal communications between campaign staff and the outside individual or group may constitute associated efforts.

Since the FEC has concluded that links constitute in-kind contributions, candidates will probably also have to report the personal information of any Web site operator that links to the candidate Web site.

Web sites that announce the availability of linked images or html code for linking to their Web site could run into trouble when they are not informed that other sites have decided to link to their site.

The prohibition on links from corporate Web sites creates problems for any site linking to candidate Web sites. Additionally, if individuals and small groups register their advocacy sites with the FEC, linking to those Web sites may constitute reportable in-kind contributions to private political committees. This extra layer of potential reporting means that Web sites would never know whether with every hyperlink they are making a prohibited or reportable contribution.

If candidate Web sites are difficult for users to find, citizens will find the wealth of information on the Web overwhelming and cumbersome to navigate. Internet users are currently frustrated by the number of parodies and non-official sites that have taken the domain names where they expect to find the official Web site.

The Internet's way of solving for such problems without reducing the number of participants in the debate or closing down important efforts by third parties is to allow Web site operators to link to the official site. Citizen efforts, search engines, ISPs, non-profit groups, and individuals can point users to the official site while perhaps also providing links to their favourite independent efforts. Commentators have even suggested that the FEC provide links to candidate Web sites or free space on its server.

The FEC has not only refused to include these links on its Web site, it has erected barriers to others' linking to candidate Web sites. For online politics to truly become an important force in voter decision- making, links to official Web sites need to be encouraged, not discouraged. Ensuring that each candidate has a voice through free links might reduce the influence of money in politics; candidates would be able to buy banner ads on other sites but anyone who wanted to compare candidates could easily find all positions.

On the Internet, however, drawing the distinction between individual and corporate speech may be difficult. For example, is it a corporate contribution if an ISP or a provider of free Web site hosting allows the posting of statements supporting candidates on Web sites, chat rooms or bulletin boards, especially if the ISP or other service provider is not a common carrier but retains some control over the content of information? Another FECA distinction rendered obsolete by the Internet is the distinction between media and non-media. To meet the FEC's definition for the "media exemption," one must meet several requirements: the content must be a news story, editorial, or commentary from a qualified press entity using the press entity's routine means of distribution.

The Internet has fostered an explosion of alternative news providers, some of which become absorbed into the mainstream media, while many have only an online presence. The current definition of media assumes the model of traditional mass communicators. Even as governments around the world acknowledged the difficulties inherent in censoring the Internet, legislative proposals continued to threaten free speech. While human rights and civil liberties groups pointed out the global implications for the rights to privacy and free expression represented by such proposals, regulators around the world were quick to refine online monitoring, screening, and other controlling technologies. Arguing that national regulatory frameworks are not appropriate to the global nature of the Internet, industry leaders joined forces to create an international Internet content rating system to "protect children and free speech" on the Web. In May they formed the Internet Content Rating Association (ICRA) to facilitate the development of an integrated self-regulatory approach to dealing with "harmful and illegal" content on the Internet. Human Rights Watch, along with other members of the Global Internet Liberty Campaign (GILC), argued for more deliberate consideration of so-called self-regulatory approaches to Internet content control.

The Global Internet Liberty Campaign Member Statement further emphasized the danger that rating and filtering systems could, in fact, facilitate government censorship. The wide-scale deployment of rating and blocking systems could be used by regulators to stifle expression and marginalize any Web sites that failed to adopt ratings. The existence of a standardized rating system for Internet content-with the accompanying technical changes to facilitate blocking-would allow governments to require Internet service providers (ISPs) and other content access providers (public libraries, schools, etc.) to employ such regimes. Exemplifying this possibility, the Australian government on June 30, 1999 approved the Broadcasting Services Amendment (Online Services) Act, which would force Australian ISPs to remove objectionable material from Australian sites and to block access to similar sites overseas. Material suitable for blocking was to be identified based on existing national film and video classification standards. The new law placed sweeping restrictions on adults providing or gaining access to material deemed unsuitable for minors. In Bahrain, Iran, Saudi Arabia, the United Arab Emirates, and Yemen, ISPs-either under government orders or pressure-all blocked Web sites on the basis of their content.

At least in the first four of these countries, blocking extended to cultural and/or political content. Proxy servers such as the ones in place in the U.A.E. and Saudi Arabia could be used by authorities to track which computer terminals were accessing which Web sites and for how long. While U.A.E. authorities denied monitoring individual Web use, Saudi Arabian users who requested blocked sites received a message on their screens warning that all access attempts were logged. State-controlled or state-influenced ISPs in Tunisia, Iran and Bahrain blocked Web sites containing political or human rights criticism of their governments. Tunisia acknowledged blocking only those sites that offended moral values, but apparently this included the sites of various human rights organizations critical of the government. Videsh Sanchar Nigam Ltd. (owned by the Indian government) was the nation's largest Internet service provider and controlled the international Internet gateways used by ISPs in India. During the last week of June, at the height of the Kashmir crisis, Internet users in India could not reach the online news site of the Pakistan daily Dawn, which was known for its independent coverage of the crisis. Fearing that VSNL gateways blocked access to the newspaper site, other Web sites began posting information explaining how surfers from India could break the blockade, and a number of mailing lists began circulating articles from Dawn in text format. Radio B92, the leading independent radio station in Belgrade, Yugoslavia, was banned in March but continued to broadcast news on the Internet. Online users around the world were able to continue to access Radio B2-92's independent news via the Web as a daily digest with headline updates every hour. In late 1998 the United States Congress passed the Child Online Protection Act (COPA), making it a crime to publish "any communication for commercial purposes that includes any material that is harmful to minors, without restricting access to such material by minors." In April the U.S. Department of Justice appealed a federal appeals court ruling declaring the law unconstitutional, the result of a lawsuit brought by opponents of the COPA.

Governments rarely admit to "eavesdropping" on e-mail, and it is extremely hard to ascertain whether government monitoring is occurring when most information about monitoring mechanisms is classified. But during 1998 official disclosures in Europe and Australia provided a glimpse into one such system, a monitoring process referred to as ECHELON. According to a January 1998 report published by the Scientific and Technological Option Assessment (STOA) unit of the European Parliament, ECHELON formed part of the UKUSA spy system and wasdesigned for primarily nonmilitary targets: governments, organizations and businesses. The system operated in virtually every country and intercepted fax, e-mail and telephone messages routinely and indiscriminately. In Britain, the Home Office announced a number of proposals in a June 1999 consultation paper on the interception of communications. Future laws based on these proposals would require "communications service providers" to integrate government interception facilities into their networks, including the Internet, at their own expense. These proposals followed the specifications secretly agreed by European police officials in ENFOPOL plans revealed the previous year. (ENFOPOL was a standard European Commission classification for documents concerned with law enforcement matters.) The British consultation paper also argued that the maintenance of an interception capability was a basic requirement for providers of communication services in countries such as France, Germany, the Netherlands, Sweden, Canada, the United States and Australia. On April 2, the Second Chamber of the Dutch Parliament approved a new Telecommunications Act that included a chapter intended, among other things, to force ISPs to facilitate monitoring by the police and intelligence services. In April, an Internet service provider, Singnet of Singapore, apologized to its subscribers after scanning their computers without their knowledge. Singnet had asked the Home Affairs Ministry to check the computers of its 200,000 subscribers during a computer virus scare.

In Russia rules requiring ISPs to provide the security service with complete access to users' e-mail were challenged by an ISP based in Volgograd. The rules, known as System of Efficient Research Measures 2 (SORM-2), were written by the Russian Federal Security

Services and the State Communications Agency in 1998. In the Middle East and North Africa, where many governments routinely tapped the phones of potential dissidents, Internet users in many countries, including Bahrain and Tunisia, suspected that the right to privacy of correspondence was being violated by government surveillance of e-mail communications. One Bahraini spent more than a year in jail on suspicion of e-mailing "political" information to dissidents abroad. Under India's License Agreement Provision of Internet Service, ISPs had to maintain logs of all Internet users and the service they were using. These logs, as well as copies of all the packets originating from the customer premises equipment (CPE) of the ISP, had to be available in real time to the government telecom authority.

China continued its crackdown on Internet dissent by explicitly prohibiting the transmission or posting of what the government considered "anti-government propaganda." In January 1999, a computer technician, Lin Hai, was sentenced to two years' imprisonment by a Shanghai court for giving the e-mail addresses of 30,000 Chinese subscribers to a dissident site that published an online magazine from the United States. In a worrying development, Internet providers and telecommunications companies in many countries could be forced to build special data taps into their Internet servers to allow government security agencies real-time monitoring of every e-mail message and Web page sent to or from their servers. This could allow government agencies to circumvent national privacy laws, allowing them to rely on surveillance mechanisms in other countries. Citing national security concerns, governments continued to avoid releasing information on monitoring mechanisms.

The development of and freedom to use encryption software could provide substantial protection for the privacy of online users. Yet contrary to the spirit of international norms that recognize privacy as a fundamental human right, governments continued to use export controls or other national laws limiting the public's access to encryption technologies and inhibiting the development of new encryption products. In December 1998, the Wassenaar Arrangement announced, largely due to United States pressure, new guidelines that would authorize restrictions on the export of most commercial cryptography products above a fifty-six or sixty-four bit strength. But there were other, more encouraging developments in this area. In Germany, an export license was no longer required for the export of encryption products to third-country markets. Ireland, counter to the wishes of its E.U. neighbors, was willing to adopt policies that favored the use of strong encryption to encourage Internet trading. The French prime minister announced in January that due to the threat of electronic espionage and other dangers to privacy France would allow encryption strengths up to 128 bits, and would remove the compulsory or third-party escrow of encryption keys.As should be evident, the field of Internet regulation and surveillance was still very much in flux in 1999. It was clear, however, that the privacy and free expression rights of users of this global medium would be shaped by a multiplicity of regulations and policies, including self-regulatory approaches promoted by Internet industry leaders as well as myriad national and international rules on surveillance and encryption.

Privacy on the Net

As a mass medium, the Internet can enable anyone to receive and to disseminate alternatives to state-controlled information at a low cost. While few individuals and groups have the means to publish books or newspapers, make a film, or air a radio or television program, any person with access to a personal computer and modem can communicate with a huge international audience. A connection to the Internet can increase access to information in less-developed countries by putting within easy reach one of the world's great repositories of information, much of it free and continuously updated, and by making that information more easily manageable and transferable. Such benefits do not depend on a large number of persons having the means to purchase their own equipment and Internet accounts.

A government policy of making computers available to the public at libraries, schools or community centers, or the presence of privately run "Internet cafés" or "cybercafés, can help to democratize use of the Internet even in relatively poor countries. In light of the Internet's vast potential for empowering people to exercise the right to free expression, some have argued that governments have an affirmative obligation to facilitate Internet access for all segments of the population on terms of nondiscrimination. Some have also contended that the Internet can significantly assist governments in enabling citizens to exercise the right, under article 25(a) of the International Covenant on Civil and Political Rights, "to take part in the conduct of public affairs, directly or through freely chosen representatives." The exercise of this right is enhanced by providing citizens access to all draft and effective laws, transcripts of parliamentary debates, and other information relevant to civic affairs.

New communications technologies are providing developing countries with an unprecedented means to leapfrog antiquated communication networks. Limits on access are imposed by governments for a variety of reasons, including economic gain and political control. Some governments, including India and Saudi Arabia, have chosen to control the liberalizing effect of the Internet by denying access to entire segments of their populations, either through exorbitant charges or by confining access to select populations, such as universities. Rather than attempting to extend the Internet to a diverse group of citizens, these governments are striving to reap the economic benefits of Internet access without making it available to economically, socially, and politically disadvantaged groups, for whom it has the greatest potential for positive change. In some countries, such as Saudi Arabia, individuals who have Internet connections through foreign-owned corporations are able to elude these restrictions.

Privacy issues are closely related to the regulation of content and access. On-line communications are particularly susceptible to unauthorized scrutiny. Encryption technology is needed to ensure that individuals and groups may communicate without fear of eavesdropping. The Internet has the potential to be a tremendous force for development by providing quick and inexpensive information, by encouraging discussion rather than violence, and by empowering citizens, to cite but a few examples. But this potential can be realized only if it becomes a truly global effort. Policy makers must make every effort to ensure that internationally guaranteed rights to free expression are extended to on-line communication and call for the repeal of censorship legislation. Without such commitments, individuals face the danger of seeing their rights eroded by the very technologies they are embracing.

A government agency can violate the privacy of e-mail correspondence just as easily as it can tap a person's telephone in order to listen to conversations or intercept faxes. The equipment needed is neither costly nor complicated to operate. Authorities can monitor by tapping an individual phone line and intercepting data streams as they are sent and received. If a user has Internet access via a private ISP, employees of that ISP can open and read e-mail sent through it or allow police investigators to do so, unless special safeguards are put in place to protect privacy. If authorities have access to an ISP's server or the country's telecommunications network, they can capture e-mails while they are in transit. Authorities can read, block, or delete messages based on such criteria as the e-mail address of the sender or the recipient, the Internet Protocol addresses identifying the sending computer and the destination computer(s), or the presence of specified character strings in the body of the message--say, the words "Emir" and "corruption" in close proximity. Such a system is analogous to a postal delivery system in which all pieces of mail are first delivered to a single location, where officials can inspect items at will.

Although data is broken up and sent in "packets," each packet contains Internet Protocol (IP) addresses. Packets can easily be reassembled while en route with the aid of eavesdropping tools. An eavesdropper can generally identify the computer terminal that is sending or receiving data, but not the person who is typing on its keyboard. For this reason, some governments are uneasy about allowing computer terminals with Internet access in places where extra effort would be required to monitor who is using each terminal, for what, and when. A contract provided by Tunisia's state-run Agence

Tunisienne d'Internet (ATI) requires institutional Internet subscribers to refrain from offering anyone remote access via their computers without prior authorization, and to declare to the ATI the names of all persons having accounts on, or access to, the computers and to inform the agency of changes in the user list.

Expression via the Internet includes the use of means that are private and others that are public. E-mail is private in the sense that the sender specifies the persons and addresses to whom it will be sent. By contrast, launching an open-access web site or posting a comment in a public newsgroup are acts of public speech since they are viewable by anyone who wishes to visit the web site or newsgroup. Computer users have various means to protect their privacy and anonymity, some more effective than others. At the low-tech end, a user can try to avoid surveillance by using a computer terminal or e-mail account that is not being monitored, for example, one belonging to a friend. These techniques may help users escape identification if they are not already under surveillance, but they are no insurance against interception if a user's computer communication is being monitored. Experts agree that there are basically three methods that, for the time being at least, make surveillance extremely difficult: direct-to-satellite and other forms of wireless transmission, anonymous re-mailers, and encryption. Small dishes are available that enable users to transmit and receive data directly via satellite, bypassing the ground-based telecommunication system. These fit into a suitcase-sized carrying case and can be placed discreetly on a balcony while in use. They resemble in size the "pizza" dishes used to download satellite television broadcasts, but are capable of sending as well as receiving.

Some countries of the Middle East and North Africa either ban or require permits for direct-to-satellite dishes. Cost also puts this technology beyond the reach of most individuals and nongovernmental organizations in the region. But as they grow more affordable and widespread, wireless communications offer a potent means of evading government monitoring and censorship. Encryption, on the other hand, costs nothing or next to nothing. Strong and easy-to-use encryption software, such as the "Pretty Good Privacy" (PGP) program, can be downloaded for free from the World Wide Web and stored on a laptop or personal computer.

While experts using powerful computers have been able to break strong encryption codes, the process requires considerable resources and time and is impractical for routine monitoring. Users should nevertheless pay attention to developments in the field--as well as to local laws governing the use of encryption. The Global Internet Liberty Campaign maintains a country-by-country review of legislation. The right to encrypt messages is of particular importance to the protection of human rights. In many countries human rights organizations use PGP to protect the identity of witnesses and victims when sending data electronically. Rights groups in Guatemala, Ethiopia, Haiti, Mexico, South Africa, Hong Kong, and Turkey are among those that use encryption, according the GILC survey. Some groups use cryptographic techniques to digitally sign messages that they send over the Internet to ensure their integrity and authenticity, that is, to prove the messages are indeed coming from them and have not been altered in transmission. The power of encryption to foil monitoring has led a number of governments to impose restrictions on the use, sale, and export of encryption software. Tunisia, Saudi Arabia, and Israel are among those countries that ban the use of encryption without prior authorization. Encryption has an Achilles heel: it may effectively shield a message's contents from an eavesdropper but not the fact that something has been encoded. This alone may lead to harsh consequences if the authorities wish to punish the sender or recipient, or coerce them to disclose the message's contents or their "private keys." Upon obtaining the latter, authorities could then read every message encrypted with the user's "public key" or use the compromised private key to impersonate that user in corresponding with others.

One way to circumvent this danger is to camouflage encrypted messages by using steganography. This type of program hides one form of data inside another in such a way that makes it more likely to escape detection by interlopers. For example, a sensitive document proving that a police unit moonlighted as a death squad can be encrypted and embedded in a photograph of a soccer team, and then e-mailed to a person outside the country who has the means to extract the document. Steganography software can be downloaded for free from the World Wide Web. However, some experts warn that sophisticated eavesdroppers can detect when a file has something steganographically hidden in it. The third anti-surveillance strategy is to route communications via secure and trusted web-based re-mailing services that forward them to the designated recipient only after expunging the original address and other identifying data. To reduce traceability further, users can select re-mailers that keep no records of the addresses from which they receive, and to which they send, data. They can also program messages to pass through more than one re-mailer; some re-mailers do this automatically.

Protecting Freedom of Expression on the net

In 1948 proclamation of the international human right to freedom of expression, the citizens of the world have the ability to exercise that right on a truly global basis, "regardless of frontiers." With the advent of the Internet, methods of accessing and disseminating information have been fundamentally changed, with profound implications for individuals, civil society and governments.

Like no medium before it, the Internet permits any individual with a computer and a gateway to the Internet to communicate instantaneously with others worldwide. The Internet offers educational institutions, businesses, and non-profit organizations an opportunity to exchange ideas and promote scientific, cultural, and economic progress. Traditional forms of media can greatly expand their audiences at nominal cost.

The Internet is global in its reach. To a degree that no other technology can, it transcends national borders and eliminates barriers to the free flow of information. These unique features of this new technology, if properly supported, can foster the freedom of expression essential to democratic rule and civil society in ways previously impossible.

The Global Internet Liberty Campaign is a group of human rights and civil liberties organizations that advocate the following:

— Prohibiting prior censorship of on-line communication.

— Requiring that laws restricting the content of on-line speech distinguish between the liability of content providers and the liability of data carriers.

— Insisting that on-line free expression not be restricted by indirect means such as excessively restrictive governmental or private controls over computer hardware or software, telecommunications infrastructure, or other essential components of the Internet.

— Including citizens in the Global Information Infrastructure (GII) development process from countries that are currently unstable economically, have insufficient infrastructure, or lack sophisticated technology.

— Prohibiting discrimination on the basis of race, color, sex, language, religion, political or other opinion, national or social origin, property, birth or other status.

— Ensuring that personal information generated on the Internet for one purpose is not used for an unrelated purpose or disclosed without the person's informed consent and enabling individuals to review personal information on the Internet and to correct inaccurate information.

— Allowing on-line users to encrypt their communications and information without restriction..

Governments, however, have already begun to impose controls on the Internet, threatening the potential of this new medium. Some governments have enacted laws prohibiting certain content on the Internet and have sought to prosecute users and service providers. Others have tried to control access, by insisting on the installation of national "proxy servers" and requiring the blocking of targeted web sites.

And in other countries, governments have encouraged forms of "self-regulation" that are in fact intended to enlist service providers to control the behavior of their customers.

An increasingly well-established body of international law protects the right to freedom of expression. As we shall see, various human rights instruments are diluted by exceptions and may be difficult to enforce. Moreover, not all countries are parties to a binding human rights agreement.

But international human rights law undoubtedly has advanced the cause of free expression and undoubtedly applies to the Internet and other digital media. Given the broad language of international and regional human rights documents, there is no doubt that government measures to control the Internet are subject to challenge under international law.

The technology itself both demands and can support fuller protection of free expression: The borderless nature of the Internet requires that the phrase "regardless of frontiers," which appears in the key international human rights instruments, be applied with a fresh eye.

The concept of a right to "impart" information takes on new meaning when anyone can be a publisher. Since censorship in one country may constitute a direct infringement on the right of persons in other countries to "impart" information "without regard to frontiers," the traditional deference given to local norms should be less relevant to the Internet.

The decentralized nature of the Internet makes government controls less effective, because Internet users have numerous ways of circumventing them. At the same time, the user-controlled nature of the technology means that government controls are less necessary in some contexts.

Furthermore, given the essentially unlimited capacity of the Internet, there is less need for government intervention to ensure fairness or balance or to protect reputation. On the Internet, the marketplace of ideas can function with less regulation since good ideas can always achieve the space they deserve. Mistakes can be corrected and the right of reply can be effectuated instantaneously.

Under international law, necessity, proportionality, and efficacy are key concepts in judging the validity of restrictions on freedom of expression. If government regulation of content on the Internet is not likely to succeed and not necessary, then it becomes less supportable under international rules.

Applying international human rights principles to the Internet requires an appreciation of the fundamental characteristics of the digital on-line media. The unique qualities of the Internet justify according the strongest protection to free expression on-line and should prompt a new vision of the right to receive and impart information "regardless of frontiers."

The Internet is really a network of networks and is comprised of a number of different technologies and infrastructures. Viewed as a whole, it is uniquely:

— *Global* - The Internet provides immediate access to information from around the world. With simple e-mail, it is as easy to send a message to another continent as it is to the building next door. Through the World Wide Web, thousands of newspapers and tens of thousands of other information sources are available from around the world. While access is still not available to most of the world's population, the fastest rates of growth are in less developed countries.

— *Decentralized* - The Internet was designed by purpose to be decentralized, to work without gatekeepers, and to accommodate multiple, competitive access points. The absence of gatekeepers of the kind that exist in broadcasting, cable television, or satellite transmission, the availability of numerous hosting sites, and the irrelevance of geographic location mean that material can almost always be published outside the control of governments, monopolies or oligopolies.

— *Open* - The Internet has low barriers to access. Service can be priced very inexpensively. The costs of creating and disseminating content are extreme-ly low. Because of the Internet, anybody who has a computer and a modem can be a publisher - a digital Gutenberg.

— *Abundant* - The digitization of information and the ability to transmit it over the telephone network, combined with the decentralized nature of the Internet, mean that the Internet has essentially unlimited capacity to hold information. In economic terms, the marginal cost of adding another web site, sending another email message, or posting to a newsgroup is essentially zero.

— *Interactive* - The Internet is designed for bi-directional communication: All Internet users can be both speakers and listeners. The Internet allows responsive communication from one-to-one, from one-to-many, and from many-to-one.

- *User-Controlled* - The Internet allows users to exercise far more choice than even cable television or short wave radio. The user can skip from site to site in ways that are not dictated by the content providers or by the access provider. User can control what content reaches their computers.
- *Infrastructure independent* - The Internet is not linked to any infrastructure other than the telephone system. Dial-up access is available from any telephone that can make an international call. Access to the Internet can also be wireless and satellite based and therefore further removed from effective control of governments. Courts and other institutions that have considered in depth the question of Internet regulation have recognized these unique features.

A unique characteristic of the Internet is that it functions simultaneously as a medium for publishing and for communication. Unlike in the case of traditional media, the Internet supports a variety of communication modes: one-to-one, one-to-many, many-to-many.

An Internet user may "speak" or "listen" interchangeably. At any given time, a receiver can and does become content provider, of his own accord, or through "re-posting" of content by a third party. The Internet therefore is radically different from traditional broadcasting. It also differs radically from a traditional telecommunication service."

The United States Supreme Court, in ruling that the Communications Decency Act was unconstitutional and that the Internet merited the strongest protection of free expression, based its judgment on the conclusion that the Internet was "a unique and wholly new medium of worldwide human communication."

The Internet Promote Democracy

The vast new potential of the Internet for expanding access to information and participation in government and civil society has already begun to show itself with concrete contributions to democracy and human rights.

The bi-directional nature of the Internet has tremendous potential for fostering democratic participation, giving voice to the voiceless. The Internet could allow citizens to communicate with their government, to pose questions to their elected representatives, and to submit comments on pending issues. While many governments have been slow to take advantage of the democratic potential of the Internet, some harbingers of progress can be seen.

The Costa Rican government, to make voting more convenient, is working to shift to an electronic voting system. Taking advantage of a literacy rate of 94% and the fact that about 50% of grade schools have Internet-connected computers, Costa Rica hopes to run an entirely electronic balloting in 2002. International bodies also use the Internet to promote public participation in their activities. For example, last year the EU conducted an online forum regarding illegal or harmful content on the Internet. Grassroots organizations can use the Internet to mobilize voters to be active on issues.

One of the most important potential benefits of the Internet is the ability to provide rapid access to the full text of government documents. If a government is willing, it can provide its citizens access to enacted and proposed laws, regulations, government reports and statistics, transcripts of parliamentary debates, judicial decisions, all searchable by word or concept.

Information previously available only to experts, usually only in the capital city, and often only with great expenditure of time and money can now be made available to individuals in the smallest rural town and at public libraries in the poorest neighborhoods. This vast openness need not be the luxury of only wealthy nations.

Strengthening civil society through the building of networks among individuals The Internet has opened up new opportunities for discourse, on matters political, intellectual, and personal. The Internet's architecture allows for a diversity of views and exchange of information that is simply not possible in any other media. As of August 1998, one service identified 29,000 IRC (Internet Relay Chat) channels, 30,000 Usenet newsgroups, and 90,095 mailing lists - each one representing a network of individuals worldwide interested in a particular subject.

Among the first to use the Internet were human rights activists. In 1992, the International Freedom of Expression exchange (IFEX) was established to provide accurate and timely information regarding censorship and attacks on journalists. The primary method of transmitting information is by e-mail: whenever there is a serious threat to freedom of expression, the IFEX action alert network sends out detailed information on the case via e-mail to participating organizations and individuals, who in turn mount international protests from their own regions. The Internet has been at the forefront of democratic uprisings. In Indonesia, "Bypassing the government-controlled television and radio stations, dissidents shared information about protests by e-mail, inundated news groups with stories of President Suharto's corruption, and used chat groups to exchange tips about resisting troops."

The Web has become a place where there is ready access to newspapers and other publications. A wide range of print publications are available on-line, and many broadcast media now have on-line services that allow searching of past broadcasts, a capability previously available only to governments and a few research institutes.

Information is exchanged via a centrai computer located in Paris. AIM texts are available in Serbian, Croatian, Bosnian, and a choice of texts is available in English. Subscribers to AIM regularly receive the whole production of AIM via e-mail. The China News Digest makes available news from non-official sources. While the site is sometimes blocked by the Chinese government, users in China have found ways to access it. The service also uses e-mail to disseminate its news within China.

With the Internet, it is increasingly difficult for governments to control content. The Internet offers creative ways to disseminate information around the controls of censors. Once an issue is ready to be published, it is secretly delivered to the United States and then emailed back to China from an anonymous address.

The technology of the Internet frustrates control in other ways. Proxy servers purportedly block access to web sites known to contain objectionable content and thus preclude such content from being accessed. Such servers fail to achieve their goal, however, because:

1) web site operators whose sites are targeted as containing undesirable content can simply change their web site address; and

2) an Internet user in a country imposing controls can simply dial into a server outside the country and

access the desired information, thereby avoiding the proxy server altogether.

Given the global nature of the Internet, content can be published from anywhere in the world. When a government tries to prosecute a content provider or force the withdrawal of material, there are others around the world prepared to copy or mirror the information on their own sites, in countries where the information is legal.

Governments' Control on Internet content and Access

Despite the power of the Internet - or perhaps because of that very power - governments have sought to restrict it. Government actions infringing freedom of expression on the Internet take many forms:

— *Internet-specific laws*: Some governments have criminalized certain types of speech on the Internet. Such criminal penalties may come in the form of laws whose expressed intent is to protect minors from certain material regarded as "harmful." However, as the United States Supreme Court recently found, requiring that Internet speakers shield certain populations from their speech is effectively a total ban on that speech.

— *Application of existing laws*: Governments can act to restrict speech without specifically enacting laws targeting Internet-based speech. For example, German government action against CompuServe for providing access to material illegal under German law did not require enactment of new law, merely the assertion by government agents that certain Internet speech violated the existing laws.

— *Content-based license terms applied to Internet users and service providers*: Several countries have already established licensing systems that require Internet users and/or service providers to agree to refrain from certain kinds of speech, or block access to speech as a condition of having a license to use the Internet or provide access to the Net. China has issued rules requiring anyone with Internet access to refrain from proscribed speech. And the Singapore Broadcasting Authority requires all Internet Service Providers to abide by licensing terms demanding that they block access to foreign web sites and newsgroups deemed harmful to national morals.

— *Compelled use of filtering, rating or content labeling tools*: Blocking, filtering, and labeling techniques can prevent individuals from using the Internet to exchange information on topics that may be controversial or unpopular, enable the development of country profiles to facilitate a global/universal rating system desired by some governments, block access to content on entire domains, block access to Internet content available at any domain or page which contains a specific key word or character string in the address, and over-ride self-rating labels provided by content creators and providers. Where any such mechanisms are required by public authorities or otherwise forced on users, they constitute serious threats to human rights.

Over the past half-century, international human rights law has enshrined the rights to free expression, access to information, and privacy of communications, creating a strong presumption against governmental intrusions. These rights are reflected both in the provisions of numerous international and regional agreements and in decisions rendered by human rights tribunals. These human rights doctrines protecting freedom of expression are fully applicable to the Internet. Indeed, these protections may offer especially strong protection to the Internet, given its unique features. These human rights instruments have their limitations. The Universal Declaration has been accepted in effect by all 185 Member States of the United Nations, but not all of its provisions have become binding.

The International Covenant on Civil and Political Rights is binding, but its enforcement mechanisms are limited. While there are binding regional agreements for the Americas, for Europe, and for Africa, there are none for Asia or the Middle East. Enforcement mechanisms are available under these regional agreements, but they are limited too. Where individual review is available, the time required to pursue a case all the way to the international level may be substantial. Most importantly, these instruments, particularly the European Convention, are burdened with exceptions that have been seriously criticized as over-broad.

Nonetheless, these human rights agreements have served to expand freedom of expression worldwide, becoming part of international law and affecting the domestic laws of many nations. The numerous international and regional instruments discussed herein provide substantial evidence that the principle of free expression is a well-settled principle of international law.

The collection of treaties, agreements, and international tribunal decisions also evidences an international consensus on the scope of this right: it applies to all forms of media, it applies to the ability to receive and to impart information, and it is subject to only limited restrictions. The advent of the Internet raises the question of how these human rights instruments apply to the new communications media. The answers are in some respects encouraging: the instruments are drafted with very forward-looking language, with powerful implications for a medium that operates "regardless of frontiers."

The international community has stated its commitment to the right to free expression in a series of fundamental agreements, including the Universal Declaration of Human Rights, the International Covenant on Civil and Political Rights, and the International Covenant on Economic, Social and Cultural Rights. The right of free expression was first proclaimed an international norm by the then-members of the United Nations in the 1948 Universal Declaration of Human Rights. Taken together, Articles 19, 12, and 27 of the Universal Declaration constitute a blueprint for the protection of free expres-sion on the Internet. Article 19 of the Universal Declaration proclaims: "Everyone has the right to freedom of opinion and expression; this right includes freedom to hold opinions without interference and to seek, receive and impart information and ideas through any medium and regardless of frontiers."

Article 12 of the Universal Declaration provides: "No one shall be subjected to arbitrary interference with his privacy, family, home or correspondence." The language of this provision is broad enough to encompass all communications directed to an individual or group of individuals, including electronic mail and newsgroup communications. Finally, the right to seek, receive and impart information guaranteed in Article 19 of the Universal Declaration is reinforced by Article 27, which upholds the right of each individual "freely to participate in the cultural life of the community, to enjoy the arts and to share in scientific advancement and its benefits." Given that the Internet's roots are in the exchange of scientific information, Article 27 seems particularly apt to the protection of communications on the Internet. The foresightful language of Article 19 ("through any medium") makes it clearly applicable to expression via the Internet. The rights to "seek" and "impart" information seem particularly relevant to "surfing" the 'Net and posting information on Web sites for all to read, while the right to "receive" information encompasses the exchange of electronic mail and the downloading of information.

Article 29(2) provides: "In the exercise of his rights and freedoms, everyone shall be subject only to such limitations as are determined by law solely for the purpose of securing due recognition and respect for the rights and freedoms of others and of meeting the just requirements of morality, public order and the general welfare in a democratic society."The Universal Declaration is not a treaty. It was adopted by the United Nations General Assembly as a resolution having no force of law on its own. However, over time the Declaration has become a normative instrument that creates some legal obligations for Member States of the UN. Many of the principles established by the Universal Declaration have since entered the corpus of international law as evidenced by an overwhelming consensus of opinion and practice among states. This consensus is illustrated in subsequent international and regional treaties and agreements, decisions of international tribunals, and domestic constitutions and legislation. Further, the Declaration has served as an inspiration for other human rights agreements of more direct effect.

The United Nations Commission on Human Rights was created in 1946 under Article 68 of the UN Charter. States name representatives to the 53 member Commission, where they serve as instructed governmental delegates. The Commission prepares reports and coordinates an expansive network of working groups and rapporteurs with thematic or country mandates. It has been criticized for being politically motivated and selective in approach, but it serves as the principal UN forum for addressing charges of human rights violations and as a focal point for broadening the human rights agenda of the UN.

International Covenant on Civil and Political Rights The principles first enunciated in the Universal Declaration are reiterated and expanded upon in the 1966 International Covenant on Civil and Political Rights ("ICCPR"), which took effect in 1976 and has now been ratified by 140 nations. Article 19 of the ICCPR restates Article 19 of the Universal Declaration almost verbatim. It declares: "Everyone shall have the right to hold opinions without interference. ... Everyone shall have the right to freedom of expression... ." In words somewhat more expansive than the Universal Declaration, Article 19 of the ICCPR expressly states that the freedom of expression extends to all forms of media: "this right shall include freedom to seek, receive and impart information and ideas of all kinds, regardless of frontiers, either orally, in writing or in print, in the form of art, or through any other media of his choice." The ICCPR also reiterates the crux of Article 12 of the Universal Declaration: "No one shall be subjected to arbitrary or unlawful interference with his privacy, family, home or correspondence." The ICCPR defines the scope of limitations that could be imposed on the freedom of expression. Consistent with the law of most if not all nations, the ICCPR recognizes that freedom of expression may be curtailed under certain circumstances. The ICCPR requires, however, that restrictions on free speech be narrowly defined and not arbitrary. Article 19(3) of the ICCPR provides that restrictions on the freedom of expression are valid only where such restrictions are "provided by law and are necessary: a. For respect of the rights or reputation of others; [or] b. For the protection of national security or of public order, or of public health or morals."

The essence of applying the ICCPR involves interpreting this limitation. It has been urged that this provision means that laws restricting freedom of expression must be "accessible, unambiguous, drawn narrowly, and with precision." Moreover, the burden of demonstrating the validity of a restriction on free speech should lie with the government. The key hurdle for governments is the requirement that restrictions be "necessary;" this has generally been interpreted as a high standard. The ICCPR includes several other provisions relevant to freedom of expression. Article 17 provides, "No one shall be subjected... to unlawful attacks on his honour and reputation. ... Everyone has the right to the protection of the law against such... attacks." Article 20 states, "Any advocacy of national, racial, or religious hatred that constitutes incitement to discrimination, hostility or violence shall be prohibited by law."Under the Covenant, States Parties are required to submit reports every five years on the measures they have taken to protect and advance human rights. The Covenant established a Human Rights Committee, one of the principal functions of which is to examine these reports. The Committee makes conclusions on individual state reports and also issues general comments, which serve as advisory opinions on the Covenant. In 1976, an optional protocol went into force which enables private parties to file individual complaints against States Parties that have ratified the covenant. The protocol is itself a treaty, and therefore binds the states that have ratified it. Complainants must exhaust domestic remedies first. Once a complaint has been admitted as properly drawn, the Committee brings the matter to the attention of the state involved, which has six months to respond. The Committee, after considering all the written communications on the matter, issues its "views." The Committee has no power to enforce its findings, but it does require States Parties to indicate in their periodic reports what measures they have taken to give effect to the Committee's recommendations. "In particular, the State Party should indicate what remedy it has afforded the author of the communication whose rights the Committee has found to have been violated."

Restrictions on the Internet also implicate rights established by the International Covenant on Economic, Social, and Cultural Rights ("ICESCR"). Echoing Article 27 of the Universal Declaration, Article 15 of the ICESCR recognizes the important "benefits to be derived from the encouragement and development of international contacts and cooperation in the scientific and cultural fields." Accordingly, the 136 signatories pledge to "diffuse science and culture" and to "respect the freedom indispensable for scientific research and creative activity." These provisions articulate that free expression across borders must be respected to realize social, scientific, and cultural advancements. To take advantage of such progress, Article 15 of the ICESCR establishes that all individuals are entitled "to enjoy the benefits of scientific progress and its applications." One of the most effective means of doing so is through Internet communication, which enables people in distant and diverse countries to share valuable scientific research and social insights.The ICESCR does not establish any interstate or individual complaint system. It only requires the States Parties to submit "reports on the measures which they have adopted and the progress made in achieving the observance of the rights recognized herein." Art. 16(1). Regional human rights agreements in Europe, the Americas, and Africa establish the right of free expression for all individuals and privacy in their communications with others. Such freedoms are protected in all forms of media and "regardless of frontiers." These regional agreements are especially important because of the opportunities they offer for international judicial review of actions restricting free expression.

The European Convention for the Protection of Human Rights and Fundamental Freedoms ("European Convention") was adopted in 1950 by members of the Council of Europe. Article 10 states in full: "(1) Everyone has the right to freedom of expression. This right shall include freedom to hold opinions and to receive and impart information and ideas without interference by public authority and regardless of frontiers. This Article shall not prevent States from requiring licensing of broadcasting, television or cinema enterprises. "(2) The exercise of these freedoms, since it carries with it duties and responsibilities, may be subject to such formalities, conditions, restrictions or penalties as are prescribed by law and are necessary in a democratic society, in the interests of national security, territorial integrity or public safety, for the prevention of disorder or crime, for the protection of health or morals, for the protection of the reputation or rights of others, for preventing the disclosure of information received in confidence, or for maintaining the authority and impartiality of the judiciary." The European Convention thus establishes that the right of free expression pertains to cross-border communication, which naturally applies to much of the content available on the Internet. Closely linked to freedom of expression are additional rights in the European Convention: the right to respect for correspondence and privacy, contained in Article 8; [24] the right to freedom of peaceful assembly and freedom of association, contained in Article 11; and the right to manifest one's religion or belief, contained in Article 9. Article 10 is not stated in absolute terms. The second paragraph specifies that freedom of expression can be curtailed in furtherance of a series of enumerated interests.

It has been widely debated whether these exceptions are too broad. But even in the U.S. and other countries with constitutional free speech provisions, restrictions are permitted through judicial interpretation. Supporters of Article 10's approach argue that Article 10 is preferable because the catalogue of possible restrictions is limited and because Article 10 also establishes that any restriction on the exercise of the freedom of expression must be "prescribed by law" and "necessary in a democratic society" to serve one of the enumerated interests. In specific situations, it has been found that there was no violation of Article 10 in: the application of blasphemy laws to seize a film, the UK's ban on broadcasting interviews with representatives of the IRA, prohibitions on Nazi material, laws against obscenity, even state disciplinary measures against a lawyer who used aggressive or insulting language.Article 10 must be interpreted in light of other Articles, notably Article 17, which states that nothing in the Convention creates a right to engage in activities "aimed at the destruction of any of the rights or freedoms set forth in the convention." Article 17, it has been held, was intended "to prevent totalitarian groups from exploiting, in their own interests, the principles enunciated in the convention." Accordingly, for example, the Court has concluded that it was not a violation of the Convention for the Netherlands to convict extremist right-wing Dutch politicians for distributing racist leaflets. Other provisions affecting the freedom of expression include Article 6, which guarantees the right to a fair trial, and the right to personal privacy in Article 8, which protects a person's honor and reputation against attack, both of which concepts are also reflected in Article 10(2) itself.

Most European countries that are party to the Convention have made it part of their national law, meaning that it can be invoked in the national courts. For many years, the UK declined to do this, but the Convention will be fully incorporated in UK law when the Human Rights Bill 1998 is enacted. The European Convention has an explicit enforcement mechanism based on judicial review by an independent regional tribunal, the European Court of Human Rights, located in Strasbourg. The most important feature of the Court's jurisdiction is that individuals can bring complaints against Contracting States alleging violations of the Convention. It is sufficient to note that individuals may bring their cases before the Court after exhausting local remedies and that an application must first be presented to the European Commission on Human Rights. The Commission decides on the admissibility of the complaint. Article 10 has a potential role in connection with competition law and rules on the free movement of goods and services. In addition, in its legislative capacity, the Council of the European Union has referred to Article 10 as a relevant norm for EU legislation. The Court's judgments on the merits are binding but declaratory in nature. The Court has no power to quash the impugned decisions of the national authorities. The Court may, however, award "just satisfaction" in the form of financial compensation. In most cases, States have been reasonably swift to make the changes in their laws and practices necessary to bring them into conformity with the Court's decision.

The European countries manifested their commitment to free speech in the Council of Europe's 1982 Declaration on the Freedom of Expression and Information. This Declaration reaffirms Article 10 of the European Convention and proclaims that the freedom of expression is "a fundamental element [of] the principles of genuine democracy, the rule of law and respect for human rights." The Declaration also provides that the freedom of expression and information is "necessary for the social, economic, cultural and political development of every human being, and constitutes a condition for the harmonious progress of social and cultural groups, nations and the international community." The Council of Europe Declaration thus recognizes that the freedom of expression serves not only an individual interest, but the interests of nation states and the international community as well. Significant in the context of Internet communication, the Council of Europe Declaration recognizes that "the continued development of information and communication technology should serve to further that right, regardless of frontiers, to express, seek, to receive and to impart information and ideas, whatever their source." To achieve this high level of protection, the Council of Europe member states agreed to the following objectives:

— "absence of censorship or any arbitrary controls or constraints on participants in the information process, on media content or on the transmission and dissemination of information;

— "the availability and access on reasonable terms to adequate facilities for the domestic and international transmission and dissemination of information and ideas; [and]

— "to ensure that new information and communication techniques and services, where available, are effectively used to broaden the scope of freedom of expression and information."

The 55-member Organization for Security and Co-operation in Europe ("OSCE"), formerly known as the Conference on Security and Co-operation in Europe, sponsored the 1990 Charter of Paris for a New Europe. Signed by 31 countries from Europe, Russia, Canada, and the United States, the Charter proclaims: "We affirm that, without discrimination, every individual has the right to freedom of thought, conscience and religion or belief, [and] freedom of expression." The OSCE's 1994 Budapest Summit Declaration, "Towards a Genuine Partnership in a New Era," complements the Charter by asserting that participating members "take as their guiding principle that they will safeguard" the right to freedom of expression and recognize that "independent and pluralistic media are essential to a free and open society." The Internet is the most "independent and pluralistic" of all media; it should therefore benefit from the strongest protection against restrictions on the free flow of information.OSCE member states also have committed to making "efforts to facilitate the freer and wider dissemination of information of all kinds [and] to encourage co-operation in the field of information." In accordance with this commitment, and in recognition of commitments made under the Universal Declaration and the ICCPR, the OSCE declared that its member states "will ensure that individuals can freely choose their sources of information."Finally, countries of the OSCE reaffirmed the ICCPR's limitations on the scope of permissible restrictions on the right of free expression. The 1990 Conference on the Human Dimension concluded that any restrictions on fundamental rights and freedoms must be (1) provided by law; (2) consistent with obligations under international law, particularly those made pursuant to the ICCPR and the Universal Declaration; and (3) must relate to one of the objectives of the applicable law and be strictly proportionate to the aim of that law.

Regional agreements from the Americas also explicitly embrace the freedom of expression. The American Declaration of the Rights and Duties of Man was the first international human rights instrument, predating even the Universal Declaration. Article IV of the American Declaration states: "Every person has the right to freedom of... expression and dissemination of ideas, by any medium whatsoever."The American Convention on Human Rights ("American Convention") was adopted in 1969 and entered into force in 1978. It is worth quoting in full, for several of its provisions are of particular relevance to current debates concerning the Internet:

"1. Everyone has the right to freedom of thought and expression. This right includes freedom to seek, receive, and impart information and ideas of all kinds, regardless of frontiers, either orally, in writing, in print, in the form of art, or through any other medium of one's choice.

"2. The exercise of the right provided for in the foregoing paragraph shall not be subject to prior censorship but shall be subject to subsequent imposition of liability, which shall be expressly established by law to the extent necessary to ensure:

a. respect for the rights or reputations of others; or

b. the protection of national security, public order, or public health or morals.

"3. The right of expression may not be restricted by indirect methods or means, such as the abuse of government or private controls over newsprint, radio broadcasting frequencies, or equipment used in the dissemination of information, or by any other means tending to impede the communication and circulation of ideas and opinions.

"4. Notwithstanding the provisions of paragraph 2 above, public entertainments may be subject by law to prior censorship for the sole purpose of regulating access to them for the moral protection of childhood and adolescence.

"5. Any propaganda for war and any advocacy of national, racial, or religious hatred that constitute incitements to lawless violence or to any other similar action against any person or group of persons on any grounds including those of race, color, religion,

> language, or national origin shall be considered as offenses punishable by law." As is the case with the international and European counterparts to these agreements, the plain language of the American Convention is clearly applicable to the Internet.

The American Convention has several features that go beyond other human rights instruments. For one, the American Convention explicitly states that the exercise of the right of freedom of expression "shall not be subject to prior censorship." The rule against prior censorship is also reinforced by Article 14, which provides for a right of reply by anyone inured by inaccurate or offensive statements or ideas disseminated to the general public. In a provision that may be relevant to the problems posed by Internet "self-regulation," the American Convention applies to private action and makes it clear that the right of expression may not be restricted by indirect methods or means. Article 13(3) provides that the "right of expression may not be restricted by indirect means, such as the abuse of government or private controls over newsprint, radio broadcasting frequencies, or equipment used in the dissemination of information, or by another means tending to impede the communication and circulation of ideas and opinions."

The American Convention, in language identical to the ICCPR, sets forth a list of permitted grounds for restriction, a list narrower than that in the European Convention: restrictions on speech must be "expressly established by law to the extent necessary to ensure [either] [r]espect for the rights or reputation of others... or [t]he protection of national security, public order, or public health or morals." Article 11 of the American Convention, like other international agreements, protects the privacy of personal communications: "No one may be the object of arbitrary or abusive interference with his private life, his family, his home, or his correspondence."

Undertaking a judicial case in order to advance the cause of human rights is always a risky business. It requires careful selection of the complainant, the respondent, and the forum. It calls for a clear-eyed weighing of the chances of success. A poorly conceived case can yield an adverse decision that represents a set back for the cause of liberty. Mindful of these concerns, it is clear that the international human rights instruments offer opportunities to NGOs seeking to challenge governmental regulation of Internet content and access. In some cases, the most promising venues may be under the regional agreements.

Under human rights principles, expression on the Internet will still be subject to restriction, but without the "margin of appreciation" that has supported restrictions in so many cases. The Internet requires the adoption of a true international standard of review, one that must look to consensus rules generally. The rise of the Internet also requires a reexamination of the meaning of the concept to "seek and receive" and to "impart" information. National restrictions on local speech have a direct and negative impact on the ability of Internet users around the world to "seek and receive" information and ideas, as well as their right to "impart" information. For example, if citizens of one country are prohibited from discussing political issues critically online, then not only are their rights infringed upon, but also the right of others around the world to "seek and receive" that information is directly implicated. Internet Service Providers (ISPs) play a special role in the operation of the Internet. While ISPs differ in nature from country to country, most people most of the time access the Internet through an ISP. The crucial role ISPs play in providing access to the Internet has made them the target of some governments' efforts to regulate content on the Internet. Those countries have assumed that if they can control ISPs, they can control content on the Internet. ISPs do not fit any of the existing media paradigms. They are very distinct from broadcasters. For this reason, it is not legitimate to subject them to regulatory structures designed for other technologies. There are two sets of arguments against making ISPs responsible for content they do not create. First, trying to make ISPs responsible for information that flows over their systems (but which they did not create) would fundamentally change the nature of the Internet and could destroy its power. Second, there is growing recognition that ISPs cannot technically assume responsibility for content they did not create. The task of sifting information is impossible. It would be so easy to encrypt content, to change addresses, to send images by email.

Technical factors prevent a service provider from blocking the free flow of information on the Internet. First, an Internet service provider cannot easily stop the incoming flow of material. No one can monitor the enormous quantity of network traffic, which may consist of hundreds of thousands of emails, newsgroup messages, files, and Web pages that pass through in dozens of text and binary formats, some of them readable only by particular proprietary tools. A number of countries have recognized, after considerable study and debate, that ISPs should not be liable for content they did not create. This reflects a judgment that while ISPs ought to provide law enforcement reasonable assistance in investigating criminal activity, confusing the role of private companies and police authorities risks substantial violation of individual civil liberties. In 1997, Germany adopted a Multimedia Law which provides that access providers are not responsible for any third-party content to which they only provide access. Providers also are not responsible for "any third-party content which they make available for use unless they have knowledge of such content and are technically able and can reasonably be expected to block the use of such content." In the United States, section 230 of the Communications Act, 47 United States Code sec.230, states "No Provider or user of an interactive computer service shall be treated as the publisher or speaker of any information provided by another information content provider." In adopting this provision, Congress specifically found that "the Internet and other interactive computer services offer a forum for a true diversity of political discourse, unique opportunities for cultural development, and myriad avenues for intellectual activity," and it said that its goal was "to promote the continued development of the Internet." In the EU and in a number of other countries, "self-regulation" has been offered as a viable alternative to governmental control of Internet content.

The use of the term "self-regulation" is a misnomer in the context of controlling speech on the Internet. In the normal sense of the phrase, "self-regulation" is when a group of people or companies decide that, in their own best interest, they should themselves regulate how they go about their joint interests. However, what is being suggested by the term "self-regulation" as applied to the Internet is not that ISPs as a group should regulate their own behavior, but rather that ISPs should regulate the behavior of their customers by taking down offensive websites or blocking offensive content. Under international law, privatized control may be harder to challenge. However, in a number of cases, it may be clear that the ISP is acting under pressure from the government and has, in essence become the agent of the government for carrying out a government policy. What is often promoted as Internet "self-regulation" is actually "privatized censorship." It is consistent with the fairly common occurrence of having a formerly direct government function turned over to a private business. The backing is still state power and government threat, but the actual implementation and mechanics of the suppression of material is delegated to a trade group. When ISPs come together to self-regulate certain classes of content in exchange for some limit on their liability for that content, the overwhelming tendency will be to censor more material, rather than less, in an effort by the ISPs to be certain that they have removed any material that might be illegal. Where ISPs are dependent on government grants of liability limitations, their "self-regulating" actions must satisfy the perceived demands of law enforcement, even if this results in removal of legal, protected speech.

5

Global ICT Scenario

Information and communication technologies (ICT) pursue two main goals: processing information (i.e. presenting it in various forms, storing it, searching for it, reproducing it, etc.) and transmitting information from one geographical point to another, from one person to another, to a group of people or to the whole community. So in a certain sense the development of ICTs reflects the development of human beings throughout history.

The second half of this century has witnessed the global phenomenon of an information explosion. The development of different electronic technologies has made it possible for millions of people to have fast access to huge information resources stored in different places on the planet, to communicate with each other and to handle information presented in various forms (text, graphics, video, sound, etc.).

Yet for the great majority of people in the world, traditional information technologies (postal services, press, radio and television) are still playing and no doubt will continue to play in the near future a much more important role than the ICTs such as electronic mail, multimedia and global computer networks. There are two main reasons for this : on the one hand, the use of these ICTs requires certain investments (the purchase of a computer, for instance) that still are too high in relation to average incomes in poor countries and, on the other hand, the ICTs need an adequate communication infrastructure, including telephone lines in sufficient number and quality.

The relations between the various technologies are complex. Postal services, for example, provide a channel for press distribution, in the same way that telecommunications channels provide an infrastructure for digital networks. Some technologies are more concerned with transporting information, while others are more concerned with its production.

Radio and television simultaneously produce and convey information, and are therefore of a different nature. The Persians were the first to establish a formal network to transmit messages across their empire, so the postal service is an ancient working technology.

It also plays an important role in the life of contemporary society because it is not only a media for a person-to-person communication, but also a media for the distribution of printed materials (newspapers, journals, magazines, advertising material, etc.). Clearly, the significance of postal service as a means of person-to-person communication is steadily declining, since contemporary technology offers much faster, more reliable and cheaper solutions.

For example, it takes only a few hours, or even just minutes, to deliver an e-mail message over the ocean, and it costs a few cents. Sending the same message to the same address by postal service takes days and costs dollars. The mail function of the postal service will, nevertheless, continue to play an important role at least in the near future, even in highly industrialized societies, as it is the only communication technology which can ensure the delivery of originals documents. Of course, modern Internet technologies also offer some solutions in this area, such as the delivery by e-mail of digitally signed messages, but these solutions are yet to be legally recognized by the great majority of countries.

The second function of the postal service as a means to distribute newspapers and other printed material in a community will no doubt survive, despite the development of modern technologies. Even the most devoted Internet users can hardly imagine themselves at the breakfast table looking at a computer monitor, rather than a newspaper, for a news item. One of the main indicators of the state of the postal services in a given region is the number of letter-post items posted per capita.

The exponential development of ICTs in industrialized countries has had practically no effect on the domestic postal service: the number of letter-post items posted per capita by the domestic services in industrialized countries has been growing steadily since 1985. However, the slight reduction in the number of international post items in industrialized countries could be a consequence of the development of Internet mailing and fax messaging.

A sharp disproportion between industrialized and developing countries in the availability of postal services. This could be the result of a whole group of factors, one of which is the higher illiteracy rate in some developing countries. The economic importance of the postal service should not be underestimated. As a public service, it has been considered for many years to be a state monopoly. However, the recent development of private delivery services has certainly created an entirely new situation, which puts strong pressure on traditional services.

The printed press is quite another type of information technology. Whereas the postal service is primarily used for of person-to-person communication, the main goal of the press is to deliver information to a large group of people, such as the population of a town or country.

Daily newspapers may be considered as a most significant part of the press, because they offer the latest information. The publishing of daily newspapers requires a highly-qualified staff of journalists and editors, as well as important infrastructures for the quick printing of a huge quantity of material, and fast and reliable delivery services. For this reason, the number of titles of daily newspapers as well as figures for their total circulation are good indicators of the situation of the press in the various regions of the world.

Today, telecommunications are one of the most important of the contemporary ICTs. They include wired and wireless telephony; different mobile services, such as cellular telephones and paging; voice and data transmission; and Integrated Services Digital Networks (ISDN), which provide a very high quality of voice as well as high data communication rates. Existing telephone networks are now also used as a compiement to computer networks, including the Internet and other wide area networks (WAN).

Yet since their very origins at the beginning of this century, the main goal of telecommunications has remained that of providing better, faster and more reliable person-to-person communication. This is why radio paging is usually considered to be a telecommunications service, in contrast to videotext for example, which is considered by many experts to be a television service. Telecommunications are a rapidly developing and highly profitable business.

International Telecommunication Union (ITU), in 1996 the world total telecommunication investment was about $109,670 million, whereas the world total telecommunication revenue was about $515,490 million. Telecommunications revenues are generated mainly by two sources: equipment trading and communication charges.

According to the International Trade Centre data, the top ten major world exporters (manufacturers) of telecommunications equipment are: the United States, Japan, Germany, the United Kingdom, Sweden, Singapore, France, China, the Republic of Korea and Canada. It may be noted that the list of the top ten major exporters and importers of telecommunications equipment is identical, except for Hong Kong, which replaces Sweden in the list of the top ten main importers.

The development of the global situation concerning the availability of telecommunication services may be characterized by the growth in the number of telephone lines (both main and cellular) per capita in different geographical regions. Cellular telephony is becoming more and more popular throughout the world, mostly in the developed countries.

In 1997 according to data from Ericsson, one of the world's leading manufacturers of telecommunication equipment, the total number of cellular subscribers in the world increased from 70 million to 207 million. Among them more than 112 million are subscribers to digital cellular networks and about 9 5 million are subscribers to analog cellular networks. The highest number of cellular networks subscribers is in North America, with about 60 million, followed by Western Europe with 57 million, Asia and the Pacific with 40 million, Japan with 29 million and Latin America with 13 million. The rest of the world numbers 8 million subscribers.

There will be 830 million subscribers to cellular networks by 2003, and an average annual growth rate between 1998 and 2003 of 27%. By the end of 2003 nearly 15% of the world's population will subscribe to cellular telephone networks. Among them will be almost 60% of the population of Japan, more than 50% of the population of North America and about 50% of the population of Western Europe.

Another popular mobile telecommunication service is radio paging. It is cheaper than mobile telephones, which usually include a radio paging mode. Radio paging is most popular in Asian countries. In 1996, according to the ITU data in 1996 Singapore and the Republic of Korea had the highest number of radio paging subscribers per 100 inhabitants - 35 and 28 respectively.

In comparison, for Hungary which has the highest number in Europe. It is interesting to note that the ITU data show that normally in those countries where figures of cellular subscribers per 100 inhabitants are high, the corresponding figures for radio paging subscribers are relatively small, and vice versa. The situation in the European countries confirms this observation. Cellular telephones and other mobile services are now a top advantage of telecommunication technology.

Integrated services digital networks (ISDN) are another leader. As with cellular telephones, the use of ISDN in a given region reflects the state of development of the most contemporary telecommunications technologies.

There are 22% are in the United States and 3% in the rest of the world. The world leader in the number of ISDN channels and subscribers, in 1996, was Germany, with 5,150,000 channels and 1,945,000 subscribers. There is very slight development in the rest of the world, and a sharp disproportion between industrialised and developing countries in the availability of telecommunication services, even such traditional ones as wired telephony. However, the example of China shows that some developing countries have great potential in manufacturing telecommunication equipment, and are thus capable of improving the availability of telecommunication services. The development of telecommunication services in a given region has a vital impact on the development of the Internet for which they provide the necessary infrastructure, as they do for other wide area networks (WANs).

The Internet and other Networks

Digital networks include the Internet, intranets and WANs and share several features including the large amount of data transmitted, the high speed of transmission and the use of digital technologies and data transmission protocols. While these features make digital networks different from the other telecommunication networks, they are not isolated from them. For instance, the 'last mile' by which a user reaches the Internet is often the common telephone wire.

Furthermore, it is convenient to distinguish the Internet, which is based on the TCP/IP protocol, from other WANs, which are most often based on other protocols such as X.25 or the asynchronous transmission protocol (ATM). There are also gateways among the networks. For instance, a subscriber to America On Line (AOL), which is a private commercial WAN, can access the Internet, and conversely Internet users can, under certain conditions, access various other WANs. Private WANs based on TCP/IP protocol are called intranets and can also be linked to the Internet and other WANs.

In an international market forecast published in 1997, the International Data Corporation estimated that the total compound annual growth rate of the purchase of products and services related to the use of Internet between 1996 and 2000 would be 49.5%. Other sources give different estimates for the Internet turnover in 1996: the total varies from $9,000 million to $10,000 million, including from $500 million to $530 million for retail trade, about $600 million for business-to-business trade, $200 million for information and the same figure for financial services.

The main indicators of the Internet and other WAN development appear to demonstrate extremely high annual growth rates, but the divergence between industrialized countries and the rest of the world still remains significant. According to various sources, the Internet is little by little becoming less exclusive.

Radio and Television

Both radio and television produce and distribute informations via their own channels. In both, although ICT production is technically separated from distribution, the two processes do coexist in these media. It may be that the educational levels of radio and television audiences are lower in comparison with those of newspaper readers or Internet users: a subscriber to a newspaper cannot be illiterate, in contrast to a radio listener or television viewer. It is also true that listening to the radio or watching television is less costly than subscribing to a newspaper or using the Internet.

Radio, for which it is sufficient to make a fairly small investment only once, is the cheapest. Finally, poor communities need not invest in their own radio or television industry since they may listen to radio or watch television programmes produced by other countries. All these considerations explain the fact that radio and television are the most available and widespread ICTs in the world, both in developing and developed countries with radio in first place.

The difference between the developed and developing countries in the availability of radio is not so sharp as in the case of printed press. Moreover, the share of developing countries in the list of the top ten world manufacturers of television receivers and radio receivers is quite large. The top ten television exporters are Mexico, the Republic of Korea, Malaysia, Japan, the United Kingdom, Singapore, Thailand, France, Germany and Spain; the top ten radio receiver exporters are Malaysia, China, Singapore, Japan, Mexico, the United States, the Netherlands, Portugal, Germany, Belgium-Luxembourg.

According to BIPE Conseil data, in the European Union Countries, television and other home appliances such as VCRs and camcorders still represent about 58% of expenditures on hardware equipment for home use, whereas expenditure on special hardware for multimedia is only 1%. This implies that multimedia per se is of very little interest for the population of this region and is more commonly used with computer equipment.

Since multimedia is basically a form of representing information, this situation is not surprising. In addition, expenditures on personal computers for use in the home are only slightly less than expenditures on television sets. This seems to indicate that the home software industry and home use of the Internet have a bright future in industrialized countries. Radio and television are clearly the most available ICTs in the world, and their development still has good prospects in both industrialized and developing countries.

Sub Saharan Africa

The sub-Saharan countries are often divided into the socio-geographic groups of East, West, Central and Southern Africa, of which West Africa is the most populous. There are also many other country groupings around areas of common interest. The most important of these are the Economic Community of West African States (ECOWAS), Common Market for Eastern and Southern Africa (COMESA), Southern African Development Corporation (SADC), Central African Customs and Economic Union (UDEAC), East African Co-operation, the Customs Union of the Southern Africa, L'Agence de la Franco-phonie, the Commonwealth and the Lomé Convention African Caribbean and Pacific (ACP) countries.

The region's population was estimated at 636 million people for 1998 - about 9% of the total world population of 5.7 billion. Nigeria has by far the largest number of people at 122 million. Ten countries have populations above 15 million, with the five largest countries comprising 50% of the subcontinent's total population. Growing at 3% annually, an additional 20 million people a year are being added to the subcontinent. Population density is relatively low - only 24 people per square kilometer - compared to a world average of 43 and an Asian average of 110. At the same time, the degree of urbanization is low - only 32% of the region's people live in cities, as compared with 78% for high-income countries.

There is a high level of ethnic and linguistic diversity: several thousand identifiable ethnic groups and about 1,300 distinct spoken languages characterize this region. The national boundaries of most of the countries were imposed by the colonial powers and as a result language groups overflow them.

Information and use of communication tools in SSA have until very recently been almost entirely in the hands of state monopolies. Now that the trend towards democracy and more liberal market-oriented policies has become established on the continent, there has been a marked improvement in the availability and diversity of information and communication channels. Rates of telephone line growth are at their highest levels ever, hundreds of new media outlets in print, radio and television have emerged in the last couple of years and in 1998 the Internet was locally available in the capital of every country in Africa. These changes coincide with an estimated average 4.7% growth in Gross Domestic Product (GDP) in 1998.

After years of stagnation, these growth levels are close to those in Asia, and in the wake of the Asian financial turmoil, it is likely that Africa may even surpass Asia as the fastest growing region in the world. The information revolution is often said to be Africa's 'last chance to catch up' and it is already clear that a number of African countries have committed themselves to joining the Global Information Society.

Most of the advances have taken place only in the latter half of this decade and are not yet reflected in many of the official statistics available, for which 1995 is the latest year published. As a result, the degree of change is not been as evident as it should be. This has in part given rise to efforts by progressive African leaders such as Presidents Museveni and Mandela to declare an 'African Renaissance' which, if present trends continue, suggests a degree of optimism for the future of the African public that is unsurpassed in recent history. Nevertheless, change is occurring from an extremely low base, and the subcontinent has a daunting degree of transformation to effect before living standards come even close to world averages. The region has 33 of the 48 countries classified as 'least developed'.

There are no 'high-income' countries and the only countries classified as 'upper-middle income' are Gabon, Mauritius, Reunion, Seychelles, and South Africa. There are six lower-middle income countries (Botswana, Cap Verde, Djibouti, Namibia, Senegal, and Swaziland) and by far the majority of countries in the region - 39 of the 48 nations - are classified by the World Bank as 'low income'. Development statistics for the region often include South Africa and North Africa and as these are much more developed areas, their inclusion can obscure the true extent of the development gap.

ICT Infrastructure

Although encouraging trends have emerged in the last few years, the differences between the development levels of SSA and the rest of the world are even wider in the area of ICTs than they are when more traditional measures of development are used. The majority of the population has never even made a telephone call, only 2.5% of the world's televisions are on the subcontinent, and just one person in 9,000 has access to the Internet compared to a world average of one in 38. Irregular or nonexistent electricity supplies are a common feature of the sub-Saharan landscape and a major barrier to an increased use of ICTs, especially outside the major towns.

Many countries have extremely limited power distribution networks, which do not penetrate significantly into rural areas, and power sharing (regular power outages for many hours) is a regular occurrence, even in some capital cities such as Accra and Dar es Salaam. Furthermore, most tax regimes still treat ICTs as luxury items, which m a kes these almost exclusively imported commodities all the more expensive, and thus unobtainable by the majority. It is not therefore surprising that radio is still by far the most dominant mass medium in Africa with ownership of radio sets being far higher than for any other electronic device. In 1995, radio ownership was estimated by UNESCO at close to 18% of the population. It should also be noted that many people listen to the same radio or watch a television at the same time.

In fact, large scale sharing of information resources is a dominant feature of the African media landscape - readership of newspapers is often above 10 and it is not uncommon to find most of a small village crowded around the only TV set, often powered by a car-battery or small generator. It has been estimated that over 60% of the population of the subcontinent are reached by existing radio transmitter networks, while national television coverage is largely confined to major towns.

Some countries still do not have their own national television service. Following liberalization of the sector in many countries, an increasing number of commercial stations are being established. However, the news and information output of these commercialisation is usually either a re-broadcast of the national (state-controlled) news, or that of an international broadcasting service or news agency.

Local news and current affairs, especially that focusing on events outside the capital, is rarely broadcast. Community radio has been slow to take off in the region. Genuine community radios are often seen by governments as a threat. Pressure is also being put on community radios - usually by the donor organizations which helped to create them in the first place - to become financially sustainable. Among the multinational broadcasters, the BBC World Service radio programming is the most widespread, redistributing its signal locally on FM and AM bands in 25 countries and 46 towns in the sub-Sahara.

The BBC's coverage is followed by that of Radio France International (RFI) and the Voice of America, all three of which are actively competing for the African radio listener via terrestrial re-broadcasting. The battle is being carried to the satellite television market as well, with the BBC and Canal+ focussing an Anglophone and Francophone audiences respectively. Portuguese colonial history is similarly reflected in services of the national television, RTP, being re-broadcast in the Lusophone countries.

For many years the South African company MultiChoice has been distributing its South African subscriber channels (M-Net) through local terrestrial broadcasters in 39 countries in SSA. Its recently launched music channel, Channel O, claims to be the most watched television station in Africa.

In 1995 M-Net launched the world's first digital direct-to-home subscriber satellite service called DSTV which carries over 30 video channels and 40 audio programmes on C-band to the whole of Africa and on low-cost KU-band to Southern Africa south of Lusaka. This year the South Africa public broadcasting Corporation (SABC) launched Channel Africa, a new satellite-based news and entertainment channel aimed at the subcontinent.

However, the audience for satellite broadcasts are confined to the elite who can afford the equipment and subscription fees. In 1998 some parts of northern sub-Sahara started receiving DTH Television broadcasts from Nilesat, the continent's first locally owned geostationary satellite, operated by the Egyptian Radio and Television Union (ERTU). World-Space has finalized its digital radio service, which began broadcasts in early 1999 and will make a suite of five audio channels available to anyone on the continent who can afford $200 for the special digital radio that has been manufactured.

In most sub-Saharan countries the telecommunication networks are being expanded and modified, with the number of main lines growing at about 10% a year. Nevertheless, the overall teledensity in 1996 was still only about one telephone line per 100 inhabitants. In addition, much of the telecommunication network is analogue and many sections are operating at saturated capacity or are highly unreliable, especially during rainy seasons.

On a worldwide basis, the sub-Saharan countries can be seen to have by far the least developed infrastructure. In 1996 the region contained almost 10% of the world's population, but only 0.4% of the world's telephone lines. The penetration of phone lines on the subcontinent is five times worse than for the average low-income country. However, there is a high level of variability among countries in the state of their existing telephone networks.

Some such as Botswana and Rwanda have made telecommunications a priority and are installing digital switches with fibre optic intercity backbones and the newest cellular and mobile technology. At the other end of the scale, countries like Madagascar and Uganda have largely unreliable analogue telephone systems and poor national links between urban centres. Surprisingly, the proportion of digital lines on the subcontinent in 1996 was 69%, close to the world average of 79%.

On a sub-regional level, the countries of the Sahel and Central Africa, such as Mali, the Niger and the Democratic Republic of the Congo have less than 2 telephone lines for every 1,000 people. North Africa and South Africa have a teledensity of around 35 per 1,000, West and East African coastal countries have densities of between 2.5 and 10 per 1,000. A much smaller proportion of the population can actually afford their own telephone: the cost of renting a connection averaged almost 20% of the 1995 GDP per capita, as compared with a world average of 9% and only 1% in high income countries.

In 1996 the average sub-Saharan business connection cost $112 to install, $6 a month to rent and $0.11 per 3-minute local call. But installation charges were above $200 in some countries, line rentals ranged from $0.8 to $20 a month, and call charges varied from $0.60 an hour to over $5 an hour. Local call tariffs in some countries have increased even further, to over $10 an hour, making extensive residential use of the World Wide Web (WWW) in these countries unaffordable to all but a tiny elite. Because of high tariffs and the large number of international calls, telecommunications operators enjoy above-average profits on their lines.

Mobile cellular telephony has experienced very rapid growth in the SSA. As well as providing an alternative to the limited public telecommunications networks, the cellular market has usually involved the private sector which has been able to institute more aggressive start-up plans. Cellular services are now available in 38 countries, supplied by over 65 operators who provide access mainly in the capital cities but also in some secondary towns and along major trunk routes.

The number of cellular subscribers in 1997 was estimated by the International Telecommunications Union (ITU) at over 225,000 outside of South Africa, where the cellular market outpaced all expectations, reaching over 2 million in 1998. Traditional data communication services based on X.25 are available in half the countries, most prevalently among those which are francophone where the use of the Minitel was adopted before the Internet became available.

SITA, the airline co-operative, has by far the largest X.25 network in Africa. SITA's commercial division, SCITOR (recently renamed Equant), which was formed to service the non-airline market, now operates dialup points of presence in 39 SSA countries. These are used by a variety of multinational organizations.

Subscribers to Internet service providers (ISP) in Europe and North America who are members of IPASS (a group of ISPs, including SITA, who share their points of presence, or POPs) can also access their home ISPs via these points of presence for about $0.22 a minute. X.25 packet-switched based services were in the past the most popular method of establishing wide-area data networks in Africa, but because of their high-cost, traffic-based tariffs, they are now mainly used by banks and other large corporations requiring secure real-time low-volume data transactions such as credit-card verification.

By contrast, the Internet has spread rapidly through the region over the last two years: at the end of 1996 only eleven countries had local access; but by the end of 1998, according to ITU, all African countries had some access to the Internet. But Internet services are still largely confined to the capitals and major towns.

To address this situation ten countries have made the decision to provide local call Internet access across the whole country using a specific area code. A few countries (Angola, Benin, Botswana, Ghana, Kenya, Namibia and the United Republic of Tanzania) do have POPs in some of the secondary towns, and South Africa has POPs in about 70 locations.

Most African capitals have more than one Internet Service Provider (ISP), and in mid-1998 there were over 265 ISPs across the region.

The total number of computers connected to the Internet in the sub-Sahara excluding South Africa was estimated at just over 5,000 in mid-1998, but the figure may be closer to 6,000 or 7,000 due to the measurement technique, which does not count hosts which are not fully referenced in domain name servers. Africa's share of Internet host sites worldwide was only 0.025% in 1997, and this had fallen to 0.022% by the beginning of 1998 due to Internet growth worldwide.

The opening up of the Nigerian Internet market will probably change the picture as the national telecommunications operator (Nitel) has big plans to provide Internet countrywide. With a fifth of sub-Sahara's population, until mid 1998 Nigeria, which has been one of the slumbering giants of the African Internet world, had only a few dialup e-mail providers and a couple of full ISPs operating on very low bandwidth links.

The rapidity with which most African public telecommunication operators (PTOs), have established Internet services is noteworthy. In the last three years PTOs have brought full Internet services on stream in 31 countries, and similar moves are afoot in three others.

The Mauritian government has a strong commitment to increase the use of ICTs and has made a number of efforts in addressing the regulatory and legal framework for ICTs. Several bills have already been drafted, and with the passing of the Copyright Bill at the National Assembly in July 1997, the legal challenges posed by the use of ICTs will be reduced significantly.

The National Computer Board (NCB) was established by government in late 1996 as a parastatal institution whose aim is to assist in the diffusion of ICTs in the various socio-economic sectors of the country. One of the NCB's major areas of activity is the use of the Internet in government, as well as the more general issues of privacy, security and intellectual property.

The NCB has established an extensive web site which acts as the home site for information on other government ministries. NCB is the programme manager for the National IT Strategy Plan (NITSP) which is currently under active development as part of the Mauritian government's strategic objectives to move the country toward an information-age economy.

In Mauritias, Government Information Infrastructure (GII), will provide the electronic mail and publishing facilities for the Government to create a responsive and 'paperless' environment. It will also aim to provide information and services to the public round-the-clock via the Internet. Over time, the GII is also expected to evolve into an electronic backbone and infrastructure to meet the future public sector connectivity needs.

The telecommunications sector is regulated by the Mauritius Telecommunications Authority (MTA) and will be advised by a newly-created Telecommunications Advisory Council (TAC). The Public Telecommunication Operator (PTO), Mauritel/ MTS, is currently a monopoly but is engaged in a slow process of liberalization and tariff rebalancing which is expected to be completed by the end of 2004 when the entire sector will be opened up for competition as outlined in the recently published Telecommunications White Paper.

Mauritius has a far better telecommunications infrastructure than most other countries in Africa. As part of its national strategy to become the 'Singapore of Africa', it has made telecommunications and data services a high national priority for some time now, and this is reflected in the availability of ISDN services in some areas, relatively short waiting times for the installation of new telephone lines (especially for businesses) and a rapidly emerging range of data communications services such as Internet, X.25 and EDI.

Three SDH fibre optic rings have been built in Mauritius to improve the local telecom infrastructure and to provide a high-bandwidth connection to the main groundstation in Port Louis. Mauritius will be connected by fibre optic cable to the global backbone in 1999 when South Africa's Far-East (SAFE) project links Cape Town to Kuala Lumpur and Singapore via submarine cable.

Few of the countries outside of South Africa had international Internet links larger than 64Kbps until last year, but 128Kps connections are now becoming increasingly common. More than 256Kbps of international bandwidth is currently present in only eleven countries. Most of the international connections are carried via satellite. The exceptions to this are the marine optic fibre link from South Africa to the cross-Atlantic hub in the Canaries, and Djibouti which has access to the SEA-ME-WEA cable. By far the majority of international Internet circuits in the region connect to the United States, with a few to the United Kingdom and France.

Generally, ISPs must pay the entire cost of the connection to Europe or the US, which effectively gives the developed country ISPs free access to the continent's network and further increases the costs of ISPs in Africa. The United Nations Development Programme (UNDP) and the Agence de la Francophonie. They adopted a project to install a regional register for Internet addresses, AFRINIC, similar to those existing in other regions. Reflecting the high telecommunication costs and the small markets, often supplied by a single operator, ISP charges for dialup access are generally higher in Africa than elsewhere: the average cost of using the Internet for five hours a month in Africa comes to about $60 per month.

In response to the high cost of full Internet-based services, and also because of the overriding importance of electronic mail, the e-mail-only store and forward services with dialup connections to the Internet are generally continuing to attract subscribers. There is also growing interest in telecentres, kiosks, cybercafes and other forms of public Internet access, such as adding PCs to community phone-shops, schools, police stations and clinics, which can share the cost of equipment and access among a larger number of users.

Computers and data processing

Demand for various services on the Internet is expected to increase only when there is a broader penetration of computers and data processing equipment on the subcontinent. Although the limited levels of equipment penetration are readily apparent, accurate estimates of the quantity of this equipment in use are notoriously hard to gather.

There have been few effective centralized systems of monitoring, and high duties and sales taxes in many countries discourage the declaration of imports and other transactions. In addition, convergence and rapid change in the technologies makes the categorization of equipment types even more difficult. Most recent estimates for the number of PCs in the sub-Sahara put the average at about 3 per 1,000 people in 1996.

However some studies, such as the 1995 survey carried out by the Agence de cooperation culturelle et technique (ACCT), indicate that this figure may be between 3 and 6 times too high, making the average closer to less than 1 per 1,000. Some countries such as Botswana, Mauritius and South Africa have significantly higher levels of penetration, at least 5 per 1,000, perhaps to 20 per 1,000. At the same time, account should also be taken of the number of users sharing a single computer, which is much greater than in more developed regions.

Generally, the penetration of computers is much lower in the public sector, with by far the majority of PC equipment being used by the private sector for accounting and word processing. Spreadsheets are used to some extent for forecasting or as a simple database application. The small number of database systems often use Microsoft Access, but many national documentation centres and archives, as well as small university and NGO libraries, use the UNESCO-developed micro CDS/ISIS package for bibliographic data, or the functionally similar package of International Development Research Centre (IDRC). Geographic Information Systems (GIS) and digitization facilities are beginning to be installed by planning departments and municipalities.

Outside of South Africa, there are only a handful of mini- and mainframe computers, and most of these are confined to Ministries of Finance for government payroll, and a few of the larger parastatal organizations, telecom operators, banks and insurance companies. The Millennium Bug, or 'Y2K problem', has gained significant attention across the subcontinent, especially because there are large numbers of older machines in use and very limited resources or skills to ensure their compliance.

The vast majority of people in the sub-region rely almost exclusively on radio for information, with smaller and more elite groups in the cities and towns also making use of television and newspapers. There were about 175 daily papers and 300 weekly or monthly general news journals in the SSA in 1996, but this number is thought to have increased substantially in the last two years.

As mentioned earlier, the majority of Africans have not yet made a phone call. But interestingly, the use of international lines is much higher than the world average, partly reflecting the large size of the African Diaspora and the arbitrary borders within the region.

In 1996 the SSA average for international outgoing calls was 233 minutes per line per year, compared to a world average of 93, and 113 for high-income countries. Current estimates put the number of sub-Saharan Internet users at about 870,000. Most of these are in South Africa leaving only about 70,000 among the remaining the 638 million people on the subcontinent.

South Africa's Internet community is 3 0 times larger than any other in Africa, being among the top 20 countries in the world when ranked by the number of Internet nodes. The definition of a 'user' or 'subscriber' may vary, however, since the number of accounts being shared in Africa may be much greater than in more developed regions.

A recent study by the UN Economic Commission for Africa (UNECA) found on average that there were 3 users for each computer with an Internet or e-mail connection. This could mean that the number of e-mail users outside South Africa is over 200,000.

The French-speaking SSA countries have a far higher profile on the World Wide Web and greater institutional connectivity than the non-French speaking countries. This is due to the strong assistance provided by the various francophone support agencies and the Canadian and French governments, which are concerned about the dominance of English on the Internet. As a result, the anglophone and lusophone countries have considerable 'catching up' to do to reach the same levels of connectivity and representation.

On a sub-regional basis, Southern Africa is the most advanced region in terms of use of ICTs, followed by East and West Africa, with Central Africa lagging furthest behind. The Library was chosen in part for its long standing experience with e-mail access and CD-ROM use, the latter which has in part been assisted by the sub-Saharan African Program of the American Association for the Advancement of Science (AAAS).

Support for the GNICC has been widespread, including from government, with participation from the ministries of environment, science and technology, education, information, transport and communication. The Ghana Government has indicated its support for promoting access to ICTs in all segments of society, particularly in the educational system. The Minister of Finance in his 1997 budget statement made the following declaration: 'In view of the positive effects of the application of information technology on development,

Government will ensure that key institutions of state machinery are linked to the Internet.

All the science resource centres will be connected to the network as and when they are commissioned. The program to link the Universities together and to the Internet will also be pursued.' UNESCO has since agreed to fund the $250,000 project, with the primary local partners being the Ministry of Environment, Science and Technology and the Ministry of Transport and Communication. One of the initial goals will be the establishment of the Ghana Academic and Research Network (GARNET). The government has requested the Bank for Institutional Development Fund to implement a network to connect the Office of the President, Parliament, the Ministry of Information and some other key ministries.

The technical subcommittee of the GNCIC has been charged with designing the specifications of a national networking backbone. Within the context of the GNICC/ GARNET project it was originally envisaged that the University of Ghana would form the hub for GARNET's Internet links to the other Universities and research centres.

The university is installing a fibre optic campus network with support from the Danish International Development Agency (DANIDA). It is located about 12 km from the centre of Accra, using a wireless link to the local Internet hub operated by NCS.

With the emergence of NCS's national Internet backbone with POPs in three cities, along with its active support for academic networking, and furthermore Gilat's interest, a joint private/public sector networking project may emerge. The Ministry of Transport and

Communications (MOTC) established the Accelerated Development Programme (ADP) for telecommunications in 1995 to address the stagnant growth in the sector. The ADP is a reform program involving the establishment of a centralized regulatory body, the National Communications Authority (NCA), as the agency responsible for regulation of the telecommunications sector.

At the same time Ghana Telecom (GT) was separated as a commercial entity from the Ministry of Posts and Telecommunications, with a 30% stake sold to a Malaysian consortium for $38 million and the availability of a second national operator's license was announced. The license was subsequently awarded to a consortium proposing a $10 million investment headed by the Ghana National Petroleum Corporation (GNPC), with the African Communications Group and Western Wireless. GNPC is working with the Israeli company Gilat to deploy a VSAT-based telephone network around the country.

The MOTC plans to divest a further 21% of Ghana Telecom. It also hopes to exploit Ghana's strategic location at the centre of the ECOWAS region and intends to position the country as a hub for trade and commerce-driven telecommunications services. Currently, Ghana's telephone network still reflects a poor state of development, but it is undergoing a process of rapid modernization. Many of the exchanges in Accra are now digitized, providing advanced services such as password, abbreviated dialing, call transfer, three-way conference, wake-up and call waiting.

Although there are a few notable government Web sites, such as those of Angola, Mauritius, Mozambique,

Senegal and Zambia, there is as yet relatively little government use of the Internet for existing administrative purposes. E-mail is used for general correspondence and document exchange, technical advice, managing projects, arranging meetings, and exchanging research ideas, although its use is still limited for accessing formal information resources.

Across the continent, users report that e-mail has increased efficiency and reduced the cost of communication, but as yet is used almost exclusively for contacting individuals in other regions, and the Web is still a relatively under-utilized resource. In the area of local content development, the SSA Web-space is expanding rapidly, and almost all countries have some form of local or internationally-hosted Web server unofficially or officially representing the country with varying degrees of comprehensiveness.

However, still relatively few institutions are well represented on the Web. While increasing numbers of organizations have a Web site with basic content and descriptive information, many are hosted by international development agency sites and very few sites actually use the Web for their activities.

There are about 120 electronic mailing lists and UseNet newsgroups on the Internet (almost entirely hosted off-continent) which discuss issues related to SSA. There is a list for almost every country as well as others on more general topics ranging from African Cinema to Post Colonialism. Two web search engines specializing on Africa have emerged over the last year: Woyaa and Orientation Africa. As with other similar services elsewhere, these are run by commercial companies which generate revenue through advertising.

The news media are now relatively well represented on the Web. The African Studies department of Columbia University in the United States has identified over 115 different newspapers and news magazines in the region that are now available on the Internet, of which over 60% are published on the subcontinent, in about half of the countries. Also of note are the efforts of the ISP Africa Online to host daily newspapers on their web sites.

There are two major continent-wide African news agencies, both of which extensively use electronic media: Inter Press Service (IPS) and the Pan African News Agency (PANA). Sub-regionally, Southern Africa has the only active news agencies using ICTs, the Southern African Broadcasters Association (SA BA) and the Media Institute of Southern Africa (MISA).

In other regions use of ICTs among the media is much lower, but in West Africa, WANAD (West African News Media and Development Centre) is assisting journalists and media outlets to adopt the use of ICTs. Of course international news correspondents in SSA are heavily dependant on ICTs to deliver material to their operations in the United States and Europe.

Cable News Network (CNN) and the other international television news companies regularly rent temporary space segments all over Africa with the local representatives of IntelSat and PanamSat to deliver reports and live coverage. Radio journalists (even freelancers) are now sending edited sound files by e-mail to agencies such as the BBC World Service. Across the subcontinent, there are as yet few locally-developed electronic information repositories of national or sub-regional significance, and none of the existing ones are currently available on the Internet. This is partly because national archive and library systems are extremely poorly resourced and many have had little opportunity to obtain ICT skills or equipment.

Although statistics-gathering operations are also at a very low level due to insufficient support, many statistical offices are now using common standards and new tools. With the help of e-mail and fax, the collection of statistical information is no longer confined to the largest urban centres. The number of studies aiming at better knowledge of the structure and functioning of the socio-economic sectors is growing and price indices now cover rural areas.

There has been a gradual wave of restructuring in telecommunication and broadcasting sectors in sub-Sahara over the past five years. Ten countries, including Cote d'Ivoire, Ghana, Guinea, Senegal, South Africa and Uganda have partially privatized national telecommunications operators and fifteen more, including Cameroon, Madagascar, Malawi and the United Republic of Tanzania, intend to do so shortly. The cellular sector, which is almost completely private, already comprises about 20% of the market. World Trade Organization (WTO) Multilateral Trade Negotiation commitments have been made by Cote d'Ivoire, Ghana, Mauritius, Senegal and South Africa.

By the beginning of 1998, twenty African countries had established independent or quasi-independent regulatory bodies for the telecommunication sector.

The liberalization of the sectors in some of the countries will undoubtedly improve the prospects for increased investment in ICTs over the next few years. However, many governments still see the media as an organ of the state and the telecommunications sector as an important part of their general revenue base. This means that public network operators are not free to reinvest their profits in network development.

Furthermore, much of the existing revenue for telecommunication operators comes as a result of the existing accounting rate system, which currently channels significant sums of international telecommunications revenue to African PTOs. The pending reform of the accounting rate system could deprive PTOs and/or their governments of vital investment capital just when they most need it.

However, the international telecommunication industry is waking up to the fact that Africa is the world's largest untapped market, and with governments desperate for ways to radically modernize telecommunications systems, new alliances are being forged between the private and public sectors.

There are nevertheless concerns that little consideration is being given to the medium- and long-term implications, more particularly because when it comes to deregulation of the telecommunication sector, the assumption of many governments is that liberalization models, which have worked in the North, can simply be applied wholesale to the South.

Moreover, commercialization of broadcasting, without adequate reform of the public broadcasting sector, has done little to promote plurality and diversity on the airwaves. Given the extent of rural poverty, profit-driven entrepreneurs have little or no interest in broadcasting to these more marginalized communities. The establishment of commercial broadcasting.

The urban-based broadcasters have then been granted re-broadcast licences to other heavily-populated areas, which increases the stations' appeal to advertisers, but contributes little to the diversification of broadcasting in the country. These new commercial broadcasters have tended to be either owned by the ruling party or by staunch supporters of that party. These public broadcasters are also increasingly under pressure to make a profit in order to save on already overstretched national budgets. In order to compete with newly-established commercial stations, public broadcasters have little choice but to act and think commercially.

Sub-regional collaboration between countries in the development of strong regulators and legislation may be one important means of addressing some of these issues. To this end the Southern African grouping of thirteen SADC countries have agreed to a legally binding Protocol on Communications which includes commitments to Universal Service and adopting the model policy and telecommunications legislation that has been developed.

ICTs are at a critical strategic entry point for development in SSA. The infrastructure is steadily improving, but not fast enough to accommodate the growth in demand for the multitude of services now available. In particular, the need for high bandwidth infrastructure for the Internet creates serious pressures on the telecommunications networks in Africa. But the Internet is just one of a number of forces that will have an impact on telecommunications operators in the region.

There are many others, such as international pressures on regulating accounting rates charges, and the growing presence of callback technology. The challenges in this area focus on issues such as expansion of the local network and tariff rebalancing (for national operators); the erosion of international revenues (through, for example, callback systems, the Internet and the breakdown of the accounting-rate system); regulatory weaknesses that need to be addressed to ensure a level playing field and to attract investment; the need to provide rural services; the shortage of skilled personnel; and the need for customer focus in terms of quality, service coverage and price.

In telecommunications alone, investments totalling at least $6,000-8,000 million would be required in SSA over the next four years to add an additional 4.5 million lines. This would improve the teledensity in a significant way, even though it will remain the lowest in the world. There have nevertheless been an increasing number of indications that the sub-region's decision-makers are committed to achieving substantial change.

One of the most important events, which helped to accelerate moves toward increased adoption of ICTs in Africa, was the Addis Abeba Symposium on Telematics for Development, organized by UNESCO in April 1995. This meeting brought together almost all of the major forces in international computer networking development projects. One of the results of this Conference was the development of a framework document entitled the African Information Society Initiative (AISI), which was adopted at the subsequent meeting of the Conference of African Ministers in May 1996.

AISI calls for the formulation and development of a National Information and Communication Infrastructure (NICI) plan in every African country, driven by national development priorities, and proposes co-operation, linkage and partnership among African countries to share successful experiences. The countries that have so far begun the process for developing in-depth national information infrastructure and communication development plans are Benin, Burkina Faso, Cameroon, Comoros, Ethiopia, Lesotho, Namibia, Mozambique, Rwanda, South Africa and Uganda.

In conjunction with efforts to built new infrastructures and improve the existing facilities, there are innovative efforts to improve accessibility to services through the use of shared public access facilities, which exploit the convergence of technologies to provide cost effective services in under-serviced and isolated areas.

Commonly called community tele-centres, the concept has received considerable support from the ITU and other members of the international community, as well as a number of national governments and PTOs. This has resulted in over 20 pilot telecentres across the subcontinent set up to test different models, means of implementation and mechanisms for sustainability.

International and Regional Co-operation and Development Assistance Related to ICT

With the worldwide recognition of the importance of ICTs in accelerating development, a number of recent international development assistance initiatives have improved the prospects for wider access to information and communication networks on the continent.

In relation to the AISI initiative described above, a study on future information infrastructure-building activities in Africa was conducted through a collaboration between IDRC, BellaNet, UNECA, UNESCO and the ITU, called the African Network Initiative (ANI).

To address the growing need for co-ordination, donors and implementing agencies involved in ICTs in Africa have agreed to establish an ongoing forum for information exchange on such projects called Partnerships for ICTs in Africa (Picta).

The overall funding coming from international and regional co-operation and related to ICT shows the importance that the international community attributes to this sector. But in Africa as in the rest of the world, the development of adequate infrastructure is only the first step in the right direction. Adequate policies should ensure that such progress will not widen the gap between the information-rich and the information-poor. The risk may be greater in Africa than in other parts of the world, since the initial situation is more critical than anywhere else.

The Status of ICT in Arab Countries

The Arab countries are are also struggling to meet the challenge of ICT's multiple impact on the social, economic, cultural and political aspects of life. The first striking feature in the Arab region is the wide variation among countries in terms of population, gross national product (GNP) per capita, education and use of ICT.

The total population is over 260 million, according to 1997 estimates. The population of individual countries ranges from 0.6 to 62.5 million, with four countries numbering over 20 million inhabitants and one country, Egypt, more than 60 million. Nine countries - Bahrain, Djibouti, Kuwait, Lebanon, Mauritania, Oman, Palestine, Qatar, United Arab Emirates - are below 5 million. Three of them are found in the Gulf area and have populations below 1 million. In the period between 1970 and 1995, annual population growth rate in the region ranged from 0.8% to 9.6%. Lebanon's rate was the lowest, but this is expected to rise after the civil war has ended.

By contrast, in Qatar and the United Arab Emirates, the annual population growth rate was very high, 6.6% and 9.65% respectively, due to the large number of immigrants needed to improve the quantity and quality of the labour force in these two oil-producing countries. Growth is expected to decline between 1995 and 2015 in all countries except Lebanon.

In such an environment, where literacy levels are also low, the new communication technologies, including television, can be very useful. Illiteracy remains a challenge for some Arab countries in spite of the campaigns which have been launched in the last few decades.

In schools, the gender balance is somewhat better. The high enrolment rate in primary education suggests that literacy rates could improve dramatically over the next generation, provided the high number of dropouts were reduced. The total enrolment rate ranges from 38% to 116%. It was above 80% in all but six countries in 1995, and higher than 90% in nine countries. The percentage of females to males is over 80% except for two countries. In secondary schools, enrolment rates decrease. In a few countries they never exceed 25% of the registration achieved in primary education.

In order to organize the presentation of ICT in the Arab countries, we have adopted the model proposed by Kobayashi which suggests five main categories. The first category, called 'human interface', covers the technologies involving interaction between the machine and human beings, such as radio, television, the telephone, personal computers (PCs) and connections to the Internet.

The second category refers to all ICT networks, including broadcasting, telecommunications and computer networks. The third category deals with ICTs used in government and administration, and the fourth concerning those found in education and research. The last group deals with information and knowledge services, such as decision support systems, the world wide web and all printed - or 'typographical' - information as it is called by Kobayashi.

In the human interface technologies, radio shows the highest penetration rates. Five countries show over 400 radio sets per 1,000 inhabitants, and four of these rise above 450 radios per 1,000 inhabitants. Only three countries are below 150 sets per 1,000. Television is the second most common communication technology, with a range of 13 to 457 sets per 1,000 inhabitants. Seven countries show a penetration rate above 250 sets per 1,000 inhabitants, and eight are below 100. Telephone lines are expanding. In 1997, these ranged from less than 1 line for 100 inhabitants in Somalia to more than 35 lines per 100 inhabitants in the United Arab Emirates.

The personal computer is the most important terminal used with a human interface: it allows for a high level of interaction, and makes it possible to do co-operative work online. It may include the use of a CD-ROM, as well as general Internet connectivity including e-mail and many other functions. Data on the penetration rate for personal computers are limited, but those available show that the level of 50 PCs per 1,000 inhabitants has been reached in two countries in the Gulf.

In many countries the number decreased, yet in one country, the United Arab Emirates, the number increased dramatically. The total number of Internet users almost doubled in most countries during the six-month period extending from July to December 1997. In the Arab countries, 98% of the Internet users are men, which is a disturbing figure. Users are evenlysplit among those who use the Internet at home and those who use it from their place of work.

Regarding electronic commerce, a survey conducted in 1998 by the magazine Internet Arab World, published by Dubai Information Technology, showed that only 4% of users in Arab countries made a purchase through the Internet during the year.

Among the factors affecting the penetration of electronic commerce, one can mention the fact that this kind of commerce is relatively new in the region, that it lacks a critical mass of consumers and has to overcome a conservative attitude regarding the security of electronic transactions. However, Arabic software companies expect to generate 33% of their sales through the Internet in the next two or three years. Some observers expect electronic commerce to grow by 100% over the next 12 months. The fax machine is complementary to the telephone, whether it is used directly on the telephone line or through a PC. As the Internet expands, e-mail may rapidly replace fax since it is more user-friendly and supports multimedia message delivery.

Available radio frequencies have reached the saturation point in most Arab countries in the last decade. On the other hand, TV channels and telecommunications have expanded greatly with the creation in 1967 of ARABSAT, the Arab Satellite

Communications Organization. The purpose of this enterprise is to invest in and operate the Arab space sector; arrange and secure extended communication of telephone, faxes, telexes, and pictures; arrange radio and TV broadcasting; offer paid consulting services in the area of satellite communication; and encourage Arab industries to invest in satellite communication.

The first satellite was launched in 1985. The available channels were used by Arab information ministries (broadcasting and TV) as well as telecommunication ministries and in co-ordination with the ground networks. ARABSAT worked as a business organization and was able to finance all successive projects. During this first generation experience it manufactured three satellites and bought two more (in orbit) to meet the increasing demand. Then it launched two second-generation satellites to expand the area covered. The first satellite of the third generation was launched on 27 February 1999 and will cover both the Arab region and Europe.

As for the cellular mobile telephone, ITU data show the total percentage increase between 1995 and 1997 in Arab countries to be 62.8%, probably due to the privatization of this service. The Egyptian satellite NILE SAT was launched in April 1998 to provide digital TV and radio broadcasting, Internet services, and distance education at different levels and in different languages. It covers the Middle East region from Baghdad to Rabat, and parts of southern and northern Europe. Several Arab countries such as Bahrain, Kuwait, Iraq, the Libyan Arab Jamahiriya, Oman, and Tunisia are channel providers.

With respect to computer networks, many organizations are moving away from centralized information systems or local area networks (LANs), a change which often implies the revision of administrative structure. Some large organizations have started thinking of establishing Intranets based on the Transmission Control Protocol/Internet Protocol (TCP/IP).

Heavy demand for telecommunication networking pushed some countries like Egypt to begin privatizing this sector. Public data networks are being enhanced from the X.25 standard to Frame Relay and Asynchronous Transmission Mode (ATM). Internet connectivity uses a variety of methods, whether through satellite links or optical fibre.

Total channel capacity to access the Global Internet has reached around 12 Mbps, of which 2.5 Mbps are used by the Egyptian Universities Network. This capacity also serves various governmental sectors, and more than 40 Internet Service Providers (ISPs) are distributed among 16 governorates.

Some of the remote ISPs in upper Egypt use very small aperture terminals (VSATs) for their local connections. A regional communication network, RITSENET, has been planned by the Egyptian government, but implementation is still in progress. Efforts to link Algeria, Morocco, Tunisia, Mauritania and the Libyan Arab Jamahiriya to the network have begun.

In most Arab countries, attempts to computerize government offices began during the mid-1980s. Since then, the building of data bases and networks within different departments and local organizations has continued to grow. Because of the non-latin alphabet of the Arab language, fax communication, introduced more than two decades ago, is still widely used despite the spread of e-mail.

The classical applications known as clerical automation and management information systems (MIS) have now matured and include accounting, inventory control, financial information, personnel and planning. The Arab League ICT Regional Arabic Institutes have tried to stimulated these countries' interest in adopting ICT through studies, workshops and conferences organized at the national level.

Geographical Information Systems (GIS) were introduced in Egypt in 1996. The systems were designed with a long-term perspective that would allow progressive implementation and continuous monitoring. Priority was given to environmental applications, infrastructure building, municipal administration, socio-economic studies, and information and mass communication.

With support from the Islamic Bank, efforts are underway to improve productivity and strengthen industrialization in the field of electronics, informatics and communication, by linking data input, operations research, modelling and implementation. Decision Support Systems (DSS) have been installed in different Arab countries since the mid-1980s. An Egyptian centre for DSS was set up in 1985 and is expanding its activities to include training and other services.

Arabization, however, is a critical factor in developing information systems, but with the increasing investment in ICT and the increase in the number of users, companies are also responding faster. Microsoft introduced an Arabic version of Windows 98 in October 1998 in Dubai, just five months after introduction of the English version. Each year there are also conferences and exhibitions in different Arab countries which address particular issues such as expert systems, modelling, virtual reality, but it is too early to evaluate the results. Finally, the number of businesses in this field is expanding and the number of software companies linked to multinational firms, or specialized foreign companies in the same sectors, such as GIS or banking, is also increasing. A high percentage of systems are designed and implemented by foreign companies.

With regard to management and administration, many national services in the Arab countries have been automated and are improving: from customs, taxes and licenses, to reservations, check payments and, to some extent, information retrieval.

National activities that have direct relation with international facilities such as airports, maritime ports and financial service cards are the most advanced in this respect since they require only a single node to be linked to a global network. National identification numbers similar to the social security number in western countries will soon facilitate the collection of statistics and improve interactions between government and the population.

Within the research community, ICT is becoming an essential tool, particularly with respect to the retrieval of scientific information. Moreover, specialized institutions involved in informatics are being established. In some cases, they participate in supervising the dissemination of scientific knowledge at the national level.

In Saudi Arabia, for example, King Abdul Aziz City of Science and Technology is supervising the introduction of Internet connectivity in Saudi Arabia. It has licensed 37 companies to provide Internet access, and 85,000 subscribers are expected by the end of 1999.

In Egypt, the Academy of Scientific Research and Technology is facilitating the access to scientific library material and patent databases. The Egyptian Universities Network is serving Egypt's top-level national administrators. The Information and Decision Support Centre (IDSC) is supervising the introduction of Internet services to the governmental sectors and also licensing Internet access to the private ISPs.

The electronic Research Institute in Cairo and the Mubarak City of Science and Technology have established special departments for dealing with Informatics. Similar examples can be found in Algeria, Morocco and Tunisia. As for university education, the task of co-ordinating information among Arab institutions is being undertaken by the Union of Arab Universities. Almost all Arab universities are connected to the Internet, although there is not yet an Arab Backbone Network.

In some countries, universities are all connected to a single network. For example, Egypt's twelve universities are linked through the Egyptian Universities Network, together with Al-Azhar and the American University. Since Tunisia, Kuwait and Egypt were the first Arab countries to have Internet connectivity, they have accumulated more experience in using this technology in the university context. Nevertheless, the United Arab Emirates and Lebanon have recently witnessed a sharp increase in Internet penetration.

Many universities already have separate departments for computer engineering and computer science. In some cases, separate colleges for Information and Computer Science have been established. Distance learning is becoming more important as pilot projects are being implemented using ARABSAT and NILESAT. For precollege education, four types of computer applications can be identified. The first type concerns the introduction of computers at schools to let students, teachers, and administrators grasp the fundamentals of information technology. The second type is the use of computers in a multimedia environment to support the teaching of different subjects and to experiment with new methods of cognitive-based education and learning. The third type is the use of Internet as a means of enhancing collaboration between Arab students and their fellows all over the world, and also to experiment with Web- based education and learning. The fourth type concerns teacher-training and the support of education administrators through the use of videoconferencing networks.

For instance, all the regional teacher-training centres in all the governorates of Egypt are linked to the main centre at the Ministry of Education through a videoconferencing network. Prototype multimedia-based educational material is being tested in Saudi Arabia and Egypt.

However, it should be emphasized that computer penetration is still low in Arab countries, and more funding and teacher training are essential. Additional efforts are required to produce educational material in the Arabic language and which reflects the cultural values of the region.

Printed products - books, newspapers, magazines, scientific periodicals, dictionaries and encyclopaedias, black and white pictures or coloured images - still represent a basic tool for diffusing information, knowledge, and news. The interaction between printing and ICT is quite strong. For instance, it is now possible to receive news on-line and in real time from all over the world, to store it, to communicate it worldwide and to make it accessible on demand. Editors and publishers can now revise in parallel with the authoring process, saving precious time.

Authors and writers now have at their disposal a number of timesaving tools for retrieving information and data, or to assist them during writing. A great number of journals are accessible on the Internet. A number of encyclopedias and dictionaries are in electronic form, some of them as hand-held devices. ICT paved the ground for remote printing, allowing newspapers, journals, and periodicals to be on time all over the world and in the form required. Libraries are also automated and equipped with CD-ROMs. The era of the electronic library is on the way. All these changes are also taking place in the Arab region.

Most of the Arab countries also import a number of magazines and newspapers from abroad, although their distribution is limited to a small number of cities. There is also a union for distributors of Arab newspapers and an Arab union of journalists, founded in 1964. The latter contributes quite actively to upgrading the profession, through a number of courses and seminars including, lately, the use of modern technology and the Internet.

Arab civilization has been closely linked with the production of books and other printed matter. Historically, its efforts in translation have been instrumental in transmitting the works of ancient writers, and Arab contributions in many fields of knowledge are well known. Today, the publishing situation is different and the basic production is translated from western sources. Most of the textbooks used at university level in certain faculties are in English or French, even if the original is Russian or Japanese.

The Arab region appears to favour the simultaneous promotion of industrialization and communication technologies. However, there seems to be more focus on ICT. ICT systems are being upgraded at many levels, but this is especially apparent in efforts to increase efficiency and thus improve productivity. Some of the countries, however, are only just now becoming familiar with ICT. Nevertheless, education at all levels is a top priority throughout the region, and computers and modern communication technologies are considered key tools in preparing all countries for the 21st century.

Below the strategic level, some organizations are studying the newly introduced data warehousing platforms, together with some data mining techniques that sometimes use expert-system methodologies. There is also an urgent need to support the creation of public information systems and to make them accessible to the general public. The launching of the last ARABSAT satellite will greatly contribute to the improvement of telecommunication, broadcasting and access to information.

Local wireless loop services may be developed as a complement. The satellite will also facilitate broadcasting news about events of common interest to Arab and Islamic countries, whether conferences, cultural events, or sports. NILESAT-2 is also expected to be launched at the end of 1999. Finally, an internal expansion of telephone subscribers is taking place in most countries of the region.

In spite of globalization, it is generally acknowledged that governments and their associated institutions have a key role to play in formulating and implementing ICT strategies. There are fundamental and complex issues that have to be addressed, and the benefits that some countries have obtained from this successful experience should be considered. Increasingly, ICTs are an integral part of the overall national strategy and this interdependence between them both is a precondition for their common success.

Arab countries rank ICTs as a high priority within their development objectives. They are seen as an essential element in education, communication, and technology transfer.

The strategic plans have to become more systematic in order to develop integrated information systems that would support greater co-operation between enterprises at different levels across the country. But in order to achieve positive results and increase efficiency, the quality of the data, their definition, and the agencies responsible for their collection and validation must also improve.

Network technologies are to be applied not only for data and information, but across the board. Some of the programmes for ICT at the European Union could be used as a model for the Arab countries. The type of co-operation that is already taking place for broadcasting should be extended. ICT is making radical changes in teaching and learning in higher education, both on campus and in distance education.

The Open University is just starting in the Arab region, but provides a model that should help modernize other sectors and promote continuous learning. Electronic commerce is new in the region and consumer resistance can be overcome gradually with appropriate information campaigns. The integration of ICT into the different activities will help ensure a positive outcome.

The Asia Crisis and ICTs

The current 'Asia Crisis' has had a negative impact on economic and social life in most of Southeast and East Asia. It has jeopardized the human development gains made in the health and education sectors in recent years. It has also brought to the fore new concerns relating to ethnic tensions, social unrest, an increased lack of peace and security, women's rights, poor health conditions and hunger as countries slip into rampant unemployment and inflation pushes millions of households back into poverty.

Despite the crisis, the use of electronic media, telecommunications and Internet are continuing to increase throughout the region as a result of globalization. Governments and business are expanding their activities in radio and television, satellite broadcasting, telecommunications and digital production, while individuals and organizations are making their own decisions about investing in various information technologies.

The prognosis is that bandwidth and new communications technologies are becoming cheaper as governments gradually liberalize their telecommunication sectors. Consequently, the foundation for distance education and open-learning systems in the 21st century will already be in place, and within the next two decades even remote Asian villages will be linked to the global communications network.

Electronic communication and programmes brought via networked media systems and instructional technology in community centres and Internet kiosks will be the new channels for educating, informing and training those in the rural and urban areas.

Since 1997, Bhutan, Papua New Guinea, Laos, Cambodia, and Viet Nam have been wired into the Internet for the first time. Apart from Myanmar, most countries in the region now have some form of presence in this global network.

India has been the largest democracy in the world since its independence in 1947. Today it is a country undergoing a massive transition with far-reaching consequences not only for its more than 900 million citizens, but for the entire globe. After a delay of nearly three years, and mired in litigation and controversy for over a year, the long-awaited ISP Policy has been announced and the process of issuing licenses has begun with gusto.

On 22 November 1998, Prime Minister Atal Bihari Vajpayee inaugurated Satyam Online, the first private-sector Internet access service in Hyderabad, and at the same time the first phase of the Hi-Tec City project near Hyderabad. The highlight of the ISP policy is that licences will be issued for 15 years and there will be no licence fee or any limit on the number of licences awarded.

The railways, state electricity boards and the National Power Grid Corporation are all allowed to provide Internet backbone services. ISPs can set up their own international gateways but require a security clearance from an inter-ministerial committee. The norms for security clearance have not yet been worked out.

India currently has an installed base of only 2 million PCs and less than 500,000 Internet users. The demand for PCs and Internet connections is expected to increase significantly due to the new services being launched. While Internet is not new in the country thanks to the efforts of the Education Research Network (ERNET) and UNDP, it has been limited to those associated with educational institutes or R&D organizations. Previously, access was highly controlled and restricted, which limited its reach.

In August 1995, Videsh Sanchar Nigam Limited (VSNL), a public-sector undertaking and the international telecom carrier, launched the first public Internet service in six major cities, which has today expanded to 42 cities and is expected to reach 70 cities by year-end. There is also a move to enable routing of calls at local-call rates from any of the 800 cities that have STD/ISD (long-distance calling) capability. Instead of setting up a local point of presence (POPs) in all cities, calls to the number 17222 will be directed to the closest Internet POP at no additional charge.

In the first year, 50,000 customers went online on VSNL's Gateway Internet Access Service (GIAS) and today the number exceeds 150,000. New Delhi and Mumbai constitute half the customers. The target is to reach one million users by the year 2000, but that seems unlikely even with the entry of private ISPs.

One of the major factors limiting the expansion of Internet in the country is poor infrastructure, with problems such as the non-availability of telephone lines and an overloading of telephone circuits that were designed for voice communication. To partially overcome this problem, VSNL has installed routers at various telephone exchanges and linked them on dedicated 2Mbps circuits, thus bypassing the congestion.

In the last five years the Department of Telecommunications (DoT) has successfully undertaken a mammoth job of converting telephone exchanges to digital/electronic exchanges and shifting to an optical fibre backbone. This has resulted in very good quality and stable connections, and a huge number of new phone connections. However, many more connections will be needed as India has achieved a teledensity of only 1%.

One of the greatest challenges India now faces is to improve penetration and broaden the access base. If the target of one million Internet subscribers is to be achieved, the entire infrastructure, especially data communication and telecommunications, will need to be overhauled. Another challenge in the short term will be a lack of expertise and talented workforce to handle ISP operations. A sizeable number of people are attracted to the field by world-wide growth figures and are thus jumping onto the ISP bandwagon, but they are often unfamiliar with the dynamics of the business.

India's software business, which relies heavily on computer networks for international operations, is reportedly poised to attain revenues of $6,000 million by the turn of the century. Exports would account for about $4,000 million of the total. Improved availability of the Internet will have a very positive impact on the software industry.

The installation of such a network throughout the region will depend on a number of factors: the regulatory approaches of governments, the number of Internet Service Providers (ISP) or web hosts and approaches to providing infrastructure. The only constant is that every country in the region carries out these activities differently and is at a different stage of development. Consider these examples. In Singapore, one of the most 'wired' countries in the region, there are only three ISPs, yet across the water in the Philippines there is a more relaxed approach to regulation that has spawned some 145 ISPs and countless walk-in access centres.

In Cambodia, the government has allowed the two ISPs to offer a full range of Internet services and has no plans to censor content, but over the border in Viet Nam the authorities have implemented a firewall that intentionally blocks access to selected sites and unintentionally has caused numerous others to become unavailable because of technical problems.

Further to the North, Laos has only just allowed its citizens to access the web after first experimenting with an e-mail-only connection. In the Himalayas, Nepal has a burgeoning Internet industry and some interesting local content programmes, while near-neighbour Bhutan is implementing an internal system · intranet - with only e-mail access to the outside world.

In Mongolia, the locals are using their high levels of literacy and technical education to create an innovative network using whatever means possible: satellite, xDSL modems, radio modem and some creative fund-raising schemes.

The list goes on throughout the region. This same diversity is present when it comes to telecommunications, broadcasting and print media, and runs parallel to developments for the Internet. The Singapore government, for example, owns the two broadcasting companies, the Television Corporation of Singapore and Singapore Television.

Competition is limited in telecommunications, which is dominated by Singapore Telecom, and there is only one print media outlet, the Singapore Press Holdings. By contrast, in the Philippines there are some 17 newspaper organizations, more than 100 television stations, and telecommunications have been opened up to foreign competition. Laos and Viet Nam, which have tried to prevent the inflow of certain content from the Internet, have similar policies for broadcasting and other media, whereas Mongolia opened up its media just before the arrival of the Internet - with the result that there are a flourishing number of print publications and satellite television channels now available in many parts of the country.

Despite this diversity, it is possible to categorize many of the countries into three broad groups. At one end are those that are moving to some form of broadband access and encouraging the use of high-bandwidth applications such as interactive multimedia and e-commerce.

A second tier of countries have a well-established presence on the Internet and a diversified number of access providers, content providers and users. This group would include the Philippines, Indonesia, Thailand, Sri Lanka, China, India, Pakistan and Nepal. Finally, there are those countries that have only recently joined the Internet community. These third-tier countries have a very limited number of ISPs, few examples of local content, and access is confined to one or perhaps two main cities rather than throughout the country. Included in this group are Viet Nam, Bhutan, Laos, Papua New

Guinea (PNG) and Cambodia. Existing media structures, broadcasting facilities, telecommunications infrastructures and regulatory environments tend to conform to this classification of Internet connectivity.

Nevertheless, some countries do not fit neatly into one of the three tiers, and even when they do, diversity is still the key feature, with each country taking its own culturally specific route to enter the information age.

Viet Nam, Bhutan, Laos, Papua New Guinea and Cambodia are all characterized by monopoly telecommunications carriers, low telephone densities, and government regulators who take a dim view of foreign ownership and outside influences. Because of this strict regulatory regime, there have been no private sector initiatives to connect to the Internet until recently. Even the academic sector - one of the catalysts for Internet access in the West and more developed Asian countries - has been slow to act. By contrast, the development sector has been very active.

Four of the five countries mentioned - Viet Nam, Bhutan, Laos and Cambodia - all received support to connect to the Internet from Canada's International Development Research Center (IDRC) under a programme called Pa n Asia Networking (PAN). The programme was launched in 1994 to promote South-South and North-South Internet networking. In the case of Papua New Guinea, the government started by opening up Internet access provision to the private sector.

The most recent entrant to the Internet, Bhutan, is not surprisingly the country that is perhaps the least open to the outside world. Bhutan has long had a policy of limiting tourism and has only allowed television transmission since 1997. The adoption of Internet is following this cautious approach, with the first connections allowing only e-mail access to the outside world and web access restricted to local sites.

All telecommunications services in Bhutan are operated and maintained by the Ministry of Communications' Division of Telecommunications. The current telecommunication network is digital and is capable of supporting data communications and other non-voice services without major problems. Laos also took a tentative approach to the Internet and started with e-mail-only services. More recently, GlobeNet, a subsidiary of Philippines-based satellite provider Globecom, has started to provide full Internet access in conjunction with the Ministry of Information and Culture.

A massive effort in training and in technology transfer is needed to develop a self-sustainable Laotian IT industry. Although such help is readily available in the Lao expatriate and resident IT communities, it does not seem to be readily accessed. There has been some urgency for Laos to adopt some effective means of mass communication, particularly as the offices of the Association of Southeast Asian Nations (ASEAN) have adopted the Internet as the standard means of communication.

Nevertheless each of the countries has a limited number of Internet service providers and coverage. Full Internet services arrived in Cambodia in May 1997 with the establishment of CamNet, a joint venture between the Ministry of Posts and Telecommunications of Cambodia (MPTC) and IDRC. Shortly after, a second ISP, Big Pond Cambodia, a subsidiary of the Australian carrier Telstra in co-operation with MPTC, entered the market. As part of the license agreement with Telstra, MPTC is not allowing new ISP players until 2002. MPTC is both the telecommunications operator and the regulatory body.

At present, there are no specific laws in the country relating to the Internet. The number of users hooked up to the two main e-mail-only servers, Open Forum Information Exchange and WorldMail, is low, numbering about 2,000. However, like other countries in the region, walk-in access centres are becoming a feature and will allow more widespread use in future.

CamNet operates two public Internet centres, one to serve Cambodian research organizations and another aimed at expatriates and tourists. CamNet is working with various Cambodian organizations to publish their own material on the Internet.

Viet Nam first allowed commercial Internet services in late 1997, following more than eighteen months of indecision. An Internet Steering Committee has been set up, headed by the Minister of Science, Technology and Environment and representatives from the Ministries of Security, Culture and Information, Education and Training as well as the Directorate General of Posts and Telecommunication.

Four companies were awarded licences to become Internet Service Providers: NetNam, Viet Nam Data Communications (VDC), Financing and Promoting Technology (FTP) Corporation and the Saigon Post Company. The ISPs must go through the monopoly gateway operator, VDC (a subsidiary of the country's monopoly carrier VNPT) for international connections and are not allowed to lease their own lines. A PAN project is also currently underway to help develop Vietnamese content and is being co-ordinated by NetNam in collaboration with organisations such as the National Centre for Scientific and Technological Information and Documentation (NACESTID) and the Ministry of Culture and Information.

Like other countries in Asia, a significant problem in presenting local information on the world wide web is the lack of a unified coding standard for the local character set. NetNam has designed a utility that recognizes the various codes in use to display Vietnamese text. The utility can detect the six (out of about ten) most common formats that are in use.

In many areas, the final link is provided by High Frequency (HF) radio which can be unreliable for data transmission. The Pacific Islands offer a complete contrast to the vast majority of Asian countries. Despite high levels of aid, the Pacific Islands region has experienced low growth and economic stagnation. This problem is attributed to high population growth, rural-urban migration, the restricted economic conditions of atoll life combined with the need to import a large number of goods and, finally, to high vulnerability to natural and economic disasters.

Government is the major customer, employer and supplier of services in the islands, maintaining in many cases a monopoly. Given the unique geographical dispersion of theses countries, Information and Communication Technologies, particularly telecommunications, offer a real opportunity to diminish the adverse effects of isolation.

The physical infrastructure for telecommunications seems well established. Three satellites can be accessed from every country, while other systems, such as telex and data transmission, cover only some of them. With the exception of emerging arrangements in mobile markets, telecommunication services are provided under state monopoly. But operations seem often to be inefficient. Coverage is poor in remote areas and consumer dissatisfaction is high. Teledensities are relatively low, with large differences between urban and rural areas.

One of the largest potential user communities for Internet is within the university sector. The University of Papua New Guinea (UPNG) and the University of Technology have recently commissioned fibre-optic campus networks that support Internet/Intranet services. In 1998, IDRC and the South Pacific Centre for Communication and Information in Development at the UPNG launched a project to establish a country-level information server that will carry PNG content from many PNG partner institutions.

One country that has recently made the transition from state-controlled and restricted media, broadcasting and information technology to a more liberalized communications policy is Mongolia. While infrastructure in rural areas is still limited and competition in telecommunications not quite a reality, the country has made great strides in providing informations technology to its people in recent years. In 1990, Mongolia switched from a communist state- E-mail services are popular with business customers and the extended family networks resulting from significant population movements.

Every Pacific Island country receives international radio. Some of them also have local radio stations. Most countries produce local television content, although in many countries this is limited to a few hours per day. The penetration rate for personal computers may vary between 1 and 30 personal computers per 1,000 inhabitants, with the exception of Niue, which has almost reached a rate of 80/1,000. There are no statistics for Fiji, the Federated States of Micronesia, Nauru and Palau. The University of the South Pacific provides distance education services using dedicated leased lines.

Additional sites are planned in Kiribati and Samoa. But the limited communication infrastructure means that visual content cannot be distributed. Pacific Islands consumers pay high prices for international and domestic phone services, leased lines and Integrated Services Digital Network (ISDN) services. The monopoly situation and/or the small margins impose prices which are 25% to 58% higher than those prevailing in other environments.

There is an overwhelming consensus in multilateral agencies and regional political groupings to endorse liberalization of telecommunications in order to attain better pricing, service quality and access. Benefits would extend to both public and private institutions as well as the general public.

Sixteen independent states located in the Pacific Ocean are grouped in the South Pacific Forum, an intergovernmental organization which includes the thirteen island states described in this box in addition to Australia, New Zealand and Papua-New Guinea. In addition to the regular budget made up of assessed contributions, eight developed countries and the European Union provide funding for operational assistance controlled economy to a democratic, market-based economy. Since then, the government has liberalized many sectors of the economy including data communications and the media. For a country that until recently had a heavily regulated media, the number of publications and available television stations in the country in 1999 is quite extraordinary.

In information technology as well Mongolia has made great progress in catching up with other countries in the region. At the end of 1996, through assistance from IDRC's PAN programme and a government loan, the local networking company Datacom Ltd set up a satellite earth station and initiated the country's first Internet connection. Since then, a number of projects have seen Internet's reach extend in terms of coverage, usage and the amount of local content.

For example, Datacom has been connecting Mongolian institutes and universities to the Internet through high speed radio modem links. Secondary schools are also being connected via satellite, with support from an IDRC grant. Part of this project will be an Educational Web Centre and an experimental information broadcasting network for provincial schools.

The Philippines and Thailand are examples of other countries that have a wide range of projects that aim to make greater use of information technology and to expand its reach to the general population. However, each country is achieving this end by different means. In the Philippines, where there has been a very open media sector and a dynamic private sector, it is not surprising that the government has taken a hands-off approach to the Internet.

As a result, the private sector is the dominant force when it comes to providing Internet access, and unlike many countries in the region, it has been given a relatively free hand in establishing services and initiating international connections.

The result is some 145 Internet access providers, many of which have countrywide points of presence, a burgeoning array of cheap, walk-in access centres, and some vibrant local content. This situation mirrors what can be seen in the print, broadcasting and telecommunications industries. There are 45 private telecommunications organizations as opposed to 7 public organizations; 86 private television stations compared with 33 government-owned stations; 466 commercial radio stations; and more than 20 daily newspapers.

The Philippines came to the Internet by a traditional route, with the initial connection being a product of the academic sector. The country's first Internet network, PHNET, was initiated in 1994 by the Department of Science and Technology and a consortium of Philippine universities and institutions. It is still the main academic backbone in the country and most recently is proposing to expand its coverage to 2,000 schools by the end of 2000. The resulting network will become the Philippine Science Academic and Research Network (RP-SARNET). In the long run, Internet in the Philippines is expected to be structured around several national backbones - one for government, one for schools and one commercial - each of which will be connected to the other.

In Thailand, the government has played a more direct role in providing access to information technologies within the country. National IT initiatives are formulated within the IT-2000 plan, which was put forward by the National IT Committee and approved by the National Economic and Social Development Board as part of its eighth national development plan.

The three broad aims of IT-2000 are to build an equitable national infrastructure, invest in people and enhance government services and the information industry. National projects such as the academic Internet backbone, a government information network, and a proposed Thailand Software Park are all part of the IT-2000 plan.

Similarly, the government dominates Thailand's broadcasting industry, controlling nearly all radio and television stations, while telecommunications is split between two main government carriers (Telephone Organization of Thailand (TOT) and Communication Authority of Thailand (CAT)) and two private carriers.

The monarchy also plays a major part in the country's development, and in accordance with a long historical tradition a number of IT projects have been initiated by the king and other members of the royal family. Indonesia has traditionally also taken a government-led approach to communications, but has suffered most from the economic crisis owing to internal political unrest and a devastated economy.

Extending telecommunications to all 27 provinces and each main island is a daunting task, yet one which Indonesia has traditionally embraced as a means of creating national cohesion. This recognition of the need for communications for development and modernization occurred more than twenty years ago, in 1976, with the launch of Indonesia's domestic satellite, PALAPA. Indonesia's national information infrastructure is being created under a programme known as Nusantara 21 which calls for all major islands and cities to be linked either by submarine and terrestrial cable, or by satellite, by the year 2001.

However, the current economic crisis has added a level of uncertainty to this project and to many government and business initiatives. The education sector in Indonesia is active in information technology and has suffered less from the economic fallout. More than half of the country's universities are connected to the Internet exchange of the Institute of Technology Bandung, which is connected via a 1.55 Mb/s link to the Asia Pacific AI3 backbone. Despite government backing for Internet and other information technologies, the second-tier countries are still held back to varying degrees by regulatory provisions. These provisions are designed to protect monopoly telecommunications interests and lessen government fears about the impact of the Internet and other outside media. This approach can be seen in countries as diverse as Nepal, Bangladesh, Pakistan, India, China and Sri Lanka.

In nearly all of these cases, Internet access must go through a monopoly carrier or designated gateway, resulting in increased costs to both ISPs and, ultimately, users. The situation is compounded by the lack of telephone lines that can be supplied by monopoly providers. For example, in Bangladesh, a country with only 0.4 telephone lines per hundred people, ISP networks are saturated due to a lack of access lines - and this is in the capital city, Dhaka. Trying to provide services to most remote villages is presently impossible owing to a lack of infrastructure.

A fibre-optic communications network owned and run by the Bangladesh state railway has been viewed by some ISPs as a possible means of gaining widespread connectivity. The transmission lines run alongside the major rail corridors and connect most major centres in the country, but its capacity is underutilized. However, the railway authority has been reluctant to let others use its dormant capacity.

In Sri Lanka, the government imposes a licence fee of Rs3 million, which ensures that ISPs are operated only by large organizations. Many local observers have suggested that this prevents smaller niche players from providing services, many of whom would be able to start in smaller areas that are ignored by the larger organizations. There are currently eight licensed Internet Service providers in Sri Lanka and many more value-added resellers, although with only an estimated 12,000 users by June 1998.

Despite these regulatory impositions, there are signs that countries in this second category are gradually liberalizing telecommunications, broadcasting, and media - albeit slower than many in the private sector would like.

In Nepal, for example, the government has recently allowed the private sector to operate its own satellite facilities rather than go through the monopoly provider, Nepal Telecommunications Corporation (NTC). This follows the setting up of an independent regulator, the Nepal Telecommunication Authority (NTA), in April 1998. One of the first decisions of the NTA was to open the market for very small aperture terminal (VSAT) satellite facilities, which will allow ISPs to obtain their own international bandwidth at a cost well below that offered by NTC.

The regulator has indicated that other aspects of telecommunications will also be opened up to competition in the next two years, although there is no indication that broadcasting will also be liberalized.

Nepal's four television stations and seven radio stations are all government-owned. By contrast, the Internet in Nepal was first introduced by the private sector, in 1993, and has flourished without any sort of public assistance.

While there are only three ISPs, there are literally hundreds of walk-in access centres, a pattern that has previously been established for telephone and fax services, where Public Call Offices (PCOs) offer walk-in services. A group of more than 30 Nepali research organizations is also networking together to provide local research and development information on NepalNet, a PAN project.

In most of the countries mentioned, there are indications that telecommunications and the media are slowly being liberalized, with governments in the process of overhauling their regulatory structures to make way for the new information environment.

In Bangladesh, control over regulatory matters was recently moved away from the state-controlled Bangladesh Telephone and Telegraph Board (BTTB); China has recently restructured and merged its regulatory environment; India has removed the monopoly for providing Internet services enjoyed by the state-owned carrier, VSNL; Pakistan is privatizing its telecommunications carrier, and the list goes on. While some governments are slower than many in the private sector would like, the momentum to liberalize will certainly continue, in a manner deemed appropriate by each country.

It is not surprising that those countries moving to broadband infrastructure based on technologies such as ATM (asynchronous transfer mode) networks · which allow for the convergence of voice, data, video, and

Internet - are also moving at a more rapid rate towards the full deregulation of the media, telecommunications, and the Internet.

The economies in this category - Australia, New Zealand, Singapore, Malaysia, Hong Kong, South Korea, and Japan - are also the most developed and prosperous in the region and have well-developed infrastructures and well-educated technical work forces. Each of these countries is also vying to become a regional hub for broadcasting and information technology, a fact which seems to further encourage liberalization and investment in infrastructure and services.

In recent years, Japan, Australia, and New Zealand have opened up their markets for telecom- munications services, while in Singapore, Malaysia, Taiwan (China), Hong Kong and the Republic of Korea this process is well underway and in some cases has been accelerated. In terms of Internet access, Japan, Australia and New Zealand are all in the top tier of nations globally. When the ratio of host computers is compared to GDP, New Zealand is the second most wired nation in the world, behind Finland.

The New Zealand city of Wellington, according to the January 1998 survey by United States-based Network Wizards, is the world's most Internet-connected city, with 4,70 2 Internet-connected computers per 100,000 people. In Australia, according to the latest figures from the Bureau of Statistics, almost a third of Australian adults, or 4.2 million people, use the Internet, while the number of households with access to the Internet increased by 46% last year to almost 1.25 million (18% of households), giving it one of the highest Internet penetration rates in the world. This increase is backed up by the number of

Internet hosts, which has been consistently among the top five nations, even though the population base is a mere 18 million.

In Japan, there were some 2,600 registered ISPs and 13 million users as of October 1998. In the year 2000 the number of users is expected to rise to 20 million. One feature of the Internet in Japan has been its spread into virtually all areas of the countryside through a multitude of small niche-market providers. Similarly, Japan's media and telecommunications industries are notable for the array of choices and the number of small players.

For example, there are 121 daily newspapers in circulation as well as 291 community papers and 528 town papers, while in telecommunications there are some 4,726 providers of varying sizes and descriptions.

In Singapore, Malaysia, Taiwan (China) and the Republic of Korea the government has historically taken a prominent role in guiding the use and spread of broadcasting and media for both political and economic reasons. The introduction of Internet has followed this pattern, although there are increasing signs that these governments recognize the need to open up more than in the past.

Nevertheless, the public sector is still instrumental in propelling these countries towards an information society. For example, Malaysia has made a number of well-publicized initiatives aimed at placing itself at the forefront of the global information economy, particularly through its Multimedia Super Corridor (MSC) project. The MSC is Malaysia's hope for becoming a knowledge-based society having developed country status by the year 2020.

MSC incorporates two 'smart cities', an advanced telecommunications infrastructure and seven flagship application areas in government, education, medicine, finance, manufacturing, R&D and marketing. As part of its efforts to attract electronic commerce projects to the MSC, it is in the process of introducing cyberlaws that aim to create a regulatory framework for information and e-commerce services. Malaysia has approximately 205,000 Internet users.

Malaysia has partially deregulated its media and telecommunications industries but government influence is still strongly felt in all sectors. In telecommunications, deregulation has been limited to a handful of large players, while in broadcasting a number of private radio and television stations have emerged, although the government stations are still in the majority. In 1996, Malaysia launched its own satellite, the Malaysian East Asian Satellite (MEASAT).

Malaysians can receive satellite transmissions only through this domestic service, rather than from other sources as an open policy would permit. In Singapore, IT 2000: a vision of an intelligent island' is a masterplan for the introduction of IT into every aspect of Singaporean society. Initiatives such as the Singapore ONE broadband network are part of IT 2000 and are aimed at turning the country into an IT and broadcasting hub. The backbone of this network uses state-of-the-art asynchronous transfer mode (ATM) switches connected via fibre optic trunks that thread through the central business districts and residential neighbourhoods.

Access to the network for individual users will be via asymmetric digital subscriber line (ADSL) modems and hybrid fibre-coaxial (HFC) cable modems, both of which can deliver Internet access at bandwidths of 2 Mbps or better. Once implemented, the network will be available to 90% of all homes. The total number of Internet users in 1998 was estimated at more than 400,000. In keeping with its approach to media in general, the government of Singapore has taken a hands-on approach to the regulation of Internet content.

The Singapore Broadcasting Authority (SBA) regulates both ISPs and Internet Content Providers through the Internet Class Licence Scheme, which requires all providers and resellers to follow the SBA's Internet Code of Practice. Under the obligations of the code, Internet access providers are required to deny access to sites that have been prohibited by SBA.

In the Republic of Korea, the IT and electronics industries have been a successful part of the economy with many large high-tech manufacturers and exporters. The government is also involved in building capacity through the Korea Information Infrastructure (KII). The KII is intended as a broadband infrastructure and comprises two networks: a public network for the private sector and a government network for government or public institutions.

The Ministry of Communications and Information plans to put this broadband infrastructure in place by 2010 through a combination of private and public sector investment. The number of Internet users was 2.5 million at the end of 1997. In advertising, there are approximately ten active companies and many others preparing to enter online activities. In publishing, book stores are opening cyber facilities, while data communications companies are also opening cyber bookstores as part of cyber shopping-mall initiatives. In the media, 'Internet only' journals that do not publish regular paper journals are also beginning to appear.

Basic telecommunications infrastructure in Taiwan (China) is well advanced and dominated by Chunghwa Telecom Co., which is in the process of being privatized. There are over 9 million telephone sets, extensive microwave radio relay trunk systems on the east and west coasts for domestic connections, satellite earth stations and submarine cables to Japan, Philippines, Guam, Singapore, Hong Kong, Indonesia, Australia, the Middle East and Western Europe.

Currently, there are over 500,000 users from around 400 academic institutions, colleges and universities in the island who benefit from the Taiwan Academic Network's free services to promote academic research. The island's National Information Infrastructure (NII) plan was introduced in 1994 with the following priorities: network construction, education and training, electronic government, electronic commerce, social welfare, life long learning, Chinese culturalrelics online, the study and revision of related laws and regulations and internationalization of Chinese networks.

Today, libraries must redefine their roles if they are to survive and prosper in the new age of information-based societies. The dramatic capacity increase of digital media, the convergence of telecommunication and broadcasting, and the availability of information resources accessible through the Internet have driven home the realization that libraries must reposition themselves. The new vision sees libraries as part of networked environments, and the promotion of IT is an integral part of library services in meeting the changing information needs of users.

Thus, the focus has been on developing the digital library, which includes identifying repositories of multimedia digital information resources and integrating the country's libraries and knowledge-based institutions through networking; establishing information resource networks or 'libraries without walls'; creating local content or databases - text (reports, publications, bibliographic databases), audio, video, maps, pictures, graphics - in digitized form, using image processing and character recognition among the technologies employed; making information resources accessible on the Internet; marketing library services through web pages; and providing Internet facilities and stimulating an Internet culture among the public.

Satellite television is one of the obvious areas of regional activity and its reach and influence has been dramatic. In recent years a large number of local, regional and multinational satellite television companies have been set up in Asia. Prominent among these is Hong Kong-based Star TV, which beams programmes to 220 million households in the Asia-Pacific region.

Increasingly, many of the programmes and channels are localized and broadcast in a variety of Asian languages. However, the use of such regional services varies from country to country, with some, such as India and Japan, welcome foreign programmes while others, including China, Malaysia and Singapore, restrict the entry of foreign programming.

In terms of telecommunications, satellite facilities are also providing regional coverage, most notably through regional systems such as AsiaSat, Apstar, as well as through international systems such as PanAmSat, Intelsat and the forthcoming Iridium and similar low-earth orbit

(LEO) schemes. Taiwan (China) and Singapore have also co-operated to launch the ST-1 telecommunications satellite in 1998.

Telecommunications networks using fibre-optic cable are also coming to the fore. Prominent among these are Fiber Optic Link around the Globe (FLAG), which links the rest of the world with countries including Korea, Singapore, Hong Kong and China, and SEA- M E - W E 3 , which in Asia connects Singapore, Australia, Korea and Japan. Another regional telecommunications project known as ACASIA comes from ASEAN countries. It is aimed at providing multinational corporations with cross-country private network services.

Development agencies have been instrumental in helping developing countries in Asia adopt information technologies. IDRC's PAN programme, mentioned earlier, promotes South-South and North-South Internet linkages, while the UNDP also implements numerous technical co-operation programmes throughout the region. The UNDP's Asia Pacific Development Information Programme (APDIP) based in Kuala Lumpur, Malaysia, promotes the use of IT in the region and also focuses on Internet governance issues.

Another regional body involved with Internet governance and infrastructure issues is the Singapore-China, officially the People's Republic of China, is the world's third largest country by area and the largest by population. Covering a total area of 9,596,960 square kilometres, China encompasses a diversity of landscapes extending from the Tibetan Plateau at the southwest extremity to the deserts in the Mongolian borderland of north central China and to the sub-tropical fertile plains of the Canton Delta to the south.

China's population density is relatively high. Distribution, however, is uneven: the coastal areas in the east are densely populated, with more than 400 people per square kilometre, while the plateau areas in the west are sparsely populated, with fewer than 10 people per square kilometre. Telecommunication is one of the fastest growing industries in China.

Domestic and international telecommunication services are increasingly available for private use. By the end of 1997, the number of telephone lines had expanded to 120 million, with 9.55 telephones per hundred persons. The domestic system serves principal cities, industrial centres, most townships and is fast reaching villages. By 1997, 55.6% of China's villages were connected to the public telephone system.

By 1997, 14 inter-provincial fibre-optic trunk lines had been installed, while mobile communication networks and international services have been expanding rapidly. The Chinese government encourages the development of Chinese software and formatted fonts facilitate the use of Chinese characters for digital communication. It is estimated that Internet users in China will exceed 2 million by the end of 1998 and reach 5 million in the year 2000.

Yet considering China's population of 1.2 billion, the percentage of people accessing the Internet is and will be very small. For the whole nation to become 'wired', the geographic, professional, gender and economic obstacles to accessing the Internet would need to be addressed. In China, major metropolitan cities and economically more advanced regions tend to have the best network facilities and therefore it is not surprising that most Internet users are based in Beijing, Shanghai and Guangzhou. Beijing also has the most ISPs.

Ordinary people are still not very aware of the Internet, and current users are mostly in computer-related professions or have higher education qualifications. The average user is young - 80% are between 21 and 35 - and 88% of Internet users in China are male. Placing great emphasis on the strategic importance of information/communication technologies to the modernization of China's economy, the Chinese government has made it a priority to build the national information infrastructure (NII), especially national economic computer network projects in the country's Ninth Five-Year Construction Plan (1996-2000).

The government supports the expansion of Internet into China, though it maintains close control over content. While foreign ownership of any Chinese telecommunications and information infrastructure is strictly prohibited, the government actively seeks foreign investments to fund the rapid development of China's information infrastructure. The four major Internet backbone networks are all government sponsored and must use China Telecom links to connect to Internet sites in other countries. All ISPs must register with the police.

The Temporary Provisions of Internet Administration of the Computer Information Communication network of the P.R.China'. This mandated that the four established Internet networks - ChinaNet, CHINAGBN, CERnet and CASnet - should be separately administered by the Ministry of Posts and Telecommunications, the Ministry of Electronics Industry, the State Committee of Education, and the Science Institute of China.

In June 1998, the government restructured its information and telecommunications authorities. The

Ministry of Information Industry (MII) was established by merging the Ministry of Electronic Industry and the Ministry of Post and Telecommunications.

The new ministry is responsible for invigorating the manufacture of information products, telecommunications and software; formulating sectoral programmes, policies and legal codes; mapping out an overall plan for telecommunications trunk networks (including local and long-distance telecommunications networks), broadcast and television networks (including radio and cable television networks), and special-use telecommunications networks for military and other departments.

At the opening of the 7th Annual Conference of the Asian Media Information and Communication Centre in May 1998, UNESCO's representative Mr Claude Ondobo observed that in education, information technologies must better respond to the different learning and training needs of society; in culture, multimedia technologies must promote cultural and linguistic pluralism; and in science, information highways must improve both access to scientific information and the sharing of research facilities on a large scale and in a more interactive way. This Asia-Pacific ICT report card seems to demonstrate these ICT goals.

ICT and Central and Eastern European Countries

All Central and Eastern Europe (CEE) countries are undergoing a process of fundamental political and economic transformation that interacts with changes in social structure and, in many cases with the need to redefine territorial and cultural boundaries. Economic policy has focused on social, economic and labour problems resulting from the crises provoked by the collapse of the old system and the accompanying need to dismantle and/or modernize inefficient and unproductive industries. Consequently, little attention has been paid to promoting forward-looking policies in information and communications technology (ICT) and progress has been slow.

Central and Eastern European countries entered the 1990s with broadcasting and telecommunications infrastructures inherited from the communist era when they were underdeveloped and tightly controlled. Now, however, big changes are underway.

The direction and the pace of change differ greatly from country to country, depending on the general political and economic context. In some of the more advanced countries, a dual system of private and public broadcasting is already operating in ways similar to the pattern prevailing in Western Europe. Elsewhere, the state monopoly of broadcasting has been preserved to all intents and purposes, with the old state broadcaster still operating and dominating the scene.

Central and Eastern European countries represent a wide variety of social and political environments, as well as different levels of economic and technological advancement. Reliable data for some of them are very hard to obtain. The following overview, therefore, cannot claim to be complete. In some cases, data from several sources and for different years have been used to provide as full a description as possible. More detailed information is generally available for Central European countries, and therefore much of the attention will be focused on them.

Progress in new information and communication technologies is determined to a very large extent by the level of economic and technological development, as well as the size of the market and the purchasing power of the population. Therefore, discussion of ICTs in Central and Eastern Europe would be incomplete without at least a cursory examination of these structural factors.

In low-income countries, the volume is insignificant, indicating that telecommunications are not yet an important part of the economy. There are also clear differences in the level of telecommunications revenue and investment between more and less advanced countries in the other income brackets.

To take one example, Lithuania is one of many CEE countries where the existing quality of local communications does not satisfy the users' requirements. Therefore, plans call for replacing analogue telephone centres with digital ones - to be completed by 2015 - and for setting up of a telephone subscriber information system, with the gradual introduction of special equipment, such as voice simulation, automatic system control, and communication with other countries' systems. By 2000, existing coin-box telephones will be replaced by card-operated ones; card telephone control and diagnostics centres will be established in all branches of Lithuanian Telecom.

Rapid development of the fibre-optic cable line network is planned. In 1996, a fibre-optic line from Kaunas to Klaipëda via Panevëpys and Diauliai was introduced, with digital 155 Mb/s multiplexing systems. Lithuanian telecommunications will be provided with a second international communication line via Latvia; it will be possible to connect twelve Lithuanian cities by means of a high-capacity transmission system. The same fibre-optic lines will be used for the setting up of a national public data network.

At the 1996 Central and East European Information Society Forum it was pointed out that penetration targets for fixed telephone lines set for the year 2000 range from 18.9% for Romania to 50.0% for Latvia. To meet those targets, CEE telecommunications would need to install new lines that are at least 50% faster over the next five years.

The total investment required in all ten CEE countries together to achieve those targets would be about $20,000 million, or $4,000 million per annum. Those targets are high compared with an annual investment rate of $1,600 million for the four years up to 1995 during which the three International Financial Institutions (IFIs) provided at most $440 million per annum.

In some countries, pay television is available and spreading. As with cable, reception of Direct to Home (DTH) satellite television and VCRs, the appearance and development of pay television is determined by the size of the market and living standards (including discretionary purchasing power) prevalent in a particular country. For this reason, pay television can be found mostly in Central European countries.

Spending on hardware, software and services is another important difference between the less and the more advanced countries. The country-level markets of Central and Eastern Europe remain heavily oriented towards personal computers and PC-related technologies. These accounted for the largest percentage of IT hardware spending during the 1996-1997 period.

By contrast, in the Czech Republic, personal computers and related hardware represent less than 35% of IT spending, with the remainder being shifted to implementation services, networking applications, development and support. Elsewhere, the low-end office equipment market, local area network (LAN) hardware and the LAN server market have experienced considerable growth over the last several years. However, the computer systems segment (mainframes, servers, workstations) has stagnated in several countries due to reductions in funding for public IT projects.

Particularly strong growth is being seen in the market for packaged software, such as PC applications software, enterprise resource planning (ERP) applications, and application tools for database development and management. Demand for basic services such as IT consulting, contract programming and software design is also strong. Most growth in the software and services sector is derived from large-scale projects in banking, financial services, government administration, telecommunications and industry. Local firms play a role of growing importance as system integrators, value-added resellers, software developers and training centres.

New information and telecommunication technologies are gradually being introduced into all spheres of life in Central and Eastern Europe. In Estonia, for example, a national school computerization programme, known as 'Tiger Leap', has been launched. In 1997, 25% of all schools were connected to the Internet. By the year 2000, all the schools are scheduled to be on the Internet.

A similar project, School-Net, was inaugurated in 1996 in Hungary, with a view to providing direct access to the Internet for about one thousand schools by 1 September 1998. As a result of this project, schools are being equipped with computer laboratories incorporating 6 to 18 multimedia computers per laboratory.

In Estonia, computer workplaces installed in national public administration authorities (PAAs) were expected to achieve an average of almost 90% by the end of 1997. Some branches were expected to reach 100%. Local area networks (LANs) are rapidly being adopted in Estonian PAAs. In 1993 there were only 15 networks in operation and 23 uninstalled network kits; by the end of 1997 the estimated number of LANs was expected to reach 431. However, the LANs used in these administrations are usually not large. The average number of workstations connected into a public administration LAN is 14.5, including 56 in networks of supporting structures, 17 in ministry networks, 12 in national board networks, 6 in inspectorates and 15 in county government networks.

In Lithuania, due to the limited funding available from the state budget in 1993-1995, only the most important technology projects were selected for investments. These included the integration of computer networks for public institutions, the state register system and geographical information systems, and networks for local authorities and customs. Altogether, 46 institutions were united into the Public Institutions Computer Network (VIKT): the Seimas (Parliament), the Government, the Ministries of Economics, Finance, Communications and Informatics, Foreign Affairs and Internal Affairs, the Customs and Statistics Departments, the Vilnius Municipal Office and similar bodies. They were also provided the opportunity of connecting to the

Internet. LITNET, a Lithuanian science network, has been an official member of the Internet since 1994.

LITNET allows the multimedia exchange of texts, graphs, signals, static and moving images among subscribers from 173 countries of the world. The network's services are used by 10 universities and academies, 14 research institutes, and about 140 other schools, libraries, public institutions, and healthcare establishments. LITNET consists of over 2,000 computers and the number of users exceeds 10,000 people.

There is a co-ordinated effort to develop computerized information systems (IS) that help manage government departments like the Ministry of Internal Affairs, the State Control Department, the Ministry of Finance, and the Ministry of Social Security and Labour. An X.25-standard data communication network, Vilniaus DATAPAK, with 240 connection ports, is operated by Lithuanian Telecom. It is used by the Customs IS and the Bank IS. The examples of Estonia and Lithuania illustrate the increasing use of ICT in Central and Eastern European countries, where they are among the most developed in the region.

Broadcasting monopolies are a thing of the past in Central and Eastern Europe, but political and economic circumstances in individual countries have shaped broadcasting systems differently. In most Central European countries, a dual system of public and private broadcasting is operating at the national and also, in some cases, at the sub-national level.

In the Commonwealth of Independent States (CIS), the situation is different. In these countries the private sector is non-existent: there are, in most cases, no independent or commercial stations at the national level, and 'authorities have retained control over important state-owned media. If they have not outlawed independent or opposition altogether . . . they have retained important levers: they may withdraw subsidies, increase the rent of editorial premises, refuse to print or distribute a paper, delay registration, deny a licence or frequency to a broadcaster, increase tariffs, restrict access to information or file libel suits'.

Economic factors also weigh heavily on growth prospects for the media in most CEE countries. Larger or more buoyant markets attract foreign investors and generate relatively high volumes of spending on advertising. On the other hand, underdeveloped and stagnant economies are not capable of sustaining extensive media growth: there is neither start-up capital, nor sufficient advertising to finance such activity.

Central European states resulting from the demonopolization of television at the national level. Practically everywhere in CEE countries cable television is in private hands, with foreign companies sometimes holding a majority stake. Progress is also being made, albeit at a slower pace in some countries, towards the liberalization of telecommunications. No doubt this is aided by the fact that many Central European states aspire to membership in the European Union (EU) which requires policies in harmony with those of the EU.

In traditional telecommunications services, the market in many cases is still closed, or open only to limited competition. Even where telecommunication companies have been privatized, many of them have been given exclusive long-term licences. Full liberalization will come only when these licences have expired. As far as new services - Global System for

Mobile Communication (GSM), Nordic Mobile Telephone System (NMT) 40, Digital Cellular System (DCS) 1800, satellite communications, radio paging, data transmission, Internet service provision - are concerned, the market is open in most cases and they have been launched from the start by private companies, many with significant foreign shareholders.

Bulgaria and Romania have yet to liberalize their telecommunications. Poland has begun a process of privatization of Polish Telecom (TP S.A.) by selling a part of its shares on the stock exchange. A strategic partner is to be chosen in 1999. Several countries have decided to choose international operators as strategic investors by partially privatizing their telephone companies. Several local telephone operators have been licensed. New services are provided by private companies, many with foreign shareholders.

The Estonian government sold 49% of Esti Telefon to a Scandinavian consortium. The private investors have been given management control with a 25-year concession to operate the national network, as well as an exclusivity period of eight years to provide long-distance service.

Hungary at first sold 30% of its national operator MATÁV to a consortium of Deutsche Telecom and Ameritech. MATÁV obtained the right to operate long-distance and international services as well as two-thirds of the local areas with an exclusivity period of eight years for public telephone services. Later, Hungary sold a further 37% of MATÁV's shares to Deutsche Telecom and Ameritech.

The government's share holding is now down to 25% so that the foreign consortium has both majority ownership and full management control. The remaining local areas have been sold to several smaller operators under similar conditions. The private investors have management control with an 8-year concession.

Latvia sold a 49% stake of Lettelkom to a consortium led by Finland Telecom and Cable & Wireless, with a 10% equity stake bought by the International Finance Corporation. Lettelcom has a 20- year concession to provide domestic and international telecommunication services.

In Lithuania, the market is theoretically open, but in most areas there is only one operator, Lietuvos Telekomas (LT). It is foreseen that a new telecommunications law will grant LT exclusive right to provide some services until 2003. The Czech government allowed SPT Telecom A/S to increase its capital by creating new shares which were sold to Tel Source. This consortium, which includes the Dutch telecommunication and postal group (KPN) and Swiss Telecom, owns 34% of SPT and has management control. The arrangement helps finance the company's modernization plans.

Central and Eastern European countries which are associated with the European Union have been able to benefit from the Phare Fund. This Fund is available for upgrading the knowledge and practical experience of staff who handle the operational and regulatory aspects of improved telecommunications systems.

Other projects have concentrated on facilitating investments, on providing aid for setting up independent telecommunications regulatory authorities and on developing licensing guidelines and expanding services. Additional funding has been earmarked for restructuring the transport, energy and telecommunications sectors in

CEE countries to help them play a larger role in a market economy.

For example, assistance has gone towards eliminating bottlenecks at some of the important border crossings and towards developing a more rational and efficient use of resources. The old system's artificially low prices for energy had encouraged inefficient production techniques and high consumption, which in turn led to serious environmental degradation. To address these problems, the European Union has supported the setting up of commercial companies to manage energy production, telecommunications services, privatization of road transport, restructuring of rail companies and the preparation of a regulatory framework for both the telecommunications and transport systems.

Since 1995, the European Commission has organized annual European Union/Central and Eastern European countries (EU/CEEC) Information Society forums whose goal is to integrate candidate CEE countries into European and international efforts towards the Global Information Society. Policies and strategies for implementation have been developed through a series of meetings.

In 1996 the second Forum created four panels which dealt with strategy and policy formulation for the Information Society; implementation of demonstrations, pilot projects and other actions; education and training for the Information Society; and the application of information and communications technologies in public administration. At the same Forum, an Action Plan for Information Society pilot projects in CEE countries was adopted. It was based on the conviction that 'for the CEE countries, the information society is a top priority in order to improve competitiveness and enhance the efficiency of public administration.

Even though some important political decisions have yet to be made, and the financial resources available are severely limited, it is still crucial to send positive signals about the information society in order to raise public awareness. For this reason, this set of ideas has been put forward in the form of an action plan. . . . The action plan has identified thirty themes covering the areas where pilot projects will be particularly effective.'

The 'informatization' of Central and Eastern European societies has been both a top-down and a bottom-up process. It began only after 1989 when political and administrative constraints on access to, and use of, information and telecommunication technologies were lifted. Considering these inauspicious beginnings, CEE societies have indeed made great strides in the past decade.

Nevertheless, it is clear that Central and Eastern European countries are only at the beginning of their journey towards the Information Society. In 1996, Panel A, Financing of Infrastructure, of the Central and East European Information Society Forum, concluded that 'in most cases, the governments of CEECs are not organized in such a way as to enable them to monitor the evolution of the "Information Society" as an economic sector [and] specific new responsibilities are needed.

To be effective, such responsibilities would have to operate across the boundaries of existing government ministries and other agencies'. Even more importantly, many of those governments have yet to focus fully on the issue of the Information Society, preoccupied as they are with the job of creating a market economy and dismantling the legacy of the centralized economic system. For many, economic underdevelopment and crisis/stagnation have created immediate and pressing challenges which direct attention away from the promise of the Information Society.

Nevertheless, a number of countries have adopted action programmes oriented towards laying the groundwork for the creation of the Information Society. In Hungary, a National Information Infrastructure Development Programme had been operating for more than ten years in 1997. Hungary has established a Governmental Committee on Information and Telecommunication Technology and has developed a 'National Informatics Strategy'.

In Lithuania, the task of the Ministry of Communications and Informatics is to form and to implement the Lithuanian communications and informatics strategy, to organize postal, telecommunications and informatics activities, and to co-ordinate the operation of public telegraph, telephone, data transmission, information, radio and television facilities and networks belonging to enterprises, institutions, organizations and individuals. The Ministry of Communications and Informatics co-ordinates the development of the national data transmission networks and state databases, registers and information systems.

In Estonia, a development plan for Estonian informatics has been adopted. It includes a package of documents describing Estonia's information policy: 'Fundamentals of the Estonian Information Policy', an 'Action Plan' and 'Proposals to the Government of the Republic'. Similar documents developed in the past have had little impact.

By the year 2005, the plan calls for extending the information infrastructure to the countryside and for advancing informatics in Romania to the level required for integration into the European information society. The Polish government has adopted a 'Telecommunications

Development Policy' and has before it a number of draft documents concerning ways of moving towards the Information Society. The third EU/CEEC Information Society Forum (1997) invited CEE governments to ensure that their national Information Society strategy and related action plan contain chapters specifically devoted to such important areas as national budgetary provision, the pro-active role of government, protection of personal data, information security and cryptography, education for the Information Society, promotion of cultural and linguistic diversity and international co-operation in statistics.

Impact of ICT in Latin America and Caribbean

The situation of information centres and libraries and the networks being set up within Latin America and the Caribbean to link them together, with the support of the Organization of American States (OAS) and the Hemisphere Wide Inter-University Scientific and Technological Information Network (RedHUCyT). Thirdly, we shall consider communications, touching briefly on the situation of mass print media, and referring to the extraordinary growth of telecommunications in the region.

The worldwide expansion rate of Information Technologies has been increasing rapidly, and the Latin America and Caribbean region is no exception to this trend, although the regional growth rate is generally below that of the developed countries and of the world as a whole.

In the Information Society Index (ISI) designed by International Data Corporation, the region ranks close to the world average for a number of social criteria (freedom of the press, civil liberties and secondary education), for one computing infrastructure criterion (percentage of PCs in networks) and for one information infrastructure criterion. For the remaining factors, it is below the world average, and far below the position of develcped countries such as the United States.

The Latin American and Caribbean region contains approximately 6% of world population and accounts for 3% of world IT investment, whereas North America, with 5% of the population, accounts for 45% of world IT investment. The relative position of the region in this respect is similar to that of Africa/Middle East. All other regions outstrip Latin America, with the exception of Asia and the Pacific (excluding Japan).

The Latin American IT market represents 3% of the world market, but growth in Latin America is above the world average, being twice as high in the period 1995-1996, and almost twice as high in 1996-1997. For the period 1997-2002, growth in the Latin American market is forecast to be 51% higher than the world average.

Information and Library Services

In general, libraries in Latin America and the Caribbean have sought to adapt to new technological developments, while their efforts have been concentrated on meeting local needs. Traditionally, however, co-operation initiatives, which are a top priority for modern information services, have been few and far between.

Institutions such as the OAS and UNESCO have been supporting the creation of networks between libraries in the region, as a way for these to cater for the growing demand for information services in spite of increasingly tight budgets. As a result, there has been progress in setting up local, national and regional consortia to develop library tools and thereby meet more of the requirements that have been created by the Information Age.

Academic and research libraries have been the most successful in entering into co- operation networks and they have received the most international support. It is on the basis of these networks that other libraries will be seeking to create networks among themselves. Consequently, we shall concentrate here on academic and research libraries.

Although the idea of co-operation between libraries was frequently discussed in the 1960s and 1970s, it was a long time before it became a reality in the region, owing to poor telecommunications infrastructure and to restrictions on computer imports in certain countries. These negative factors managed to overwhelm the strong common regional heritage of language, religion and history, which had created a territorial situation probably unique in the world.

The Costa Rican National Research Network (CRNet), supported by the RedHUCyT, is the mainstay of the trunk network which will link up the networks of the Central America region. The first connection was made in November 1996: Costa Rica and Nicaragua were interconnected directly by digital link. Since then, the other countries have also been interconnected. RedHUCyT is supporting the process and providing technical consultancy services to El Salvador, Honduras, Nicaragua and Panama. In March 1997, an agreement was signed with the University of Costa Rica to provide technical assistance to other countries in Central America and the Caribbean.

With the process of creating a trunk network thus under way, Internet use has gained momentum, and this has been reflected in the substantial rise in the number of hosts since 1996. Even so, the number of hosts per capita has remained very far below the regional average, and is falling farther behind all the time. Cellular telephony has always been below the regional average, and is likewise dropping ever farther behind. As regards the number of personal computers (PCs) per capita, the gap with the region is very large indeed, although there could be some uncertainty about this as our source does not have data for certain Central American countries.

In the process of setting up co-operation mechanisms, a number of information networks have emerged, with many of them relying on the CDS/ISIS software distributed by UNESCO which was prepared especially for developing countries.

Among the new fields of operational information there are networks for public administration (CLAD), social sciences (CLACSO), health sciences (BIREME), education (REDUC), planning (INFOPLAN and CARISPLAN), and Major contacts and arrangements are currently being made to connect the Universidad Estadual Minas Gerais and other institutions to the Internet with the support of the RedHUCyT project. This network was one of the joint sponsors and organizers of the First Network Forum in Latin America, together with the National Research Council/National Research Network (CNPq/RNP).

Although progress of this kind had already been achieved before the Internet boom of recent years, the extraordinary growth of Internet use is definitely strengthening co-operation among libraries in these countries.

The Inter-University Network

With the new opportunities generated by the Internet have come new initiatives to support the creation of Latin American information networks that can provide the basis for greater co-operation among libraries in the region. Of these initiatives, particular mention should be made of the RedHUCyT project (Hemisphere Wide Inter-University Scientific and Technological Information Network), launched by the OAS, which began in 1991.

Its main objective is to 'connect Member States to the Internet, forming an electronic network for the exchange of scientific and technological information. The project provides high-tech equipment and technical support, and sponsors technical workshops and seminars in the region to prepare technical projects, improve skills, share technical knowledge and train network managers in the countries'.

The importance of this type of information infrastructure was recognized by the 34 American heads of State at the Summit of the Americas held in Miami in 1994. The Plan of Action signed by them emphasizes the importance of telecommunications and information infrastructure, an entire chapter being devoted to the subject. They state: 'The telecommunications, information technology and broadcasting infrastructure of a country is an essential component of political, economic, social and cultural development.

The Governments of the Americas propose to meet these needs by undertaking a wide range of actions,' in which it is stated, and highlighted in bold, that Governments 'will urge the main universities, libraries, hospitals and governmental organizations to link up to these networks by taking advantage of the OAS Hemisphere Wide Inter-University Scientific and Technological Information Network'. Again, the RedHUCyT has received the backing of Ministers of Science and Technology who, at their Cartagena Meeting in 1996, undertook that their respective countries would 'Promote active participation by the countries of the region in the construction, design and standardization of the Global Information Infrastructure, and encourage them to link up through regional networks such as RedHUCyT'.

In turn, the General Assembly of OAS, meeting in Panama on 3 June 1996, once again stressed the importance of RedHUCyT, with the participants resolving to 'Strengthen regional networks such as the Hemisphere Wide Inter-University Scientific and Technological Information Network (RedHUCyT)'. As a result of the undertakings and support provided on these various occasions, more and more countries in Latin America and the Caribbean have come to participate in the RedHUCyT, constructing their own national networks and connecting them to others.

With this ongoing support and encouragement, the RedHUCyT has been carrying out important activities. During the first stage of the project, the focus was on setting up the basic infrastructure needed to provide academic institutions in the region with access to the Internet. Many of these connections are made via the PAS-1 satellite operated by the Panamerican Corporation of Florida, which provides a direct link-up to the NSF node in Florida. Latin America and the Caribbean 251 for the following countries: Argentina, Costa Rica, Ecuador, Honduras, Paraguay, Peru and Venezuela. The other countries of the region make the connection through operating companies.

The following objectives were set for the second stage of the RedHUCyT project, here quoted verbatim:

— International expansion of Member States' intercommunication and value added networks: the new and increasingly large applications being introduced into electronic networks require high communication speeds. Immediate action is needed on this, as numerous requests for support have already been received.

— Increase in the number of connections and points of presence available nationally for the electronic networks currently in use in member countries. Although most of the countries in the region have some kind of electronic network connectivity, there is a need to create or expand national backbones so that a greater number of institutions can be interconnected. Likewise, local networks within institutions need to be expanded so that a greater number of final users can be reached.

— Assistance for other non-academic sectors, such as: government agencies, particularly those that have databases of interest to the scientific community, and other sectors such as trade, promotion of democracy, human rights, environment and others.

Compuserve Global Data Communication to connect up to the OCLC (Online Computer Library Center) Network. As the RedHUCyT project advances, increasing use will be made of OCLC services in the future. Now that OCLC is using Internet TCP/IP, replacing the proprietary communication protocols with which it began when it was set up in 1970, it is easier and easier to gain low-cost access to libraries connected to the Internet.

Information Services and Libraries in Latin America and the Caribbean will turn this advantage to increasingly good effect. Thus, WorldCat (the OCLC online union catalogue), the Inter-Library Loan System and the FindSearch service, which have yielded such good results in the United States, will be used more and more in the region.

The tide of democracy in Latin America and the Caribbean has generated hopes and expectations of greater freedom of expression and an expansion of the press, radio, TV and other mass media. Although the fall of dictatorships and the emergence of governments elected by popular suffrage do not necessarily guarantee adequate press freedom - as is illustrated, for example, by what has been seen in Guatemala, Peru and Venezuela - they do open the way for a process leading to greater social, political and economic openness, which will gradually foster greater press freedom and freer speech through the media.

Privatization, deregulation and a growing influx of outside capital are acting as catalysts in the process that the tide of democratization made possible and set in train. They are also bringing the countries of the region into the globalization process, which is providing the underpinning for greater expansion of the media and for greater interaction between them and the rest of the world. A good image of this rapid progress towards greater openness to the world may be observed in the juxtaposition of the 150-metre high Entel Tower which dominates the Avenida Bernardo O'Higgins in Santiago, Chile, just two blocks away from the 400-year-old La Moneda Palace. This tower is the voice of the capital; with its satellite and microwave links, and with its data, video and audio communications network, it connects the capital with the rest of the country and with the world beyond the Andes and the Pacific, the geographical barriers that kept Chile isolated in the past. Something similar is happening, rather slowly perhaps, but steadily, throughout Latin America and the Caribbean.

The rapid development of the mass media in recent years has not diminished the great differences and contrasts found in this sector, and may indeed have increased them. What has come out of this process appears to be an intermixing of the First and Third Worlds. On the one hand, there are the multimedia conglomerates typical of the First World, thriving printed newspapers and magazines, television networks and production companies that export television serials and other material. These large corporations have little reason to envy their northern counterparts. The Industria de Medios Latinoamericana owns two of the world's largest and most profitable television networks.

On the other hand, there are newspapers with very

low circulation and rural areas that are sometimes served by just a single primitive radio set. Notwithstanding this contrast, the rise of the communications media would appear to be helping small firms that are effective and efficient to grow, while causing less efficient ones to perish or to be absorbed by better-performing ones.

Consequently, the trends appear to be very promising; this at least is the opinion of a number of authors who have researched the media situation in Latin America. Print media in Latin America and the Caribbean do not appear to have grown significantly in the last two decades.

Some countries, such as Argentina and Chile, have taken firm steps in the right direction; in others, such as Brazil, Colombia, Mexico, Peru and Venezuela significant progress is being made, but prospects are somewhat uncertain and the future is unpredictable enough to discourage the big operating companies from committing greater resources.

However, the great potential of Latin America is attracting more and more attention from operators willing to run the risks involved. Long-term strategies are beginning to take precedence over short-term profits. For example, Robert Meyer, the business development manager for Latin America of BellSouth International, has claimed that 'to be successful here (in Latin America) you need to have patience, and partners that understand the region'.

Two of the main factors driving growth in the telecommunications industry in the world as a whole, and in the Latin America and Caribbean region in particular, are Internet plus mobile computing technologies and wireless communications. These two areas of technology are enjoying the most rapidly accelerating growth in the telecommunications industry. The growth of cellular telephony is remarkable, particularly in developing countries like those of the region, since it is being used as a substitute for traditional telephony, whereas in developed ones it is being used to complement it. The underdevelopment of traditional telephony in developing countries, and the inadequacy of the infrastructure used to provide this service, have led to growth in cellular telephony that is as extraordinary as it is unexpected.

The use of Internet/Intranet/Extranet-related technologies is growing at an extraordinary pace in the region. Corporate spending in this area was $18,000 million in 1997, and in 1998 it increased substantially, according to the 1998 Latin American Corporate Internet Strategy and Adoption Report produced by the International Data Corporation (IDC).

Latin American corporations, however, do not yet have significant plans for electronic commerce, although 45% stated that they had electronic commerce applications. Latin American executives gave two main reasons for this, namely: the problem of security, and a perception that electronic commerce is not particularly profitable, at least for the time being. Security is an issue that has attracted a great deal of attention from Latin American corporations, as a result of which major investments are being made in firewalls and other security mechanisms.

In fact, 40% stated that they were using firewalls in their Web sites and 23% that they were using them in their Intranets. More than 95% stated that they were using some type of Internet/Intranet security mechanism.

Growth in the number of hosts in Latin America and the Caribbean is exponential, as it is in the rest of the world.

Although what has been said so far is equally applicable to Latin America and the Caribbean, except where we have referred explicitly to Latin America alone, we believe it would be useful to make some specific reference to the Caribbean subregion.

Association of National Telecommunication Organizations (CANTO) have been gradually furthering the development of telecommunications and computing in the subregion. The mission of CANTO is to promote and facilitate co-operation and integration in the development of telecommunications in the Caribbean. Its ambition is to become the backbone of the Caribbean family with its focus on human and economic development, through telecommunications.

Its aims are to exchange information, know-how and experience in the area of telecommunications; to help generate the inputs needed for orderly growth and for the formulation of appropriate policies; to consider aspects that are of mutual interest to the Caribbean countries; to develop telecommunications links between those countries; and to promote technical and economic co-operation between them.

CANTO seeks to achieve these aims by providing technical, financial and administrative advisory services, facilitating human resources training, keeping member organization in formed and aware of developments, carrying our out strategic planning, identifying and designing projects of interest and organizing conferences, seminars and exhibitions in the subregion. CANTO held its fifteenth Annual Conference and Trade Exhibition in Aruba from 16 to 20 May 1999. The Organization of Eastern Caribbean States (OECS), whose membership is made up of nine island countries of the Eastern Caribbean, has the objective of making these countries attractive to electronic equipment manufacturers, information processing companies, tourist development companies and agribusiness.

To that end they have set up the Eastern Caribbean Investment Promotion Service (ECIPS) which has recently been giving priority to its efforts in the areas of computing and telecommunications. They hope to turn the Caribbean into a major artery in the information superhighway. Their objective is gradually to build up the advantages of the Eastern Caribbean countries so that foreign companies will site their information processing operations there.

Most of the Caribbean countries now have access to the Internet. Connections to the outside are made through telephone companies. RedHUCyT has also helped arrange two important subregional seminars and financed a number of consultancy operations. In a second phase, the OAS is providing significant funding for the purchase of communications equipment, technical assistance and training, to help enable a greater number of academic, scientific and governmental institutions to connect to the Internet.

In cellular telephony they were slightly above this average until 1996. The apparent decline since then is not a real one, as several Caribbean countries have not reported data. In personal computing, the Caribbean is well below the region; in fact, together with Central America, it has the lowest values for this indicator. A number of Caribbean countries did not provide data in 1996 or 1997, which accounts for the irregular pattern of those years.

Latin America and the Caribbean aim to secure these advantages by providing member countries, which are geographically close to North America, with good-quality and reasonably priced telecommunications services, an efficient labour force with a good command of English, tax incentives, a peaceful and stable environment and pro-business governments.

These efforts are beginning to yield some initial returns. The World Bank has given the OECS countries support in building up telecommunications. Amendments to the laws governing this sector of industry have considerably improved pricing. The Cable and Wireless company is implementing major investments and technological improvements in the OECS countries, including the installation of fibre optic networks. Jamaica has just granted a licence to Globalstar Caribbean Ltd. to provide mobile and wireless communication services, both in Jamaica and in the Caribbean generally. The wireless communication services of this company are based on 48 Globalstar satellites, which send and receive signals to and from regions that are not covered by terrestrial cellular telephony.

ICTs and Western Europe and North America

De regulation of the telecommunications sector, the emergence of global markets and the convergence of media and developments in telecommunications and information technology have forced countries all over the world to face up to new challenges.

It will be less and less easy to separate telecommunications from networked computer-based communications (i.e. the Internet, electronic commerce, Internet-telephony, etc.) and electronic media and content (broadcasting, multimedia, on-line services). The convergence of electronic networks and services is a global phenomenon which transcends national boundaries and increases international competition. Furthermore, unemployment and its harmful effects on society increase the pressure to seize the new economic opportunities offered by the emerging Information society.

These developments represent a political challenge. Experts say that sustainable economic growth and prosperity can be supported by making more efficient use of telecommunications and information technology, by increasing productivity and the development of new products and services.

The development potential of new services such as digital television and the Internet offer huge scope for services that are either completely new or designed to complement existing ones. However, the process of technical convergence brought about by digitization and the merging of previously distinct areas should not lead to the assumption that future developments will be dominated solely by technical issues. Initially we are 'merely' talking in terms of technical potential.

The extent to which this potential is realized and utilized in the countries of Western Europe and North America will depend primarily on infrastructural penetration, usage rates with corresponding added value in work and daily life, and last but not least on political initiatives for the emerging information society.

The worldwide ICT market grew from 910,000 million euros to 1,225,000 million euros between 1994 and 1997, an increase of around 35%. Europe takes second place with 371,000 million euros (30%), followed by Japan with 171,000 million euros (14%). The combined total for all other countries amounted to 259,000 million euros (21%), with growth rates in Asia and Latin America being mainly responsible for the disproportionate increase in this category.

A comparison of national ICT expenditure in 1997 shows that in the United States, it reached 7.0% of GDP and exceeded 6% in the United Kingdom, Sweden, Switzerland and Ireland. In Western Europe ICT technology averaged a direct proportion of 4.9% of GDP in 1997. However, the extraordinary financial significance of information and communications technologies to competitiveness is not only illustrated by the increasing proportion of turnover that this sector represents. More important still is the fact that ICTs are an innovative interdisciplinary technology for other products (e.g. in the fields of mechanical engineering, equipment manufacturing and automotive engineering) and services (e.g. electronic commerce) and represent a high proportion of the potential added value creation of these markets.

At the same time, the extensive digitalization of content, services, networks and terminals is reinforcing the trend towards convergence in the fields of information technology, telecommunications and media (broadcasting, publishing etc.), leading to increased process and product innovation in the value-added chain of the developing multimedia markets. The ongoing process of convergence in the information technology, telecommunications and media sectors serves to reinforce the increasing significance of multimedia-related markets for overall economic development.

In Western Europe, the annual expenditure in these converging fields increased by around 21% between 1993 and 1996 from 743,000 million euros to 897,000 million euros. However, information and communication technologies continue to be the driving force for ongoing growth in the converging sectors.

A study carried out by Booz, Allen and Hamilton on multimedia-related ICT markets (content, networks, components and terminals) in the G7 countries reported a total expenditure of around $1,344,000 million for 1996. The growth rates in these markets have been approximately 10.4% each year since 1992, with the content sector (software, games, multimedia, TV/Pay-TV), which is to a large extent dependent on the software and ICT service market, showing the highest growth rate.

Basic Indicators of ICT

One of the main factors determining a country's competitiveness, its ability to develop innovative new services and content and provide equal access to the new multimedia-related markets for all, lies in the creation of an ICT infrastructure that allows these new services to be distributed among and used by large sections of the population. From a sociopolitical point of view, the problem of ensuring equal access to these markets calls for particular vigilance, because the new media, services and content on offer in an emerging information society represent much more than mere commercial products or sources of market information.

The development of multimedia is in itself a significant cultural issue and serves to express cultural identity. Therefore the extension of technological infrastructures in ICTs and multimedia is one of the main pillars for developing economic and cultural prosperity. However, willingness to invest in information and communications technology - and the financial capacity to do so - varies greatly inside Europe and between Europe and North America.

The lowest per capita ICT investment is found in Greece, Italy, Portugal and Spain. Access to electronic information and services can only be provided where the country in question possesses a network infrastructure that allows the user to connect to the various information and communications services at areas on able price. This infrastructure includes analogue and digital telephone lines, mobile telephone networks and cable and satellite Television connections.

Unlike in Africa, where there are only 2 main telephone lines for every 100 inhabitants on the average, the widespread availability of telephone lines is almost taken for granted in Western Europe and North America. In addition to individual telephony, a telephone line used in connection with the appropriate hardware provides extra functions and services (telephone answering, fax services), which are increasing in importance for both personal and business use. Furthermore, the combination of a telephone line, a personal computer (PC) and modem is currently the most important gateway to the Internet network, which is expanding very rapidly all over the world.

The United States and Canada are again among the leaders, with over 60 lines for every 100 inhabitants.

Germany is the overall international leader in this field, with 4.4 integrated service digital network (ISDN) lines per 100 inhabitants in 1997. By comparison the United States is a long way behind, with around 0.5 ISDN lines per 100 inhabitants.

However, ISDN will face increased competition from other digital transmission technologies in the future, such as Asymmetric Digital Subscriber Line (ADSL), which can multiply the transmission capacity of ISDN using the digitized telephone network. The same applies for the multifunctional application of cable and satellite television, which is currently used almost exclusively for the reception of radio and television programmes, but which will also be used for new multimedia services in the near future.

Within Western Europe, cable and satellite penetration stands at almost 100% of television households, particularly in the Benelux countries. Following close behind with over 90% penetration are Denmark, Switzerland and, with a slightly lower penetration, Germany. However, terrestrial television is still of great importance in Europe and in individual countries such as France, Italy, Portugal, Spain and the United Kingdom.

With around 66 million cable television connections in the United States and 8 million connections in Canada, North America has a very high level of cable penetration. Its lead in relation to the total figure for Western Europe of 42.5 million cable television households is considerable, despite the fact that individual countries in Europe had a higher cable penetration in 1997 than Canada and the United States.

In Western Europe 24.5 million television households received their television and radio programmes via satellite at the end of 1997, representing 16.6% of all television households. Europe is therefore a long way ahead of North America in terms of satellite penetration.

The commercial significance of digital television using broadband transmission via cable and satellite will increase in the future. The interlinking of new television services with new interactive services (Internet access, Online shopping, e-mail by television, electronic commerce, etc.) is particularly important in opening up new economic opportunities for the multimedia-related ICT industry and the media sector. The decisive advantage of digital transmission systems is that, by using compression techniques, the data quantities to be transmitted can be greatly increased, and the frequencies released in the process can be used for new multimedia services.

The current trend within the digital market in European countries shows that the countries that have traditionally been pay-television countries, such as France and Spain, have the highest digital television penetration. France, with the digital television providers Canal+ and the Television par Satellite consortium, and Spain with the providers Canal Satellite Digital and ViaDigital, are currently the only digital television markets in Europe in which there is any noteworthy level of competition.

Digital television is to be launched over the American cable networks this year after a long experimental phase, with the largest cable network operators such as TCI, Time Warner and Comcast having already ordered several million Set Top Boxes for digital reception. The software company Microsoft has also prepared itself for this development, investing around $1,000 million in the cable network operator Comcast in 1997.

This involvement should speed up the development of data and video services available via the Comcast cable network and promote the merging of PCs and televisions , as will the takeover of Web-TV, a company involved in the provision of Internet services and Internet navigation systems via the television set. In the Canadian market, two digital satellite systems have been available since the end of 1997, Expressvu, which has 30,000 customers, and Star Choice, with 50,000 subscribers.

The digital mobile telephone sector is one of the few other areas of the telecommunication sector apart from ISDN development in which Western Europe holds an edge over North America in terms of its position in the world market. This applies both to the production of hardware (e.g. Nokia, Siemens, Ericsson), the development of Global System for Mobile Communications standards (GSM) and in terms of the usage figures for mobile telephone subscribers. The Nordic states of Finland, Norway, Sweden and Denmark in particular surged ahead of North America in the number of lines.

Growth rates in the mobile telephone sector from 1993 to 1997 are impressive. The boom is particularly pronounced in those countries that had previously occupied a mid-range position, with the number of subscribers increasing between five- and tenfold in the last four years. Increasing competition, the integration of tariffs with the fixed network and new services will lead to an increase in the number of mobile telephone subscribers.

In addition, new digital network developments in the mobile telephone sector such as Universal Mobile Telecommunications Systems (UMTS), which have transmission capacities far in advance of those that can be achieved using ISDN, will promote further growth.

In the Southern countries of Europe, on the other hand, only one in ten inhabitants possesses a PC. Penetration is most advanced in North America (United States and Canada), where almost one out of two inhabitants possesses a PC.

At the heart of the multimedia-related ICT revolution is the Internet, the most dynamic market of the future from a financial point of view (electronic commerce, Internet telephony, Internet broadcasting, on-line shopping, etc.). According to figures from the Fachverband Informationstechnik (FVIT), around 89 million people used the Internet or online services on a regular basis in 1997. It is extremely difficult to measure the number of Internet users directly, because individual accounts are sometimes used by several people, and figures from Internet Service Providers (ISP) and on-line services cannot be verified with any certainty.

In both Canada and the United States almost one in four inhabitants was using the Internet at the beginning of 1998. Within Western Europe a very mixed picture emerged with large variations. In the Nordic countries of Europe, Internet use is very advanced, but in the Southern countries (Spain, Italy, Portugal, Greece) at the beginning of the year only around 3% of the population had access to the Internet.

Internet hosts are computers that are permanently connected to the Internet via a fixed Internet Protocol (IP) number and through which access can be gained to the

Internet at any time using the IP. Computers that have access to the Internet only at certain times (e.g. using telephones with alternating IP numbers) are not considered here.

The percentage distribution of Internet hosts illustrates even more clearly the large lead that the Scandinavian countries have gained over other European countries, with Finland having overtaken even the United States. The great variations within Europe have very different causes.

On the one hand, due to their economic weakness, the ability and willingness of Southern European countries to invest is much lower than that of countries with stronger economies and higher incomes.

Cost structures for Internet access are also very varied within Europe and disproportionately high in comparison with North America. The liberalization of the European telecommunications market has been an important factor in causing telecommunications costs to fall within Europe, thus reducing the costs of Internet access. This indicates that the growth rate for Internet use will increase more rapidly in countries where Internet use has previously been at a lower level than in those countries that already have relatively high Internet penetration.

For most governments, the availability of infrastructures for electronically transferring and accessing information is perceived as essential for the realization of the economic, social and cultural benefits and competitive advantages for the economy.

The well known metaphor 'Information Superhighway' is very attractive to the American public.

From the beginning, the NII initiative emphasized benefits for all Americans and stressed a broad concept of universal service and public access. The administration therefore received strong support from public-interest groups. Furthermore the Information Infrastructure Task Force (IITF), set up to co-ordinate the United States Federal Government's activities, developed at an early stage a specific programme aimed at promoting non-commercial applications for the public and non-profit sectors, called the Telecommunications and Information Infrastructure Assistance Programme (TIIAP), which serves the public interest.

In contrast the TELEMATIC application programme in Europe is not limited to the non-profit sector but also supports commercial projects to promote the competitiveness of the European Union. Western Europe and North America 273 The reform of the United States telecommunications law dating back to 1934 took place, when President Clinton signed the Telecommuications Act in February 1996.

This act primarily pre-empts state laws that prohibit entry into local telephone services; establishes the conditions for competition for local telephone services; eliminates restrictions that prevent cable and telephone companies from entering each others' business; gives the Federal Communications Commission (FCC) broad authority; requires the FCC to continue to update the definition of universal service, and to provide discounted service to schools and libraries; and makes the transmission of obscene or indecent communications to minors illegal.

As far as online communication is concerned, legal provisions of the 1996 Telecommunications Act outlaw the transmission of indecent or patently offensive material to minors over PC networks. But the Supreme Court ruled that this Commmunication Decency Act would be unconstitutional as it breaches freedom of speech protected under the First Amendment of the United States Constitution.

In a speech at the International Telecommunications Union (ITU) in 1994, Vice President Gore argued for world wide co-operation to extend the project of the NII to a Global Information Infrastructure (GII). This proposal was later endorsed at a 1995 meeting of ministers from the G7 group of leading industrialized countries. This G7 ministerial conference in Brussels was the first large international conference devoted to the information society, and bringing together political leaders on that subject.

The G7 conference outlined common principles for the worldwide information society and common guidelines for co-operation. The principles outlined were to promote dynamic competition; encourage private investment; define a regulatory framework that can change with the times; ensure open access to networks; guarantee universal supply of and access to services; promote equal opportunity for all citizens; promote diversity of content, including cultural and linguistic diversity; and recognize the need for global co-operation by paying particular attention to the least-developed countries.

This agreement was important as a means of facilitating multinational efforts to co-ordinate the work of global bodies like the World Trade Organisation (WTO), the World Intellectual Property Organization (WIPO) and the International Telecommunication Union

(ITU). The GII is regarded as a key element of economic development and industrial policy in many developed countries as it creates opportunities for reaching international markets.

The United States Administration's major programme for supporting research and development related to the NII is the $1,10 0 million High-Performance Computing and Communications (HPCC) initiative.

Since 1993 the scope of the programme has been expanded to include support for the NII applications and technologies. In October 1996, President Clinton announced the Next Generation Internet (NGI) initiative that will support universities and national laboratories with networks that are much faster than today's Internet.

The Canadian Information Highway

The Canadian Information Highway proposed three main objectives for Canadian strategies, which were to create jobs through innovation and investment, reinforce Canadian sovereignty and cultural identity, and ensure universal access at reasonable cost.

To reach these goals and to provide advice and recommendations to the Minister of Industry the Information Highway Advisory Council (IHAC), with representatives from industry, education, research, labour, consumer and public interest groups, was established at the beginning of 1994. In September. 274 1995, the Advisory Council released its final report Connection, Community, Content: The Challenge of the Information Highway, which contains some 300 recommendations for government action.

In May 1996, the Government of Canada unveiled its plan for building the Information Highway in a report, which underlined four strategic thrusts with the following policies and initiatives:

— building Canada's Information Highway by creating a competitive, consumer-driven policy and regulatory environment that is in accord with the Canadian public interest and that is conducive to innovation and investment by Canadian industry in new services on the Information Highway.

— growing Canadian content on the Information Highway, thereby strengthening the ongoing national cultural dialogue and creating economic growth and jobs.

— realizing the economic and social benefits for all Canadians of the Information Highway and allowing them to participate fully in the emerging information society.

— getting government right by ensuring better services and more affordable, accessible and responsive government and making government a model user and a catalyst for Information Highway development across Canada.

The government also expressed the intention - where market forces fail - to ensure affordable access to essential Information Highway services for all Canadians, regardless of their income or geographic location. In September, 1997, the IHAC published its second final report of its mandate to encourage continuing action with regard to these commitments.

The IHAC concentrated on two tasks, namely advancing the public policy agenda by advising the government on outstanding issues and concerns related to the Information Highway, and reporting on Canada's progress in the transition to an information society and a knowledge-based economy. The IHAC emphasized that technology-neutrality must be the central principle of policy and regulation for the Information Highway, so that no obstacles remain to using the best technology for a given application or purpose.

Access for all Canadians and Canadian quality content are seen as most important imperatives to ensure Canada's future as a knowledge society. The government instructed the Canadian Radio-Television and Telecommunication Commission (CRTC) early in 1995 to conduct public hearings on regulatory changes required as a result of the convergence of broadcasting and telecommunications.

In 1997 the CRTC adopted measures to fully liberalize Canada's telecommunication market by January 1998 and to encourage convergence between telecommunication and broadcasting. New telecommunication entrants were allowed to offer local services in 1998. As regards convergence, cable television operators were immediately allowed to offer local telecommunication services, while telecommunication companies were entitled to apply for broadcasting licenses to enter the market in 1998.

These decisions reflected the policy objectives included in the 1993 Telecommunications Act and the 1991 Broadcasting Act and, last but not least, the priority that the Canadian government has placed on the development of a competitive communications environment. The CRTC is an independent federal agency and is responsible for the supervision and regulation of telecommunications and broadcasting in Canada. The Telecommunication Act gives the CRTC a broad range of powers, including the regulation of telecommunication rates and conditions of service, approval of interconnection agreements, and quality of service standards.

In Canada, a wide range of social and cultural approaches built upon the Canadian tradition of a mixed public/private system (e.g. broadcasting) to the. Western Europe and North America NII have emerged during recent years. In order to develop the new information infrastructure, public policy promotes a new hybrid model of communication, which combines the social and cultural objectives of both broadcasting and telecommunications, and provides new regulatory mechanisms.

Information Policy for European Union

Since the early 1990s the European Union has recognized the need to act quickly to develop an Information Society in Europe. The pace of globalization is picking up and Europeans fear that they will lose ground to the United States, Japan and the new emerging industrial nations in the Far East and South-East Asia. An analysis of the policies of the European Community reveals a gradual shift taking place in strategy. In the 1980s, the emphasis was on promoting information technology. Due to its multifunctionality and cross-sector significance, information technology was designated a 'key technology' and computer manufacturing was elevated to a 'key industry sector'. The key role given to information technology was illustrated in particular by the efforts made by the EU to set up the European Strategic Programme for Research and Development in Information Technology (ESPRIT) in 1984 and the increases in budget allocation for this area in subsequent Framework Programmes. This period was followed by measures aimed at improving the communications infrastructure and accompanied by the deregulation of the telecommunications sector.

By creating a comprehensive telecommunications infrastructure the idea was to offer, by simple, cost-effective means, opportunities to companies, authorities and citizens to share multimedia information (in the form of data, text, voice, still and moving images) to a high technical standard and with no constraints of distance. The creation of a European telecommunications infrastructure featuring narrow- and broad-band networks began with the Research and Development in Advanced Communications Technologies (RACE) and continued with its successor, the Advanced Communications Technologies and Services (ACTS). Within the framework of European policy on promoting the information society, increased assistance was given in the early 1990s towards establishing a trans-European network. To help accelerate and finance this expansion of the technical infrastructure, the European community has adopted deregulation and liberalization of the telecommunications sector as a key pillar of policy with some basic rules: an important precondition in this process is the need to safeguard a universal service and maintain interconnection and interoperability in a manner which ensures open and fair competition.

The liberalization of the European telecommunications market was largely completed at the beginning of 1998. The next step was to place greater emphasis on business matters relating to new services and content in the information society (information as a commodity and factor of production markets). This issue came to the fore, mainly because of the increasing convergence between telecommunications, computing and broadcasting/media sectors. These considerations led among other things to the setting up of the Telematics research programme.

The programme placed greater emphasis on demonstration projects (i.e. in the area of transport, education, health and administration) that reflected market needs and provided assistance for products and multimedia applications likely to prove successful in the marketplace. In this context the problems facing small and medium-sized enterprises (SMEs) were given greater attention within the European assistance programmes. The 'information economy' was seen as the key area which will determine future growth and prosperity.

In December 1993, the European Council entrusted a high-level group, later known as the Bangemann group, with drafting a report. The report by the Bangemann group underscored that the private sector should be given a leading role in developing the European Information Society. In July 1994, the European Commission published a communication entitled Europe's Way to the Information Society: An Action Plan that underlined issues such as the legal and regulatory setting as well as services, applications, content and social and cultural aspects. Since the mid-1990s, new approaches in European information policy, particularly in the area of education and training, pointed to the need to consider the social repercussions of the information society. This change in approach grew from the realization that the upheavals taking place in society and business needed to be underpinned by a social framework. It was also understood that if such a social dimension were to be overlooked, growing problems of acceptance could jeopardize further progress.

The High Level Group of Experts on Social and Societal Aspects of the Information Society, set up in April 1995, and the Information Society Forum (ISF) in July 1995 focused more attention on the social aspects of the information society. However, it can be seen that from the beginning the United States gave more prominence than Europe did to the notion of supporting the non-profit-sector and of improving the ways in which democracy functions and achieving higher levels of political codetermination with the help of online technology. One of the main problems with the European approach of concentrating on individual aspects of the information society one after the other is an inability to anticipate well in advance the cross-sectoral repercussions of the various actions for society, business, law and technology, along with accompanying structural changes. Only with the Green Paper on convergence of December 1997 has the European Commission launched a public discussion regarding a more comprehensive regulatory approach in the field of telecommunications, media and information technology.

Bibliography

A. Friedlander, *Natural Monopoly and Universal Service: Telephones and Telegraphs in the U. S. Communications Infrastructure*, 1837-1940, Corp. for National Research Initiatives, 1995.

A. R. Bennett, *The Telephone Systems of the Continent of Europe*, Longmans, Green, and Co., 1895.

Anonymous, *Distributing music over telephone lines, Telephony*, vol. 18, no. 25 (Dec. 18, 1909), pp. 699-701.

B. Klopfenstein, *Problems and potential of forecasting the adoption of new media*, pp. 21-41

D. Blair, *Impact of the Internet on core switching network*, presented at ENPW '98, March 1998, Les Arcs, France.

D. Cressy, *Coming Over: Migration and Communication between England and New England in the Seventeenth Century*, Cambridge Univ. Press, 1987.

D. Gabel, *The Evolution of a Market: The Emergence of Regulation in the Telephone Industry of Wisconin*, 1893-1917, Ph.D. Dissertation, University of Wisconsin-Madison, 1987.

D. R. Irvin, *Modeling the cost of data communication for multi-node computer networks oper-ating in the United States*, IBM J. Res. Develop. vol. 37 (1993), pp. 537-546.

E. Baark, *Lightning Wires: The Telegraph and China's Technological Modernization*, 1860- 1890, Greenwood Press, 1997.

F. Cairncross, *The Death of Distance: How the Communications is Revolution will Change our Lives*, Harvard Business School Press, 1997.

F. J. Brown, *The Cable and Wireless Communications of the World,* Pitman, 1927.

H. S. Dordick, The *Information Society: A Retrospective View*, Sage, 1993.

J. Ahvenainen, *The Far Eastern Telegraphs: The History of Telegraphic Communica-tion between the Far East, Europe and America before the First World War,* Ann. Acad. Scien. Fennicae #216, Helsinki, 1981.

J. Altmann, B. Rupp, and P. Varaiya, *Internet demand under different pricing schemes,* in Proc. ACM Conference on Electronic Commerce (EC-99), ACM, 1999, pp. 9-14.

M. Blondheim, *News Over the Wires: The Telegraph and the Flow of Public Information in America*, 1844-1897, Harvard Univ. Press, 1994.

M. Castells, *The Rise of the Network Society*, Blackwell, 1996.

M. S. Baratz, *The Economics of the Postal Service*, Public Affairs Press, 1962.

P. Flichy, *Dynamics of Modern Communication: The Shaping and Impact of New Communi-cation Technologies,* Sage, 1995. Original French version published in 1991.

R. R. John, *Recasting the information infrastructure for the Industrial Age,* pp. 55-105 in A Nation Transformed by Information: How Information has Shaped the United States from Colonial Times to the Present, A. D. Chandler, Jr., and J. W. Cortada, eds., Oxford Univ. Press, 2000.

Index

Advanced Technological Education (ATE), 69
Agence de cooperation culturelle et technique (ACCT), 204
America On Line (AOL), 189
American Association for the Advancement of Science (AAAS), 206
Asynchronous Transmission Protocol (ATM), 189
Authoritarian governments, 108

Broadcasting media, 111
Bureau of Labour Statistics (BLS), 25

Cable News Network (CNN), 210
Cellular services, 198
Central African Customs and Economic Union (UDEAC), 191
Children's Online Privacy Protection Act (COPPA), 18
Common Market for Eastern and Southern Africa (COMESA), 191
Communication techniques, 108
Computer and Data Processing Services (CDPS), 51
Computing Research Association (CRA), 36
Congressional hearings, 4
Current Population Survey (CPS), 25

Department of Telecommunications (DoT), 232
Digital Entertainment Network (DEN), 10
Digital media, 3
Diverse media, 5

Economic Community of West African States (ECOWAS), 191
Egyptian Radio and Television Union (ERTU), 196
Electronic communication, 6
Electronic gadgets, 11

Federal Trade Commission (FTC), 19
Filtering software products, 4

Geographic Information Systems (GIS), 204
Ghana Academic and Research Network (GARNET), 207
Ghana National Petroleum Corporation (GNPC),208
Global positioning systems (GPS), 18

Information and communication technologies (ICT), 182
Information Society Forum (ISF), 300
Information Society Index (ISI), 270
Information technology (IT), 23
Institute of Electrical and Electronics Engineers-USA (IEEE-USA), 56
Integrated Services Digital Networks (ISDN), 185
Interactive television (ITV), 10
International Development Research Centre (IDRC), 204
International Freedom of Expression and Exchange Network (IFEX), 116
International Telecommunication Union (ITU), 186
Internet service providers (ISP), 199
Isolated ethnic communities, 107

Mauritius Telecommunications Authority (MTA), 201
Mobile communications devices, 10
Mobile telecommunication service, 187

National Computer Board (NCB), 201
National IT Strategy Plan (NITSP), 201
Network society, 116
Non-governmental organizations, 108
Northwest Centre for Emerging Technologies (NWCET), 70

One-party systems, 105

Personal digital assistants (PDAs), 9
Personal Video Recorders (PVRs), 10
Person-to-person communication, 185
Practical Work Experience Program (PWE), 69
Public Telecommunication Operators (PTOs), 200

Radio France International (RFI), 195

Scientist and Engineer Statistical (SESTAT), 26
Software Council Fellowship Program (SCFP), 75
South Africa public broadcasting Corporation (SABC), 196
South Africa's Far-East (SAFE), 202
Southern African Development Corporation (SADC), 191

Technical Teams Encouraging Career Horizons (TECH), 62
Technology-intensive companies, 60
Telecommunications Advisory Council (TAC), 201
Telephone Organization of Thailand (TOT), 243

UN Economic Commission for Africa (UNECA), 206

Videsh Sanchar Nigam Limited (VSNL), 231

Wireless Application Protocol (WAP), 8
World Trade Organization (WTO), 211
World Wide Web (WWW), 198